Sheikh Farid

Sheikh Farid

◇

The Great Sufi Mystic

Dr. T. R. Shangari

RADHA SOAMI SATSANG BEAS

Published by:
J. C. Sethi, Secretary
Radha Soami Satsang Beas
Dera Baba Jaimal Singh
Punjab 143 204, India

First edition 2015

20 19 18 17 16 15   8 7 6 5 4 3 2 1

ISBN 978-81-8466-391-4

Printed in India by: Replika Press Pvt. Ltd.

CONTENTS

NOTE FROM THE TRANSLATORS

ADI GRANTH TRANSLATIONS used throughout this book have been taken from the approved English-language versions. Because Gurmukhi, Multani, and Persian scripts all have more characters than the English script, the transliteration provided in this book is an approximation of the pronunciation of the original script. RSSB publications use simplified transliteration for easier reading in preference to an academic style. Readers are advised to refer to the original script – or an Indian language expert – for exact pronunciation.

Sweet are sugar and candy
and honey and buffalo's milk.
Yea, sweet are all of these,
but sweeter by far is God!

~ *Sheikh Farid*

PREFACE

MORE THAN SEVEN CENTURIES after his death, Sheikh Farid remains a towering figure in the hearts, minds, and imaginations of the Punjabi people. His slokas in the Adi Granth are cherished, his words are sung by popular performers, and his sayings continue to be part of everyday conversation. Even very young children in the Punjab are able to recite many of his poems by heart.

Sheikh Farid: The Great Sufi Mystic is based on the extensive research done by the author for an earlier book, *Bolai Sheikh Farid*, published in 2002 in the Punjabi language. Incorporating additional contemporary research and new English translations, it has been prepared with the assistance of an accomplished team of researchers and translators.

This is the most recent volume in a series of books published by Radha Soami Satsang Beas presenting the perspectives of mystics from different traditions. Although Sheikh Farid was a Sufi mystic from North India, his poetry is included in the Adi Granth, and his message clearly underscores the commonality found among the great mystics of the world and their mystic traditions.

We are particularly pleased to be able to publish the Persian and Multani verses translated into English, most of them for the first time. With these two additional collections of poetry, the multi-faceted Sheikh Farid comes into clearer focus: Sufi sheikh, love-intoxicated mystic, Arabic scholar, poet, and a native son of the Punjab.

Faith Singh
RSSB Publications
Beas, India

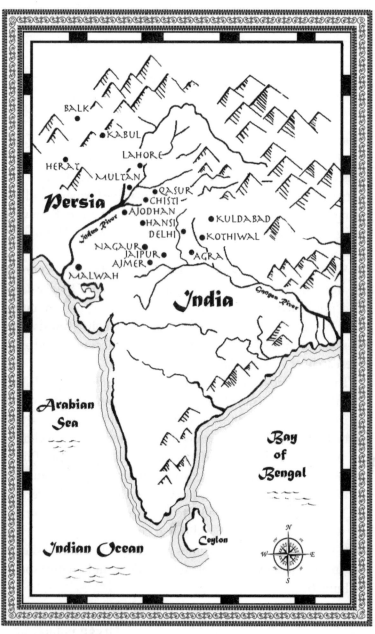

Illustration based on a thirteenth-century navigational map

INTRODUCTION

BABA FARID (1173–1265 CE), the beloved thirteenth-century saint from the Punjab, is widely known by the unusual title of the Treasure of Sweetness (*Ganj-i shakar*). Among people who come from the Punjab, even a reference to *Ganj-shakar* or *Shakar-ganj* will immediately be understood to mean Baba Farid, also known as Sheikh Farid.

Over the centuries legends have developed giving miraculous explanations for Farid's title. For example, one of these legends has it that after fasting for forty days, Farid broke his fast with a lump of mud. In response to his extraordinary austerity, a voice from the heavens said, "You have been included in the category of mystics that spout sweet words, and from today you will be called *Ganj-i shakar*, the Treasure of Sweetness." Another legend tells that when Farid tripped and fell on the road, a piece of dirt entering his mouth turned into sugar. His master heard of this and quoted a verse from Sanāī:

> A stone turns into a pearl in your hand,
> The poison becomes sugar in your mouth.[1]

Balwant Singh Anand, a twentieth-century biographer of Farid, suggests a less miraculous explanation: It was probably "the sweetness of his words, the kindness of his actions and the warmth and affection he displayed towards one and all that earned him the

1

INTRODUCTION

title of *Ganj-i shakar*."[2] Certainly, all descriptions of Sheikh Farid's manner of living support Anand's conclusion. Many anecdotes that record his interactions with disciples, visitors, and even belligerent enemies refer to Farid's kindness, warmth, and affection. His generosity was such that he routinely starved himself while giving all he had to feed the poor. Seemingly tireless, he made himself available at all hours for those who sought his help.

Perhaps Sheikh Farid's humility and simple practicality also contributed to the ineffable sweetness people associate with him. Though well educated in Persian and Arabic, he reached out to the local Multani people in their own language – a language which up to that time had no written form. Far from confusing them with the ornate courtly images and complex, layered symbolism of the Persian poetry that seemingly flowed from his lips as easily as breath, Baba Farid spoke to them simply. In rhyming couplets, he used images from the parched landscape they knew: birds, river banks, trees, desert thorns, grass and dust underfoot, fire, crops in the fields, torrential rain, and mud.

This book is the result of the efforts of an extensive team of researchers and translators. Finding accurate, historical sources for the life of this medieval saint is challenging. Our goal is to present a rich and vibrant picture of Sheikh Farid, as depicted in the most reliable sources. We begin sketching his life by piecing together anecdotes and recollections, relying particularly on the accounts of people who had direct contact with Sheikh Farid.

Next, we discuss his mystical teachings. Sheikh Farid was the third Sufi master (sheikh or pir) in the Chishti lineage in India.*

---

* See the Glossary for explanations of unusual usage, technical or Indian-language terms. Islamic names and terms in this book are spelled in the simplest possible way, leaving out most diacritical marks. Within quoted material the same name may have been spelled in a wide variety of ways. We have selected one spelling and used it throughout the book, including a change of Fareed to Farid in the English translations of the Adi Granth.

2

In the verses and sayings attributed to Sheikh Farid, we can glean a few fundamental aspects of the teachings he passed on to his disciples. By going beyond his own words to include the teachings of other Sufi masters in the Chishti lineage – particularly Sheikh Farid's own pir, and the pir of his pir – our intent is to attain a clearer and more detailed discussion of his teachings. Throughout this book we refer to locations using the place names that were current during Sheikh Farid's lifetime.

Following a section on his life and teachings, we present two collections of poetry attributed to Sheikh Farid. Each poem includes a transliteration of the original language and its English translation. This format gives readers familiar with both languages an opportunity to enjoy them in their original version as well as in translation.

The first is a collection of the verses that are included in the Adi Granth, the seventeenth-century scripture that brings together the poetry of the first five Gurus, and the ninth, in the line of Guru Nanak, as well as many other saints from different parts of India. Sheikh Farid's reputation as a poet rests overwhelmingly on this collection of verses. We present a phonetic transliteration of the original Gurmukhi script along with an approved Adi Granth translation.

The second section of poetry contains verses that are outside of the Adi Granth. All are in Persian or in the Multani language of the western Punjab. While Sheikh Farid is best known for the verses in the Adi Granth, Persian was the language he spoke with his disciples, his master, and his fellow Sufis. Like many other Sufis of his time Sheikh Farid loved to gather with his fellow Sufis for *sama*, the recitation and listening to the singing of mystical poetry in the Persian language. Some of the Persian verses presented here were composed by Sheikh Farid. Others are Persian verses he frequently recited which he may or may not have composed himself. Both those he composed and those he loved to recite add richly to our understanding of Sheikh Farid, his mystical insight, and his ardent love of God. For example, disciples report that he often recited the following poem:

> I wish to turn into dust
>> and find my abode under Your feet
> I wish to live in union with You.
> I am weary of both worlds
>> and my sole purpose here is You –
> to live for You and die for You.[3]

It is said that the final lines of this verse, "to live for You and die for You," were continually on his lips.

Most of the verses in Multani attributed to Sheikh Farid were passed down orally for centuries before they were first recorded in writing. An early manuscript penned close to Sheikh Farid's lifetime contains only a few of them. Despite the uncertainty of whether each verse was actually composed by the historical Sheikh Farid himself, we find value in these Multani verses. They reflect the rich and vibrant ongoing spiritual and literary tradition that has grown up around his legacy. Sheikh Farid remains a treasure of sweetness – that was filled to overflowing in the thirteenth century and continues infusing life with its sweetness today.

Sufism in Sheikh Farid's Time

Sheikh Farid lived in a particularly rich and vibrant period of Sufi history, as evidenced by the many great mystics who were all alive at the same time: Attar, Chishti, Ibn al-Arabi, Jilani, Kirmani, Rumi, Sa'di, Shadhili, Shams-e Tabriz, Suhrawardi, and others. The stories of their meetings with one another, their exchanges of pithy wisdom, are the stuff of Sufi lore. Sheikh Farid's lifetime also coincided with one of the great turning points in the history of Sufism.

Over the preceding 500 years, Sufis had pursued the mystical path without much formal, organizational structure. Each sheikh guided and trained his disciples, eventually naming one or more successors. To these he granted authorization to initiate and guide disciples. And so the mystical teachings were transmitted down through the generations. The group of disciples around any Sufi master was known as a circle (*halqa*) of disciples. Sufi sheikhs may have lived in Arabia or Khurasan, in North Africa or the Iberian Peninsula, but from one end of the Islamic world to the other, they all could trace their spiritual heritage through a 'chain' or lineage of Sufi masters (*silsilah*) back to the Prophet Muhammad.

Around 1200 CE, in Nishapur, in present-day Afghanistan, the great Sufi poet Abu Hamid bin Abu Bakr Ibrahim, better known by his pen-names Fariduddin and Attar, set about collecting the stories and sayings of Sufi saints from the previous five centuries. Up till then, these sayings, as well as the incidents and examples from the lives of saints, had been passed down orally and used as teaching stories by generation after generation of Sufi masters. When Attar published his *Memoirs of the Saints (Tazkirat ul Auliya)*, he captured for posterity precious glimpses of the wisdom, the humility, and the mystic insight of the early Sufis. Perhaps he sensed that the time of these informal and unstructured associations of Sufis was ending and a new era beginning.

From North Africa in the west to India in the east, Sufi masters began to form Sufi *tariqahs*, usually translated as 'Orders' by Western scholars. An Order is a lay brotherhood or sisterhood of mystical practitioners following specific rules of conduct, distinct practices, and generally bearing the name of the founder. However, to say that someone was the 'founder' of an Order does not mean that he or she was self-proclaimed. Each founder was the disciple of a Sufi sheikh who named him as successor.[4] One Order might be more prevalent than another in a certain geographic or cultural area and might lay more emphasis on certain aspects of the spiritual teachings. Yet, the Orders were not rival sects, nor are they today. A spiritual aspirant may move from one Order to another or may follow more than one Order.

Of the Sufi Orders that developed during Sheikh Farid's lifetime, those which became most important in India are the Qadiri Order, founded by Sheikh Abdul Qadir Jilani; the Suhrawardi Order, founded by Sheikh Shihabuddin Suhrawardi; the Naqshbandi Order, founded by Sheikh Abul Hasan Naqshband; and above all in terms of its influence within India, the Chishti Order, which made its home in Ajmer, Rajasthan, under the guidance of Khwaja Muinuddin Chishti. It was into the Chishti Order that Fariduddin Mas'ud, later known as Sheikh Farid, was to be initiated.

A Cultural and Linguistic Fusion

Before sketching Sheikh Farid's own life, it may help to paint a picture of the world in which he lived: the Punjab of the twelfth and thirteenth centuries. During the century before his birth, massive violence in Western and Central Asia had spurred a great upheaval and migration of populations. The Christian Crusades gripped the lands along the eastern end of the Mediterranean in perpetual battle from 1095 to 1291 CE. During the same period, Turkic tribes pushed their way across Central Asia, taking lands by conquest. The armies of the Turkic Ghaznavids razed cities, killed many, plundered extensively, and when they were finished with all this destruction, set about building their own empire. Meanwhile, Muslim artisans and farmers, merchants and scholars, poets and musicians fled eastward, seeking a safe place to live. And with them came the Sufis, the mystics of Islam.

Today the Punjab is in northern India and Pakistan. During the long span of Sheikh Farid's life – 93 years – the Punjab witnessed a steadily growing immigration of Persian-speaking Islamic populations. This area where five rivers course across the plains was a harsh landscape, with large tracts of uncultivated wilderness. Farmers and nomadic tribes alike eked out a living at the mercy of flooding rivers and scorching heat. With the influx of newcomers, the Punjab played host to one of history's great cultural fusions. This was the fertile ground that gave birth to 'Indo-Persian Sufism,' exemplified by Sheikh Farid.

By the time of Farid's birth, the major cities of the Punjab – Delhi, Lahore, and Multan – had become home to growing intellectual, cultural, and spiritual communities of Muslims under the rule of the Ghaznavid Empire. The Ghaznavids had conquered territory that stretched from present-day Iran to the Punjab. Though their original language was Turkish, they had a passion for Persian poetry and literature, and under their rule Lahore became a centre for literary and cultural affairs, as well as for religious and legal studies.

In 1175 CE, two years after Farid's birth, the army of the Ghurid Empire advanced past Kothiwal, the village where he lived, and captured the nearby city of Multan from the Ghaznavids. By 1186, when Farid was 13, they had seized Lahore from the lingering remains of Ghaznavid power. But by the time Farid was 31, the Ghurids had fallen to another conquering Turkic tribe, the Mamluks, who established the Delhi Sultanate. In other words – to summarize an immensely complicated history – Farid's childhood and youth were spent in a region riddled with the warfare of an expanding, then collapsing, empire.

The Mamluk Delhi Sultanate, established in 1206 CE, was successful in holding back the next threat that was terrorizing Central Asia – the Mongol warriors under the leadership of Genghis Khan. Refugees poured into this haven from the ravaged lands of

Persia and Central Asia. Thus, the Punjab of Sheikh Farid's time was home to a Hindu majority living side by side with a quickly growing Muslim minority.

Ghaznavids, Ghurids, and the Mamluks of the Delhi Sultanate had much in common. All were Muslim; all had Turkish roots, all spoke Persian, and were fascinated by Persian poetry. The word Punjab itself means 'five waters' (or rivers) and derives originally from Persian. Regardless of changing dynasties, imperial patronage continued to cultivate Persian literary expression as well as to promote Arabic scholarship. These sultans ruled over a land where the languages of the educated elite were Persian, Arabic, Turkish, and Sanskrit. The many local languages of the common people had no script. One of these was Multani, the oral language in which Baba Farid composed his verses (*slokas*). It may have been the language spoken in his childhood home; it probably was the language spoken in his native village of Kothiwal.

The linguistic richness of the world Baba Farid lived in may help us to understand his extraordinary versatility. He was a scholar of Persian and Arabic, and he composed poetry in Persian. If we are to accept the first-hand accounts of his disciples, he composed graceful Persian verses orally, on the spot, with an astounding fluency and ease. The following is an English translation of one example:

> No night goes by
>   that this stricken heart does not bleed.
> No day goes by
>   that I am not robbed of my honour.
> Not a single glass of water quenches my thirst
>   that does not return to earth as my tears.[5]

Yet, he is best known today for his verses in the Adi Granth, which are rhyming couplets composed in the local dialect: Multani.

Scholars have searched for prior examples of the use of this early form of Punjabi language, but Baba Farid seems to have been the first ever to use the language for any literary expression. He is thus rightly hailed as the first poet of the Punjab, the founder of Punjabi poetry and literature.

From Sheikh Farid's time onward, Sufi spirituality influenced and was influenced by traditional Indian forms of spirituality. Similarly, Persian styles of poetic expression influenced and were influenced by traditional local forms of expression. This Indo-Persian cultural fusion ultimately gave to Sufism the distinctive form it developed on the Indian subcontinent. Historian Anna Suvorova poetically describes this process as a wave rising up first in the major cities, then flowing across the countryside:

> The powerful wave of Indo-Persian Sufism, which had risen so high in the imperial capitals, became divided, spread across the boundless expanses of the subcontinent, merged with the water of already existing springs, filled dried-up riverbeds, was absorbed by the local soil and fantastically changed the South Asian cultural landscape.[6]

Today Baba Farid is often cited as a pioneer of the unique cultural identity that unites people of the Punjab regardless of religious differences or national boundaries. In 1855, Mian Muhammad Bakhsh composed a poem celebrating the mystic poets of the Punjab:

> Many are the wise poets of the land of the Punjab,
> Whose kafis, baran-mahs, or baits and dohras shine.
> First stands Sheikh Farid, the saintly Shakar-ganj;
> Each word he uttered guides us on the righteous way.
> Then came Sultan Bahu, a special man of God,
> Whose holy dohras are so glorious in both worlds.

Bulleh Shah swam in the sea of Unity,
His kafis from the heart remove all unbelief.[7]

As Sufism spread across the subcontinent, this fusion of
cultural and spiritual traditions also spread. Baba Farid was the
first – but not the only – Sufi who is considered the 'first poet'
or the 'founder' of literature in a local, previously unwritten,
Indian regional language. Other Sufis also began teaching in a
local language where no written language existed. As a result,
each was referred to as a 'first poet' or 'founder' of literature in
that particular area.* These mystics infused their Sufi practice and
teachings with Persian poetic traditions and gave expression to
the universal love and longing for the Divine in the local language
of the land that had become their home.

A Note on Sources

Sheikh Farid did not leave any writings for future generations to
ponder. Both his verses and his sayings are part of an oral tradition.
In relying on oral transmission, Sheikh Farid was following the
pattern established by his Sufi master (pir), Sheikh Qutbuddin
Bakhtiyar Kaki, and the pir of his pir, Khwaja Muinuddin Chishti.
The decision on the part of the first three spiritual masters in the
Chishti lineage of Sufis in India not to leave anything in writing
was apparently intentional, a conscious choice to impart the
mystical teachings orally and by example, rather than through
written treatises. For us today, however, the lack of sources in

---

*Muhammad Gesu Daraz, a fifteenth-century Chishti Sufi saint, is considered
the founder of literary expression in Urdu. Similarly, in the sixteenth century
Bayazid Ansari became the first poet of the Pashto language, as did Qāzi Qadan
of the Sindhi language, Muhammad Jiv Jan of Gujarati, and Habba Khatun of
Kashmiri. In the eighteenth century, the Sufi Jam Durrek became the first poet
in the Baluchi dialect.

writing leaves us piecing together fragmentary and often conflicting information about these saints.

The most reliable sources we have about Sheikh Farid's life – his deeds and sayings – are those written closest to his lifetime, recording the memories of people who had direct contact with him. For example, the recollections of his disciple and successor Hazrat Nizamuddin Auliya provide a rare and intimate glimpse of Baba Farid. As a first-hand account we can expect it to be accurate, not only in the facts related but also in conveying the atmosphere of spirituality that surrounded the beloved sheikh. In Nizamuddin's reminiscences we catch the scent of the love between disciple and pir as the sweetness of Sheikh Farid's warmth and tender caring is revealed.

After the publication of Attar's *Memoirs of the Saints* around 1200 CE, the *tazkirat* became a popular genre of Sufi literature. In each *tazkirat* the sayings and deeds of a given saint are pieced together to create a kind of biography. In each case, these anecdotes are presented as traditions that have been passed down orally through the centuries until the time when the *tazkirat* is published. The fourteenth, fifteenth, sixteenth – and particularly the seventeenth – centuries brought a profusion of these works. Understandably, with the lapse of time after a saint's death, widely different versions of incidents are told. As always in the stories of saints, miracles begin to take a prominent place in the tales.

In the case of Sheikh Farid, books written hundreds of years after his lifetime seem preoccupied with the idea of his extreme asceticism, describing more and more excruciating forms of self-mortification. Surely it is a fact that Sheikh Farid fasted; his life was one of what we might today call 'radical simplicity.' Earlier sources, however, focus less on how little he ate and more on his unstinting hospitality, giving his all to the poor and to his disciples. As portrayed in the earlier sources, we hear less about extreme ascetic practices and more about his ardent and ever-present love of God. Sheikh Farid's verses give voice to this intense love.

Sometimes accounts in later sources display the values and prejudices of their own times. For example, texts written in the time of the Mughal Empire (two to six centuries after his death) often present dramatic legends of Sheikh Farid converting people from Hinduism to Islam, sometimes with displays of miraculous power or even violence. In the earlier sources there is no evidence that he ever converted anyone to Islam, or that he had any intention to convert people. He welcomed all people to his congregation – rich and poor, high and low caste, men and women, Hindu and Muslim.

In presenting events from the life of Sheikh Farid, we have relied on the earliest known sources. Where later sources give information that conflicts with that of the earlier sources, we have deemed the source closest to Sheikh Farid's own time the more reliable.

The most reliable source used is *Morals for the Heart* (*Fawa'id-ul-Fu'ad*), a record of conversations with Nizamuddin, the successor of Sheikh Farid. In these conversations Nizamuddin frequently refers to incidents involving his pir, often incidents where he himself was present. The conversations were recorded by Amir Hasan Sijzi, a disciple of Nizamuddin. Nizamuddin went over the manuscript with him, making corrections as needed.

Morals for the Heart was the first work of its kind. It was immediately popular among Sufi circles. The record of informal conversations between sheikh and disciples (a book of sayings called a *malfuzat*) became a common means of conveying Sufi teachings. Among these, *The Best of the Assemblies* (*Khayr al-Majalis*) may also be considered relatively reliable. Although documented two generations after Sheikh Farid, the manuscript was known to have been carefully corrected by Nasiruddin Dehlavi.

Another early source is *Disposition of the Saints* (*Siyar al-Auliya*), written by a disciple of Nizamuddin, Amir Khurd. The author's father and grandfather were both disciples of Sheikh Farid and spent much of their lives living in close company with him. Amir Khurd recorded events related to him by his father and grandfather as first-hand witnesses, as well as events related by his sheikh, Nizamuddin. Moreover, Amir Khurd himself was a gifted Sufi poet of whom it was said that his "verse exhibits the humility, the pathos and the directness of one who has travelled the Path."[8] His book captures the essence, the spiritual message, conveyed in the stories of Sheikh Farid.

Several other books written by the generation of disciples of Nizamuddin may also be considered relatively reliable. However, some obvious legendizing has already begun, and information in different accounts is contradictory. Ultimately, as much as we may attempt to paint an accurate picture of the historical Sheikh Farid, it must be admitted that, to some extent, we are dealing with his legend. None of these early sources sets out to relate a complete biography of the saint; rather they offer us incidents, events, and glimpses of Sheikh Farid, along with his sayings and his teachings.

The noted scholar, Bruce Lawrence, titled his work on the early Sufis in India *Notes from a Distant Flute*. It is an apt metaphor. Reading the verses said to have been sung by Sheikh Farid over 700 years ago, pondering the incidents and conversations passed down to us through the centuries from this long-ago saint, is rather like hearing the notes of a flute wafted on a breeze from far away. The delicate tones, muffled by the shifting breeze, speak of a beauty that stirs in us that same longing for divine union that drew disciples to Sheikh Farid in his own lifetime.

The Oral Tradition

The verses by Sheikh Farid presented in this book were composed orally and sung repeatedly. With their melodies and rhythm, these rhymed couplets were remembered and passed down orally, and have become part and parcel of Punjabi culture.

By the twelfth and thirteenth centuries, when Sheikh Farid lived, the Sufi tradition of expressing mystical teachings through poetry was already well established. Muslim singers of mystical verse (*qawwals*) travelled throughout the areas where Sufis had settled, singing verses of love and longing for the Divine. Poetry has a mysterious quality that makes it particularly apt for conveying mystical teachings. With its visual imagery and compact language, it may open the heart and allow the essence of its meaning to penetrate the barrier of intellectuality. The listener feels its impact, perhaps without always being able to articulate why. With music the impression may penetrate still deeper. We read of Sufis who enter an ecstatic state simply by hearing a particularly beautiful mystical verse being sung.

Today it is difficult for us to imagine an oral tradition that accurately passed down poems through successive generations. Perhaps, knowing that these verses were sung may make this easier to believe. Still, we know that language changes over time, and it is reasonable to assume that these verses have undergone some change. With the influence of Persian idioms on the Multani dialect, and the subsequent evolution from Multani to Punjabi, the wording in verses repeated generation after generation may well have evolved. For some of the verses, scholars have even raised questions as to which language – Persian or Multani – was the original one used by Sheikh Farid.

Aside from these questions of language, it is natural to wonder if the disciples in the lineage of Sheikh Farid have added some verses, striving to convey what they had learned through Sheikh Farid. Later sheikhs in the Chishti lineage could have added further verses in Farid's name. This is particularly plausible given the practice in many spiritual traditions for one mystic poet to attribute poetry to a revered spiritual teacher.

Scholars have debated – and continue to debate – whether all the verses ascribed to Sheikh Farid were actually composed by him. Can we trust the oral transmission of verses sung, heard, and remembered, generation after generation? When do we find the earliest record of them in written form? How reliable is the source where they are recorded? These questions are discussed in the poetry section presented later in this book. We have made every effort to meticulously select those verses of Sheikh Farid that are confirmed in the earliest texts. It may be impossible, however, to completely separate the historical individual, Sheikh Farid, from his legacy of spiritual teachings. Notwithstanding these difficulties, the poetry that has been passed down to us still serves to illuminate those high spiritual teachings.

Life & Teachings

Youth and Discipleship

FARIDUDDIN MAS'UD – better known as Sheikh Farid and Baba Farid – was born in the Punjab soon after his family arrived as immigrants.* He was descended from a long line of scholars ('alim) originally from Kufa, a city south of Baghdad.[1] From Kufa, his ancestors moved eastward to Balkh, an area in northern Iran that was home to many distinguished Sufis of the eighth and ninth centuries. Ibrahim ibn Adham (718–782 CE), the king in Balkh who left his throne to pursue the mystic path, is counted among Farid's ancestors.† By the eleventh century, Farid's family had migrated further east and settled in Kabul.

Some historians believe that Farid's grandfather, Sheikh Shu'aib, was connected to the ruling family in Kabul and may have been the son of Farrukh Shah, the ruler of Kabul. Historical accounts differ about which tribe attacked and conquered Kabul around 1125 CE and whether or not Farrukh Shah was killed in this attack, but around that time Farid's grandfather, Sheikh Shu'aib, left Kabul with "his three sons, followers, army and family" and moved to Lahore.[2]

The busy, pressured pace of life in Lahore did not appeal to Sheikh Shu'aib, nor did the jockeying for position among the

---

*His birthdate is given as either 1173 or 1175; because Nizamuddin says he was 93 years old at his death in 1265, we will use the earlier birthdate.
†The life story of Ibrahim ibn Adham is narrated by such eminent Muslim writers as al-Bukhari (810–870 CE), Attar (1142–1220 CE), and perhaps most extensively by Rumi (1207–1273 CE) in the *Masnavi*.

elite scholars. He moved his family to the quieter town of Qasur. When the ruler of the region understood the circumstances under which this distinguished family had sought refuge in Lahore, he sent a very polite message asking how he could be of service to Sheikh Shu'aib. The sheikh, who apparently had seen enough of worldly power and glory, replied, "We do not want to run after a thing which has been lost to us." The sultan then appointed him magistrate (*qāzi*) of the small village of Kothiwal, near the city of Multan.[3]

Sheikh Shu'aib's second son, Jamaluddin Suleman, who was a noted scholar in Lahore, was appointed *qāzi* of Kothiwal after his father's death. He was married to Qarsum Bibi, the daughter of Sheikh Wajihuddin, and they had three sons and a daughter. Their second son, born in 1173 CE, was named Fariduddin Mas'ud, later known as Sheikh Farid – or as he is often called in the Punjab, Baba Farid – using the respectful honorific 'Baba' to mean wise elder, father or grandfather.

Childhood

Farid's father died when Farid was quite young, but the influence of his father, an eminent scholar, can be seen in the high value he placed on education and scholarship. In Islam, it is considered a sacred duty incumbent on all men and women to seek knowledge.[4] While certain schools of Sufi thought see mysticism in opposition to scholarship, most Sufis, including Sheikh Farid, have understood the study of philosophical and religious texts as part of the discipline that supports mystical development.

The strongest influence in Farid's childhood was his mother, Qarsum Bibi. Her example of deep devotion and disciplined spirituality must have made a profound impression on the young boy's character. While raising her three sons and one daughter and attending to all the daily duties of a household, Qarsum Bibi reportedly stayed awake most of the night in prayer. Legends illustrating her high spiritual attainment have been passed down through the centuries. It is said that one night a thief broke into the house, but was so struck by the radiance that surrounded the lady as she prayed that he abandoned the idea of stealing and changed his ways. In another version of this story, the thief who entered the house was actually struck blind. Instinctively understanding that his blindness was due to the spiritual station of the lady who was deep in prayer, he pleaded for mercy. Only when he promised Qarsum Bibi he would reform was his sight restored.[5]

Qarsum Bibi's all-night praying suggests that she could have been a practising Sufi, though there is no record to substantiate this. As a devoted Muslim, she would certainly have prayed five times a day and observed all the obligations of Islamic law. It was a practice of many Sufis, however, to devote the night-time to incessant prayer. In the Chishti Sufi Order – the lineage of spiritual masters that includes Sheikh Farid – women were initiated as disciples. The Chishti masters would often say that the greatness of a person lay in the purity of their mind, not whether they were male or female.

Guided by Qarsum Bibi from a tender and impressionable age, both Farid and his younger brother Najibuddin Mutawakkil were eventually drawn to the Sufi path. While Farid was still quite young, his saintly mother apparently set out to train him to pray regularly, lovingly, and with pleasure. She told him that each time he prayed with love and devotion in his heart, Allah would put a sweet under his prayer mat. Then, while the young boy was absorbed in prayer, she would slip a sweet under the corner of the mat. And, of course, at the end of his prayers he always looked and was delighted to find the sweet, his gift from God.

One day his mother forgot to place the sweet under the mat. When she realized her mistake, she was deeply distraught and prayed fervently that Farid's faith in God would not be shaken.[6]

One version of this legend says that the young boy finished his prayers, looked under the mat and, miraculously, found a sweet. This miracle not only saved Farid's faith, but also strengthened his mother's trust and deep reliance on the Lord. Another version says that when Farid finished his prayers, he told his mother there was no need to put a sweet under his prayer mat anymore, because he was enjoying the sweetness of the Lord's presence.

Regardless of variations in the story, Farid developed an association of sweetness with the Lord from a very young age. Many years later he celebrated that sweetness in one of his best-known verses, preserved as Sloka 27 in the Adi Granth:

> Sweet are sugar and candy
>> and honey and buffalo's milk.*
> Yea, sweet are all of these,
>> but sweeter by far is God![7]

This popular verse resonates with the image of sugar that has become so much a part of his name: Treasure of Sweetness (*Ganj-i shakar*).

With the influence of his mother, a devotional bent of mind was nurtured in Farid. As a child he preferred to spend much of his days behind the mosque in Kothiwal praying rather than playing with the other children. By the time he was an adolescent, he was known throughout the village as an unusually pious boy. From the point of view of some villagers, he was even seen as eccentric or crazy to be so one-pointed in his fervent life of prayer. When a well-known Sufi, Sheikh Jalaluddin Tabrizi, passed through Kothiwal on his way to Delhi, he asked among the villagers if there were any mystics in the town. They answered that there

---

*Water buffaloes are domesticated as dairy cattle in India and their milk is highly prized for its rich quality.

weren't any Sufis, but that the *qāzi's* crazy son could always be found praying behind the mosque.

Sheikh Jalaluddin Tabrizi (from Tabriz, in present-day Iran) was the disciple and successor of Abu Saʿid Tabrizi.* One might wonder how he happened to be passing through the small, out-of-the-way village of Kothiwal, so far from his home. In the thirteenth century, Sufis often spent decades travelling to meet the great mystics of their day, to hear their discourses, to be inspired, and to continue their own learning on the spiritual path. Two close and lifelong friendships brought Sheikh Tabrizi to the area between Multan and Delhi. One was with Sheikh Qutbuddin Bakhtiyar Kaki, who was to become Farid's spiritual master. Sheikh Bakhtiyar Kaki invited Sheikh Tabrizi to Delhi, where he stayed some months with his friend. The other was Sheikh Shihabuddin Suhrawardi's young successor, Sheikh Bahauddin Zakariya, who had established his centre in Multan. On the day when Sheikh Tabrizi stopped in the village of Kothiwal, Farid would have been between eight and fifteen years old.

One of the villagers made a gift of a pomegranate to the eminent Sufi, and Sheikh Tabrizi went off to find the boy whom the villagers thought was so crazy to pray all the time. Breaking open the pomegranate, the Sufi offered it to young Farid. The boy explained that he was fasting and refused the gift. Sheikh Tabrizi was highly pleased with Farid's discipline and stayed to chat with him a while. He noticed, however, that Farid's trousers were in shreds and that the boy kept trying to hide the holes in the ragged fabric. Realizing that he was embarrassed, Sheikh Tabrizi kindly said, "There was a *dervish* (a Sufi disciple) in Bukhara who was busy in education. For seven years he had no trousers and wore only a loincloth. Don't be worried. See what happens."[8]

---

*After many years of travelling, Jalaluddin Tabrizi settled in Bengal, where he established his centre and began initiating disciples. His shrine is still visited by many pilgrims today.

After Sheikh Tabrizi left, Farid finished his devotions. When he got up to go home, he noticed that one seed from the pomegranate had fallen on the ground. He picked it up and wrapped it in his handkerchief. Later, at the time of breaking his fast, he ate the seed and experienced a sudden spiritual illumination. Realizing that the uplift and inner light he enjoyed was the result of Sheikh Tabrizi's blessing, young Farid was filled with remorse for having been so foolish as to refuse the whole pomegranate, a gift freely offered from a Sufi master.[9]

If Farid's mother had taught him the sweetness of devotion, Sheikh Tabrizi taught him the power of contact – however brief – with a Sufi master.

Sheikh Tabrizi was among the first generation of travelling Sufis who ventured into what was then called Hindustan. Khwaja Muinuddin Chishti's historic first trip into the Punjab had occurred in 1165, ten years before Farid's birth. During that journey Khwaja Chishti – who was eventually to establish the most influential Sufi Order in India – stayed in Multan, near Kothiwal, and then in Lahore. The Khwaja returned for a second journey through the Punjab when Farid was eight years old. After a stay in the Punjab, the Khwaja continued on into Rajasthan. It was on this trip that Khwaja Chishti finally settled in Ajmer and established his centre there.

Meeting His Spiritual Master

When Farid was eighteen, he left his home in Kothiwal and went to Multan to continue his education. By that time the city of Multan had become a great seat of learning. Farid joined the school (*madrassa*) in the mosque of Maulana Minhajuddin Tirmizi. In the course of his studies there, he committed the entire Qur'an to memory. He also studied various texts in Persian and Arabic, including books of Islamic law.

One day, as he was reading a book on Muslim law titled *Nāfi*, he noticed a Sufi deep in prayer. The stranger had newly arrived in Multan, and Farid did not know who he was. He was drawn by a spontaneous, inexplicable certainty that this was his spiritual master. With the book still in hand he went and sat down near the stranger and waited for him to finish his prayers.

At last, the Sufi turned toward him and, with an affectionate smile, asked, "Maulana! What book is this?" Farid told him it was *Nāfi*. The stranger, making a play on the word *naf* (benefit), said, "May there be *naf* (benefit) for you in its study." To this, Farid replied, "There is benefit for me in your mercy and blessings." He placed his head at the feet of Qutbuddin Bakhtiyar Kaki and recited the following verses:

He, who is approved by you, is approved eternally
And no one is disappointed of your blessing.
Your mere attention to any particle, even for a while
Makes it better than a thousand suns.[10]

In that moment the closest bond of Farid's life was forged, the bond with his pir. According to Sufi understanding, the spontaneous attraction Farid felt in that moment signalled an intuitive recognition of a bond that belonged to eternity, not to time and space. In the Sufi tradition, the importance of the spiritual guide – called the pir, or sheikh, or murshid – in the life of the disciple can hardly be overstated. As Sheikh Bakhtiyar Kaki himself was advised by his pir, Khwaja Chishti, "The nearness of Allah cannot be acquired without the company of a perfect spiritual guide."[11] This fundamental principle has been conveyed down through the Chishti lineage of masters to present times.

Sheikh Zahurul Hassan Sharib, a twentieth-century sheikh in the Chishti lineage, explains, "Mysticism is essentially practical in nature. It cannot be learnt from books alone. It is only in the company of the spiritual guide that one can learn, imbibe, and appreciate the implications of mysticism."[12] He draws a stark distinction between discipleship and merely following a philosophy:

> Discipleship means personal, passionate, and unflinching devotion to a person. It is important to note that devotion to a person and devotion to a principle, or to a cause, are not the same. Mysticism does not proclaim a cause. It enjoins personal devotion. To be a disciple is to be a love-slave of his spiritual guide and teacher. We may admire a man. We may pay him respect and utmost reverence, but if we are not devoted to him, we cannot be said to be his disciple.[13]

Service and obedience to the pir are key elements of discipleship. As Sheik Sharib puts it, "a disciple must submit his whole self and will to his spiritual guide and teacher. He should run at his bidding."[14] Further, he says, the base of such selfless service is love:

> Love and devotion are the fundamental planks of discipleship. Our heart, our soul, our mind, our nerves, even our own personality should blaze, glow and grow with devotion to the spiritual guide. A disciple should be consistent and firm in his devotion. It is not enough to be consistent with hard and fast creeds. No formal ceremony is necessary for initiation as a disciple. The silken cords of love and devotion are enough. They act as a cementing force.[15]

The love that spontaneously bound Farid to his pir at that first meeting set the course for his life. As a child he had learned to relish the sweetness of the divine presence in prayer. Longing for that sweet presence had driven him to a solitary childhood, teased as 'the *qāzi*'s crazy son' as he followed an irresistible pull to prayer. He now had the support and spiritual companionship of his pir. In the company of Sheikh Bakhtiyar Kaki, he was finally able to unburden his heart. He told his teacher of the pomegranate that Sheikh Tabrizi had offered him, a single seed of which had opened his spiritual vision, and of his distress and shame over having refused the whole fruit. His pir set his heart at ease, saying, "Don't worry. All the spiritual blessing for you was in that one seed. It was destined for you, and it reached you. There was nothing in the rest of the fruit."[16]

Sheikh Qutbuddin Bakhtiyar Kaki

Sheikh Bakhtiyar Kaki has been described as a reclusive, love-intoxicated mystic strongly drawn to the practice of listening to the singing of mystical poetry (*sama*)* as a means to enter deep meditative states. By character, he was probably more inclined to the private ecstasy of spiritual experience than to the large public role that his pir, Khwaja Chishti, assigned to him.

Reliable details of Sheikh Bakhtiyar Kaki's life are scarce. He was born and raised in the city of Uch (in present-day Afghanistan).† As a youth, Bakhtiyar Kaki was strongly influenced by the Oneness of Being (*Wahdat al-Wujud*) philosophy – the doctrine that God and his creation are not two separate entities, but that all being is one unity.[17]

He may have been an adolescent when he travelled to Baghdad. A number of eminent Sufi sheikhs were in Baghdad at the time, and their discourses drew large gatherings. Bakhtiyar Kaki, eager for spiritual insight, attended many of these discourses. He spent some time in association with Sheikh Suhrawardi, the founder of

---

*For a discussion on *sama*, see the appendix.
†Uch is a centre for followers of Mansur al-Hallaj who was martyred for proclaiming, "I am the Truth. I am God."

the Suhrawardi Order. Here he met his friend Jalaluddin Tabrizi, who was also attending the discourses.

Bakhtiyar Kaki had great respect for Sheikh Suhrawardi, but it was not until he met Khwaja Chishti that he recognized his own master. Little is known about his initiation or his period of spiritual training under Khwaja Chishti's guidance. Conflicting stories have been passed down to us about when and where Khwaja Chishti bestowed the *khilafat nama* (the certificate authorizing him to initiate disciples) on Sheikh Bakhtiyar Kaki. What is agreed is that he instructed him to go to Delhi and establish his *khanqah* there. A *khanqah* (literally meaning a house of prayer) is a Sufi gathering place, a hostel where disciples and visitors can stay. It would become Sheikh Bakhtiyar Kaki's home and the centre where he would initiate and guide disciples.

Among Sufis it was common for a master to appoint one or more successors during his lifetime. A master would send each successor to a different location to serve and guide the spiritual seekers who came to him there, according to a principle known as *wilayat*.* Khwaja Chishti had two main successors: Sheikh Bakhtiyar Kaki in Delhi and Qāzi Hamiduddin Nagauriin Nagaur.

Sheikh Bakhtiyar Kaki may have been reclusive by temperament, but his sheikh's instructions were to go to the teeming capital city of Delhi and feed the hungry. He was to hear the complaints of the distressed and to stand by them. Khwaja Chishti instructed him to repay any and all enmity with unstinting friendship and at all times to maintain equanimity. He was to express joy even in times of grief. All in all, he was to "become such a type of *dervish* who may pose to be rich."[18] The literal meaning of *dervish* is a beggar or a pauper; it is used to mean a mystic in the sense of spiritual poverty – one who is empty of self, empty of

---

*For more information about *wilayat*, see the section on Multan and Ajodhan: A Study in Contrasts.

the world, empty of all desires. The meaning of Khwaja Chishti's instruction was that Sheikh Bakhtiyar Kaki should be a bounteous giver; whatever came to him should be given away, no matter how little he actually had.

Sheikh Bakhtiyar Kaki went first to Multan and stayed there a while, perhaps preparing himself for the task he was to take on, before he proceeded to Delhi. When he arrived in Delhi, Sultan Iltutmish welcomed him warmly and begged him to settle near the palace. The sultan was deeply pious and may have had leanings towards Sufi spirituality himself. Sheikh Bakhtiyar Kaki, however, refused his invitation and settled on the outskirts of the city.

This was in keeping with his master's teachings. Khwaja Chishti advised his followers to avoid all dealings with rulers. Accepting favours from rulers would, he taught, invariably lead to a loss of one's spiritual independence. The Chishti lineage of Sufi masters has continued to follow this guidance. In fact, the Chishti sheikhs, including Sheikh Farid, have been adept at avoiding entanglement with the power struggles of political leaders.

Sheikh Bakhtiyar Kaki never visited the sultan's court or gave permission for the sultan to visit his *khanqah*.[19] It is said that even without this permission, Sultan Iltutmish humbly visited Sheikh Bakhtiyar Kaki's *khanqah* outside the city twice a week.[20] Once Sheikh Bakhtiyar Kaki advised the sultan:

O ruler of Delhi: It is incumbent on thee to be good to all poor people, mendicants, dervishes and helpless folk. Treat all men kindly and strive for their welfare. Everyone who thus behaves towards his subjects is looked after by the Almighty and all his enemies turn into friends.[21]

Sultan Iltutmish offered Sheikh Bakhtiyar Kaki the highly coveted honorary title of *Sheikh al-Islam*, but he refused this honour. So Iltutmish conferred the title of *Sheikh al-Islam* on another Sufi sheikh in Delhi, Najmuddin Sughra. But since the sultan and the populace at large continued to show ever more reverence to Sheikh Bakhtiyar Kaki, Sughra became jealous and he tried to undercut the influence of Sheikh Bakhtiyar Kaki. He tried to incite the religious scholars (*ulema*) against Sheikh Bakhtiyar Kaki by complaining about his practice of *sama* as a means to reach ecstatic states – a practice the scholars considered bordering on heresy.

Khwaja Chishti visited his beloved disciple and successor in Delhi twice, once in 1212, and once in 1224. During the second of these visits the tensions with Sheikh Najmuddin Sughra came to a head. Khwaja Chishti, understanding the unpleasantness of the situation, went to see Sughra, who was having a platform built in front of his house as a sign of his importance.

> He [Chishti] approached closer and said, "Perhaps the pride of becoming Sheikh al-Islam has overcome you." Sheikh Najmuddin replied, "I am still just as devoted to you but you have placed a *murid* [disciple] in this city who does not understand the implications of my position as Sheikh al-Islam." Muinuddin [Chishti] smiled and said, "Do not worry. I will take Baba Qutbuddin [Bakhtiyar Kaki] away with me."

> In those days the reputation of Qutbuddin [Bakhtiyar Kaki] in Delhi had reached the greatest heights. The whole population of the city was turned towards him. When Sheikh Muinuddin [Chishti] returned to his house, he said, "Baba Bakhtiyar, you have become so well known that people are complaining of you. Come and stay with me in Ajmer. I will serve you properly." Sheikh Qutbuddin [Bakhtiyar Kaki] submitted, "I have not the impertinence to sit before my Lord or even to stand before him."[22]

With these words he signalled his unquestioning obedience to his sheikh's order. What is delightful in this interchange is both the delicacy of Khwaja Chishti's handling of Sheikh Sughra, and also the ease with which Sheikh Bakhtiyar Kaki was ready to leave his fame – and the strife it provoked – behind him. However, as the two of them walked out of the city, word spread and soon large numbers of people, including the sultan himself, followed them.

> As Sheikh Qutbuddin [Bakhtiyar Kaki] passed, people took up the dust he had trodden on and displayed signs of worry and distress. When Muinuddin [Chishti] saw this, he said, "Baba Bakhtiyar, make this your place because the people are so sorely distressed at your departing. I do not wish to cause so much misery and heartbreak. Go, I have left the city [Delhi] under your protection.[23]

So Sheikh Bakhtiyar Kaki remained in Delhi.

Grasping the Hand of His Sheikh

Traditional accounts differ about exactly when and where Farid's initiation took place. Some say that Sheikh Bakhtiyar Kaki left Multan soon after meeting Farid, and that Farid travelled with him to Delhi where he was initiated. A long list of important Sufi sheikhs are said to have been present at the initiation, indicating its significance.

According to other accounts, Sheikh Bakhtiyar Kaki initiated Farid in Multan. Farid then accompanied him partway to Delhi – "up to three stages only" of the journey. At that point, the sheikh said, "Baba Farid! Remain busy in external education along with this other-worldliness and celibacy. Come to Delhi afterwards."[24] Farid, who was only eighteen years old at the time, returned to Multan and completed his education as his pir had instructed.

In Sufism, initiation is called *bayat*, meaning a pact, a bond, an oath of allegiance sworn between two people. Sheikh Sharib, who was an attorney by training, explains *bayat* using the language of contracts:

> The relation subsisting between the disciple and the teacher is everlasting. It is not a contract voidable at the option of either party. The dictum governing the mutual relations is that once a disciple, always a disciple, nothing but a disciple.[25]

Hazrat Inayat Khan, another twentieth-century Sufi, echoes the same sense that the oath of allegiance sworn at the time of the *bayat* "belongs to eternity":

> I heard from my murshid, from my initiator, something which I shall never forget: "This friendship, this relationship which is brought about by initiation between two persons, is something which cannot be broken; it is something which cannot be separated; it is something which cannot be compared with anything else in the world; it belongs to eternity."[26]

Colloquially, Sufis refer to initiation as 'grasping the hand of the sheikh.' This expression gives a hint of the loving relationship that is cemented by the oath of allegiance at the time of initiation: the master offers his hand to help and support the disciple; the disciple grasps his hand to accept his loving protection. Sheikh Sharib writes:

> The spiritual guide is, at once, a guide and philosopher to his disciples. By accepting the hand of his disciple, he has agreed to be responsible for the moral, spiritual, and ethical development of his disciple. The spiritual teacher must stand by his disciple and lend him his helping hand.[27]

Education and Travels

After his initiation Sheikh Farid spent some time away from the company of his pir; sources differ about how long. In some accounts, after finishing his studies in Multan, Farid went to Qandahar for further education and stayed there for five years. Only after his studies in Multan and Qandahar did Farid come to Delhi to stay in the *khanqah* of his pir.[28] Another account skips this period of his life altogether, taking him straight to Delhi.

Regardless of the version one believes of this period of Sheikh Farid's life, it is clear that he was highly educated. He is described discussing difficult Arabic or Persian texts with his disciples, sometimes correcting defective manuscripts – a skill that implies in-depth knowledge of the text. Poetry seemed to spring from his lips, both his own verses composed on the spot, as well as verses quoted from memory. In fact, his knowledge of the Qur'an and its various readings, his interpretation and commentary on its scripture, as well as his understanding of Islamic law and the subtlest points of Arabic grammar were impressive even to specialists. In general, during this period, a Sufi sheikh was expected to be highly educated, so it is reasonable to assume that he must have devoted some significant period of time to studies. Baba Farid's attitude towards scholarship illustrates this melding of knowledge, self-knowledge, and human virtue. Historian Mohamed Taher notes that:

> Baba Farid was a great lover of knowledge and scholarship. It was his firm conviction that without knowledge it is very difficult to discipline the self [the lower self, the lower mind] and to traverse the path of love. Knowledge, says Baba Farid, is a divine gift for the individual.... Therefore, one should make an earnest effort for the attainment of knowledge. He should not mind humiliation and disgrace in the way of attaining knowledge. Religion, in the opinion of Baba Farid, can be

protected through knowledge. The Prophet used to say that blessed is the man whose knowledge of his own faults and defects prevents him from disclosing the faults of others.[29]

Traditional accounts add a long series of travels to Sheikh Farid's itinerary, perhaps after his studies and before settling in Delhi with his sheikh. He is said to have travelled within the Punjab and within what was then known as Hindustan: to Kashmir, to Ajmer (in Rajasthan), and to the region of Malwa. In particular, Farid's visit to a city in the Punjab known at that time as Mokal Nagar is corroborated by many writers. This city was later renamed Faridkot in honour of his stay.

Sheikh Farid is also said to have visited such far-flung places as Ghazni, Khurasan, Baghdad, Bukhara, Badakhshan, and Kirman (cities in present-day Afghanistan, Iraq and Iran) and to have met with many highly regarded Sufis, receiving their blessings. These travels are not mentioned in the earliest sources, and most historians today doubt their authenticity. However, Sloka 20 in the Adi Granth – in which he is reminding the reader of the facts of aging and of the transience of life – indicate that he possibly did make extensive journeys on foot:

> Farid, with these small legs,
>   I crossed deserts and mountains.
> But today, Farid, my water jug seems
>   hundreds of miles away.[30]

We may not be able to answer the questions of whether Sheikh Farid travelled, or how far he travelled, but we can presume that during this period of being physically separated from his pir, Farid missed being in his master's company. For some disciples, being separated physically from one's pir ignites the fire of longing; for others, too long a separation can gradually extinguish it. Distracted from one's purpose, one can lose focus.

Baba Farid's disciple and successor, Hazrat Nizamuddin Auliya, once spoke with his disciples about how Farid made sure he did not lose focus during his long separation from his pir. According to Nizamuddin, Farid invented for himself a kind of private recommitment ceremony. He had a garment of Sheikh Bakhtiyar Kaki, presumably a personal gift from the sheikh. Keeping this garment with him, he would periodically take some time alone and solemnly re-state his oath of allegiance, the oath taken at the time of initiation. In this way he renewed and refreshed his connection with his pir. As Nizamuddin told his own disciples, Farid "renewed his allegiance to Sheikh Qutbuddin [Bakhtiyar Kaki] many times in this fashion, and I have followed his example."[31]

In turn, Nizamuddin offered his disciples comforting reassurance for those who must spend extended periods of time away from their spiritual guide. His disciple, Amir Hasan Sijzi, asked this question:

"If it happens that a disciple comes to see his master less and less, but remembers him more and more at home, what does this signify?" "It is better," replied the master, "for someone to be absent from his master and remember him than to be present with him all day yet not be touched by his love." Then this verse came to his blessed lips:

Better out than in, if out while you are in![32]

In the Company of His Sheikh
Once he had completed his education (and travels, if any), Sheikh Farid went to Delhi. Medieval accounts are unclear about how

long Farid stayed in the *khanqah* of Sheikh Bakhtiyar Kaki in Delhi. Some say he lived there for twenty years; others say he only visited in the *khanqah* on several occasions for varying periods of time.

Sheikh Gesu Daraz, a sheikh in the lineage three generations after Sheikh Farid, was asked, "How did Sheikh Qutbuddin train Sheikh Fariduddin?" He replied that Sheikh Farid had joined Sheikh Qutbuddin's discipline after he had already acquired complete spiritual ability (*ista'dād-i-tamām*). He had needed little instruction and did not stay in the *khanqah* for long.[33] There is no way to know which version of Farid's life we are to believe.

We do know that while Farid was with Sheikh Bakhtiyar Kaki, he was able to ask him questions and receive guidance on some knotty issues. The exchanges that have been passed down to us offer a glimpse into the subtle wisdom of Sheikh Bakhtiyar Kaki. Once, for example, Farid asked Sheikh Bakhtiyar Kaki: "People approach me asking for amulets. What should I do? Should I write and give them?" Seeking amulets from holy men for curing sickness or other problems was common throughout the medieval world, across many cultures. An amulet could be any object deemed to carry spiritual power from the holy person. Sheikh Bakhtiyar Kaki himself would often give as an amulet a few written words, such as a holy phrase from the Qur'an or one of the names of God. The sheikh answered Farid, "This work rests neither in your hands nor in mine. The amulet is God's name; write and give them God's word!"[34]

In the Sufi view, however, the value of being in the company of one's sheikh goes far beyond merely answering questions. As the modern Chishti Sheikh Sharib puts it, "There can be no doubt that [the] society of the spiritual guide and teacher is the best training school for the disciple.... To see the face of his spiritual guide is a great blessing for the disciple."[35]

The spiritual station of the sheikh has an influence on all who come in contact with him. Sheikh Farid often recited the following verse in Persian:*

> If your desire is to find your soul
>> look for it among the People of the Heart
>> so you too may become what they are.[36]

'People of the Heart' is a Sufi expression meaning highly advanced mystics, those who are advanced in the way of divine love. Their hearts are on fire with longing for and love of the Divine, and they radiate something of that intoxicating love and longing to those around them.

Paradoxically, given the stress Sufis lay on the value of time spent in the pir's company, the literature of this period is peppered with instances of Sufis who reached complete spiritual realization in virtually no time after meeting their pir. Such was the case of Sheikh Zakariya, Sheikh Suhrawardi's successor who established his *khanqah* in Multan.

> He had been with Sheikh Shihabuddin [Suhrawardi] but seventeen days when, on the seventeenth day, Sheikh Shihabuddin conferred on him his blessings (and dismissed him as a fully empowered disciple).... In but seventeen days ... Sheikh Bahauddin [Zakariya] obtained the blessings that other disciples had not acquired in years. So rapid was his success that some of the older disciples took offense, complaining, 'We have spent so many years in the saint's presence and yet we had no such favours conferred on us.'

---

*The author of the verse is unknown. According to Abidi, the medieval text *Rahat ul-Qulub* tells us that Sheikh Farid often repeated it. In the tradition of oral composition of poems, it could possibly imply that he composed the verse.

Their murmurings reached the ears of Sheikh Shihabuddin. He made this reply to them: 'You brought wet wood. How can wet wood catch fire. But Zakariya brought dry wood. With one puff he went up in flames.'[37]

Sufi literature of this period also offers examples of disciples who spent long years of service and uninterrupted attendance on their sheikh before – seemingly all in an instant – complete realization was given, as a gift from the sheikh. Such was the case of Khwaja Chishti himself who said:

After receiving the blessing of becoming the disciple of Usman Harwani, I spent the next twenty years in his service. Never for a second or a minute did I spend time on my own comfort rather than in his service during all those twenty years. I carried his bedding whether at home or on journeys.[38]

Khwaja Chishti's journeys with Usman Harwani were rigorous, traversing thousands of miles through deserts and rugged mountain passes. At length, however, the master, "recognizing my services and being pleased with me, at last conferred upon me such gifts which can neither be described nor circumscribed."[39]

In the case of Sheikh Farid, the medieval sources simply do not tell us how long he spent in the company of Sheikh Bakhtiyar Kaki. The only dates that seem clear and consistent are that he met his pir at age 18, and that he was aged 62 when Sheikh Bakhtiyar Kaki died, leaving Sheikh Farid as his successor and head of the Chishti Sufi Order. In between these dates, there is not enough consistency in the various accounts to map out when and for how long he was in any one place.

In the *Khanqah* in Delhi

While staying at Sheikh Bakhtiyar Kaki's *khanqah*, however, Sheikh Farid apparently spent much of his time in the solitude of his cell, devoted to the spiritual practices. He must have been strongly drawn to the silence and solitude of a reclusive life, so much so that even while living in the *khanqah* he only saw Sheikh Bakhtiyar Kaki twice a month. The other disciples joined in the communal life of the *khanqah* to a much greater extent, including visiting the sheikh very frequently.[40]

Sufi discipline advocated communal life, rather than a withdrawal into a hermitage. In the Sufi view, interacting with others was needed to challenge the disciple to develop such human virtues as patience, kindness, and generosity of spirit. As the scholar and historian Khaliq Ahmad Nizami puts it, "mystics knew that a life of solitary contemplation would not provide enough of the ordinary day-to-day contact in which we learn how to deal with the inevitable conflicts with compassion. We can only reach for the mystic ideal by learning how to rub shoulders with our fellow human beings with humility."[41]

This emphasis on communal living lay behind the establishment of *khanqahs*, which sprang up in towns and cities as each new Sufi sheikh was appointed by his master to initiate and teach disciples. Chishti *khanqahs* were especially busy, bustling places. All visitors were welcome, whether Hindu or Muslim, rich or poor, yogi adept or unlettered labourer. All who came were fed, free of charge, and this work of welcoming and caring for the visitors was a service undertaken by the sheikh as well as the disciples. Life in the busy *khanqah* may have been challenging for Farid who, by temperament and inclination, may have been more reclusive.

In Sheikh Farid's lifetime, the Muslim or Sufi image of the 'holy man' was distinctly different from the traditional Indian cultural image. The Hindu sadhu might be honoured for leaving his home and taking up a hermit's existence; the yogi adept might be revered (and feared) for undertaking the most intense ascetic disciplines and developing supernatural powers that astounded the masses. The Indian sadhu or yogi could be expected to beg for his food, and the community understood that giving to such holy men was a way to acquire spiritual merit. On the other hand, the Sufi sheikh was expected to be a well-educated scholar, to be married, to be a householder and, at the same time, to be an ardent disciple who devotes his heart, mind, and soul to the spiritual path. Not an easy balancing act! Farid, like other Sufis, was married. Though there is no record to show at what age or during which stage of his discipleship he married, we do know that he had several wives. Five sons and three daughters survived to adulthood.

Sheikh Farid belonged to the first generation of Sufis actually born and raised in what was then called Hindustan. Historians trace the influence of Sufism on Indian culture, as well as the 'Indianization' of Sufism, as a gradual process over several centuries starting in 1193 CE (at Farid's age of 20) when Khwaja Chishti first established his centre in Ajmer. Viewed in a historical context, Farid's submission to the Sufi discipline of communal life, while he was evidently longing for a sadhu's solitude and asceticism, is emblematic of a fundamental tension in Indian Sufism during this period.

One time he asked Sheikh Bakhtiyar Kaki for permission to observe a forty-day retreat of solitary fasting and praying (*chillah*). The *chillah* was a common practice in Sufism, though one would never undertake it without the permission and blessings of the pir. As Nizamuddin recalled, Sheikh Farid once told him that when he asked, Sheikh Bakhtiyar Kaki replied:

> "There is no need to do this... it will give you notoriety. Moreover, no such practice has been transmitted from our masters." I replied: "The luminous moment (*waqt*) of God's

presence is upon me, and I have no intention of seeking notoriety. I will not do this for the notoriety of it." Sheikh Qutbuddin fell silent. After this, for the rest of my life, I was ashamed of what I had said, and I have repeatedly repented of my hasty, disrespectful reply.[42]

Sheikh Farid described this seemingly harmless exchange as the one time during his life that "he himself had committed an act of arrogance toward his spiritual master."[43] This incident illuminates the master–disciple relationship: both the subtlety of Sheikh Bakhtiyar Kaki's way of guiding his disciple, and the awe Farid felt for his pir.

Siyar al-Auliya, written half a century later, adds that following the strained silence during which Sheikh Farid burned in the chagrin of having talked back to his pir, Sheikh Bakhtiyar Kaki told him that he could perform the *chillah-i-ma'kus* (inverted *chillah*). Farid had never heard of an inverted *chillah* and didn't know what it was, but his awe before his master prevented him from asking. So he went to his fellow disciple, Badruddin Ghaznavi, and asked him. Badruddin had never heard of it either, but he went and asked Sheikh Bakhtiyar Kaki. The sheikh replied, "*Chillah-i-ma'kus* means that a man should tie a rope around his feet and, suspending downwards in a well, worship God for forty days or forty nights."[44]

Much has been made of this incident in the biographies of Baba Farid. Some say he took the words conveyed to him by Badruddin Ghaznavi as an instruction from his pir and performed this feat. In one version of this incident, he searched for a suitable location, one where he would not attract the attention of curious onlookers. Finally he found a well near a mosque in the city of Uch, where a man he deemed to be discreet would do the service of lowering him into the well and pulling him out. In some traditions Farid performs the *chillah-i-ma'kus* not once, but many times. Later writers have marvelled over this feat, asking, "How is it that blood does not run out of the eyes and mouth of the person who performs it and how food and other things do not come out of him?"[45] One writer adds details such as birds building nests in his hair. Nizami points out, "This is good fiction, but not sober history."[46]

It may not be possible to ascertain whether or not Sheikh Farid actually performed this inverted *chillah*. Since Nizamuddin ends the story with the life-long shame Farid felt, he may never have done it. Or he may have taken his master's instructions as a penance for the error of being "hasty and disrespectful." But what is clear is that the Chishti teachings are decidedly opposed to extreme ascetic practices; as Sheikh Bakhtiyar Kaki put it, "No such practice has been transmitted from our masters."

> The Chishtis were 'moderate' mystics and in excessive passion for asceticism they saw temptation and arrogance, so incompatible with their propagation of humble and selfless service to God and His creatures. Encouraging self-restraint which is obligatory for a mystic, they nevertheless did not allow it to exceed the limits of the rational.[47]

Ironically, Sheikh Bakhtiyar Kaki's point – that such practices bring an unwelcome level of notoriety and fame – is borne out by Farid's experience. This *chillah* seems to be a focal point for so many of his biographers.

> The albeit apocryphal and fabricated *malfuzat* [records of conversations] which describe not so much his spiritual perfection as his physical self-tortures mean that those Sufis were right who considered that asceticism attracts the unnecessary attention of the 'simple folk' to the feats of the body to the detriment of the spiritual feats.[48]

According to Nizami, Baba Farid was never interested in 'feats of the body' for their own sake. We may not know exactly what practices he undertook, but we can be certain that his motivation was love for the Lord.

> The inspiring motive of Baba Farid's devotions and penitences was neither the hope of Heaven nor the fear of Hell. It sprang out of his intense love for his Lord. His heart was 'Love's feverous citadel' and he prayed and fasted day and night because he wanted to break all obstructions which stood between him and his Beloved. Whether in Kothiwal, Hansi, Delhi, Uch or Ajodhan he was always absorbed in his prayers.[49]

Of his yearning for union with the divine Beloved, Sheikh Farid wrote in one of his Persian poems:

> Last night my grieving heart sank in melancholy,
>   and yearning for my sweet Beloved filled my soul.
> I wanted to rush and take refuge at Your gate,
>   but my tears kept pouring and would not abate.[50]

Perhaps, in the end, the most significant point about the incident of the inverted *chillah* is not whether Sheikh Farid performed this feat, but rather what Nizamuddin focuses on: that Farid felt ashamed for the rest of his life for having answered back to his pir. Here we see the essence of discipleship: the implicit obedience even to a hint from the master, a type of submission that leaves no room for the ego-based self to assert its own wishes. It was a standard of discipleship which Farid felt he had failed to attain in that instance. Yet his reply, spoken in his enthusiasm for prayer and fasting, was hardly rude or overbearing by normal standards. Farid's sensitivity to the highest standards of discipleship was emblematic of his purity of heart. Guiding such a disciple required delicate and sensitive handling. As Nizami expresses it, "Young Farid busied himself in devotions and prayers in that lonely corner [his cell]. Sheikh Qutbuddin used to supervise his work with keen and sympathetic interest."[51]

In 1212 CE, during the first of Khwaja Chishti's two visits to Sheikh Bakhtiyar Kaki in Delhi, Khwaja Chishti met the young Farid. It is said that Khwaja Chishti asked Sheikh Bakhtiyar Kaki whether there was any disciple in the *khanqah* who was still struggling and had not yet received the blessings of spiritual realization. Sheikh Bakhtiyar Kaki named Farid as the only one so deprived. How do we make sense of this surprising revelation? Are we to believe that Farid – who was so assiduous in the spiritual practices – was the last one in the *khanqah* without spiritual realization? Or do we believe Sheikh Gesu Daraz that young Farid had come to Sheikh Bakhtiyar Kaki already possessing complete spiritual ability?

It is one of the paradoxes of mysticism that both could be true. In Sufi literature it is often noted that spiritual realization comes as a gift from the sheikh when he deems it to be the right moment. Intense and dedicated effort at spiritual practice may not earn immediate results in the form of spiritual realization. Sometimes a sheikh may withhold the gift of realization in order to intensify the disciple's yearning. Thus, even a disciple who inherently has complete spiritual ability could be struggling and striving at spiritual practice without experiencing the realization he seeks.

Clearly Khwaja Chishti recognized Farid's potential. When Khwaja Chishti met Farid he said to Sheikh Bakhtiyar Kaki, "Baba Bakhtiyar! You have caught a noble falcon which will not build its nest except on the holy tree of heaven. Farid is the lamp that will illuminate the *silsilah* of the dervishes."[52]

One of the most important incidents of Sheikh Farid's life, and certainly one of the most famous, occurred during Khwaja Chishti's visit to Delhi:

Sheikh Muinuddin [Chishti] and Sheikh Qutbuddin [Bakhtiyar Kaki] were together in the same cell. Sheikh Muinuddin said to Sheikh Qutbuddin, "O Bakhtiyar, how much longer will you burn that young man up with spiritual exercises? You must reward him with something." Sheikh Qutbuddin answered, "What power do I have in front of you?" Muinuddin announced, "This is your *murid* [disciple]."

Then he stood up and suggested that they both give him their blessings. So Muinuddin stood on the right and Qutbuddin on the left with Farid between them, and whatever blessings they had received they bestowed on him.

Farid is unique in the history of Sufism in having received such grace and blessings both from his pir and also from the pir of his pir. This extraordinary incident is memorialized in a poem by Amir Khurd:

> The two saints have bestowed the two worlds on you.
> You have received kingship from these kings
> of the age.
> The realms of both this and the other world
> belong to you.
> The entire creation in fact has been made over
> to you.[53]

The Move to Hansi

Sometime, probably when Sheikh Farid was in his forties or early fifties, he moved from Delhi to Hansi, an ancient town in the Hisar district. According to one account, Sheikh Bakhtiyar Kaki instructed him to go to Hansi. According to another version, Farid went to Sheikh Bakhtiyar Kaki to ask permission to move from Delhi to Hansi, and before he had placed his request, his pir already knew of it. While granting permission, the sheikh made it known that Baba Farid was to succeed him, and also that Bakhtiyar's own death would occur before Farid could return to see him:

> "Maulana Fariduddin!" Khwaja Qutbuddin [Bakhtiyar Kaki] addressed his disciple with tears in his eyes when the latter sought his permission to leave Delhi for Hansi, "I know that you will go to Hansi." "I will do as the Sheikh orders me to do," submitted Baba Farid. "Go," continued Sheikh Qutbuddin Bakhtiyar Kaki, "it has been preordained that you will not be present at the time of my death." The saint then asked those who were assembled there to recite the *fatihah* for the spiritual elevation of Baba Farid and bestowed upon him his special prayer carpet and staff.[54]

The gift of the prayer carpet and staff meant that Sheikh Bakhtiyar Kaki had authorized Sheikh Farid to begin initiating disciples in Hansi.

Sheikh Farid's fellow disciple Badruddin Ghaznavi had also been designated as *khalifa* (literally, representative or substitute, one who has received the *khilafat* authorizing him to initiate disciples). Sufi sheikhs often appointed several successors, but at the sheikh's death one would be named as the primary successor. Before Farid's departure, Sheikh Bakhtiyar Kaki made it clear that this was to be Farid:

> While bidding him farewell Sheikh Qutbuddin [Bakhtiyar Kaki] said that he would leave his *khirqah* [patched cloak], *dastar* [turban] and wooden sandals with Qāzi Hamiduddin Nagauri and that he would receive them from him on the fifth day of [after] his death. Then, with these words on his

lips: "My place is yours", the great Chishti saint of Delhi parted forever with his eminent disciple from the Punjab.[55]

The patched cloak, turban, and wooden sandals were symbolic objects signifying successorship. Meanwhile, the prayer carpet and staff that Sheikh Bakhtiyar Kaki gave him as a parting gift were cherished by Baba Farid all his life.

Some forty or fifty years later, Nizamuddin described watching as disciples prepared the cot for Sheikh Farid, now in his nineties and very frail. The staff was laid on the cot by his head. "The Sheikh, placing his head on that staff, would take rest, but frequently he would reach up to touch, and also to kiss, that staff."[56] The small carpet that Farid sat on during the day was laid over him, though it was not long enough to cover his legs. Sheikh Farid's final years were a period of extreme poverty, and these were probably among his very last possessions. This description has often been cited as an example of his asceticism and austere lifestyle. It may also be described as an example of his deep reverence and love for his pir.

Hansi was a military outpost, far from the crowds of Delhi, when Sheikh Farid moved there. According to most traditional accounts, Sheikh Farid went to Hansi expecting peace and quiet and long uninterrupted hours of contemplation, but it was not to turn out that way. One day a well-known mystic named Maulana Nur Turk arrived in Hansi and Baba Farid went to the mosque to hear his sermon. As he later related to Nizamuddin:

> No sooner had he arrived in Hansi and begun preaching than I went to hear him. I had a dirty and tattered cloak, and he and I had never met. Yet at the moment that I entered the mosque his glance fell on me and he exclaimed: "O Muslims, the weigher of words has arrived." After that he began to praise me with paeans such as were never addressed to any king![57]

After this incident, spiritual seekers began to gather around Baba Farid. Soon he was guiding a circle of disciples. Perhaps he was pulled to Hansi by a divine assignment, to 'offer his hand' of loving support and guidance to the spiritual seekers who were ready to grasp it. Some of the disciples who came to him in Hansi became his lifelong companions.

It was here that Jamaluddin Hansawi, a native of Hansi, came in contact with Baba Farid. Jamaluddin Hansawi was to become one of Sheikh Farid's closest disciples. He was a wealthy man who left his comfortable life to live as a disciple, often performing the most menial tasks. According to *Siyar al-Auliya*, it was due to the deep bond of love for this disciple that Baba Farid remained so long in Hansi. Some say he stayed there twelve years, but it could have been as long as twenty years.

The Death of Sheikh Qutbuddin Bakhtiyar Kaki

The story of Sheikh Bakhtiyar Kaki's death has become a part of Sufi lore, told and retold as an inspiring example of the heights of mystical ecstasy. The sheikh was engaged in *sama*, listening to a singer (*qawwal*) sing verses written by Persian mystical poets. Then the *qawwal* sang a verse from Sheikh Ahmad Jami:

> Those slain by the dagger of submission (*taslim*),
> Every moment get a new life from the Unseen.[58]

Hearing this verse, Sheikh Bakhtiyar Kaki went into a meditative trance. Lost in ecstasy, he remained in this state for four days, though he periodically returned to normal consciousness just long enough to ask to hear this verse again. On the fifth day he died. He is called a 'martyr to love,' because he selflessly gave up his life to love. The poet, Amir Hasan Dehlavi, memorialized this extraordinary event in a quatrain. This poem continues to be recited in Sufi gatherings to this day:

> That saint who gave up his soul on this verse,
> Take note: what a rare gem he was.
> Those slain by the dagger of submission,
> Every moment get a new life from the Unseen.[59]

Succession

At the time of Sheikh Bakhtiyar Kaki's death, Sheikh Farid was in Hansi. Some traditions say that he had a dream; others say that he had a vision of his pir. Regardless of how he knew of his pir's death, the next day Farid set out for Delhi, arriving four days later. Qāzi Hamiduddin Nagauri, as previously requested by Sheikh Bakhtiyar Kaki, presented him with the cloak, the turban, and the wooden sandals. After solemnly reciting two cycles of prayer, Sheikh Farid put on his pir's cloak, turban, and sandals and went to the house that Sheikh Bakhtiyar Kaki had occupied.

His stay in Delhi, however, was short – some say seven days and others say it was a mere three days. Sheikh Farid didn't like all the Delhi formalities, which created a barrier between himself and his closest disciples. His abrupt decision to leave was triggered by an incident when a disciple, named Sarhanga, came from Hansi to see him.

He came to the house two or three times, and each time the doorman would not admit him. One day, as the Sheikh was leaving the house, Sarhanga came and, falling at his feet, began to sob. 'Why are you crying?' asked the Sheikh. 'Because,' replied Sarhanga, 'while you were in Hansi, I could see you easily, but now when I come to see you

49

it is very difficult.' That same day the Sheikh said to his friends: 'I am going to return to Hansi.' 'But your Sheikh has ordered you to stay here,' counselled those who were present, 'how can you go elsewhere?' Replied the Sheikh: 'The blessing that my Sheikh bestowed on me will remain the same, whether I stay in the city (of Delhi) or return to the wilds (of the Punjab)!'[60]

So Sheikh Farid turned over the leadership of the Delhi *khanqah* to Sheikh Badruddin Ghaznavi (who reportedly had been nursing a desire for the position) and went back to Hansi.

Scholars have failed to turn up much information about the mysterious Sarhanga cited in this incident beyond a brief reference that he was an ecstatic. Since Sarhanga is not an Islamic name, it is assumed that he was one of the non-Muslim followers of Sheikh Farid.

Part of Sheikh Farid's motivation in leaving Delhi may also have been to avoid displacing Badruddin Ghaznavi, who was already a *khalifa*, empowered to initiate disciples in Delhi. If so, it was typical of his humility to step aside, rather than set himself up as a rival. In any case, the wisdom of his surprising move became apparent soon afterwards. Within months of Sheikh Bakhtiyar Kaki's death, Sultan Iltutmish also died. Iltutmish had been deeply respectful and supportive of Sheikh Bakhtiyar Kaki's *khanqah* and of Sufis in general. After his death, the sultan's court quickly degenerated into a hotbed of intrigue and conspiracies. It soon became nearly impossible for a Sufi sheikh with a large following in the capital city to maintain the strict independence from political powers that the Chishti teachings stressed.

The Move to Ajodhan

Even so, Hansi was not to hold Sheikh Farid for long. He went to his home village of Kothiwal for a while, and then moved to Ajodhan in 1235 CE, on the banks of the Sutlej River. Here he established the *khanqah* where he remained for the next thirty years until his death in 1265 CE.

Ajodhan was, perhaps, not the most obvious choice for locating a holy community, as it was a town plagued by many upheavals. Ajodhan was a strategic point on an important trade route – presiding over the main ferry route across the Sutlej River and situated at the meeting point of the two major western roads: the roads to Dera Ghazi Khan and to Dera Ismail Khan. Traders and caravans, wandering yogis, sultans travelling with the pomp of a royal retinue, and refugees from war-torn Central Asia were continually passing by this spot. Also, in those unsettled times were armies of warriors on horseback – shields and swords flashing in the bright sun – on their way to battle.

Over the millennia, Ajodhan had been destroyed and rebuilt seventeen times, victim of just such conquering armies. The name of the town changed many times, perhaps as many times as the town had been rebuilt. Even the records of the Hellenic historians mention a sequence of towns at this location. Each time the town was rebuilt over the ruins, the level of the ground rose higher, creating a hillock called the Dhakki. Sheikh Farid built his *khanqah* on the Dhakki, commanding an expansive view, 150 feet above the Sutlej River.

In spite of the town's strategic location, Ajodhan is portrayed in contemporary reports as a wild place, surrounded by deserts and teeming with poisonous snakes and wild animals. Baba Farid himself was bitten by a poisonous snake and nearly died. We might wonder why Sheikh Farid chose such a place to live and teach the spiritual path. As explained by Nizamuddin, these rough conditions suited the work he had to do:

His was a different kind of work. Removing himself from the company of people, he preferred the isolation of uncultivated regions. He settled in Ajodhan. He opted for the bread of dervishes and other things that were available in that region. He was content, for instance, to have rough wood for his tooth brush.[61]

If, indeed, he chose Ajodhan to 'remove himself from the company of people,' then his purpose was not met. His spirituality was a light that couldn't be hidden for long and, once again, disciples flocked to him. According to the Sufi poet Jami, it was a verse from the Qur'an heard by Sheikh Farid at the time of prayers that settled his decision to move to Ajodhan and establish his *khanqah* there. Whatever his reasons, his stay in Ajodhan turned out to be a blessing for this beleaguered town, both during and after his lifetime. In 1398, for instance, Timur the Lame, whose warriors terrorized all of Asia, marched to Ajodhan, but spared the town and its inhabitants out of respect for Baba Farid's tomb. In the following centuries, armies clashed nearby several times, yet the town has been left standing since the time Baba Farid built his *khanqah*, with its mud-daubed walls and thatched roof.

When Emperor Akbar made his first visit to the tomb of Sheikh Farid, the town was renamed Pakpattan, meaning 'ferry of the pure' in honour of Sheikh Farid. The name 'Farid' means 'unique.' The epitaph on his tomb reads, aptly,

"There is only one Farid, though many spring forth
from the bud of the flower."[62]

Mystical Teachings

To know the mystical teachings of Sheikh Farid we can look to his words, his slokas in Punjabi, his verses in Persian, and a collection of sayings or aphorisms. Beyond this, we have anecdotes that record what he said in conversation. We can look at how he responded to a particular situation, and in these we can see the reflection of his teachings: teachings as shown through action. Taken together, these sources leave us with an impression which is still somewhat fragmentary and incomplete.

If we look to the Sufi mystical teachings as expressed in the Chishti lineage, however, the picture begins to become more complete. Because neither Khwaja Muinuddin Chishti, nor Sheikh Qutbuddin Bakhtiyar Kaki, nor Baba Farid wrote anything down, all teachings ascribed to them represent what has been passed down through the lineage – first orally and only later in writing. When a sheikh in the lineage some centuries later quotes Sheikh Farid's or Khwaja Chishti's comments on some point of mystical teachings, we may recognize that while these are probably not the exact words, they may still convey the essence of the teachings, as passed down the lineage.

Love, the Foundation

Mohamed Taher, historian of Sufism in India, sums up the essence of Sheikh Farid's teaching simply: "The *summum bonum* of life, in the opinion of Sheikh Farid, is the realization of God....For the attainment of this cherished end, he prescribed the path of love."[63] In two of his often-repeated slokas in the Adi Granth, Farid depicted the path of love with the earthy images of a lover who braves a drenching rain and muddy path to reach the home of the beloved:

> Farid, the path is muddy
>> and the house of my Beloved is so far away.
> If I go out, my blanket will get soaked,
>> but if I remain at home, my heart will be broken. .

> My blanket is soaked, drenched
>> with the downpour of the Lord's rain.
> I am going out to meet my Friend,
>> so that my heart will not be broken.[64]

Theologians, scholars and philosophers might intellectualize about God, reality and the Divine. For Baba Farid, intellect could only lead to an abstract concept of God. Love was the portal into the actual 'experience' of God. He often used to recite the following Persian verse:[*]

> What intellect can dare
>> to dream of Your perfection?
> Where is there an eye
>> worthy of beholding Your beauty?
> Suppose You removed the veil,
>> where is there a soul to bear Your glory?[65]

According to Sufis, the capacity to behold the beauty and glory of the Lord required an inner transformation which could only come about through cultivating spiritual love. Therefore,

---

[*] It is not known whether he himself composed this verse.

Khwaja Chishti said, "The Sufis breathe nothing but love."[66] However, Khwaja Chishti also made it clear that he was speaking of a type of love far different from the ordinary "biased self-love."[67]

> The human love, which does not carry an individual beyond himself is not love at all.... It may be a feeling, it may be affection; it may be warmth of feeling, but it is not love, and it has not the true nature of love in it.[68]

In an attempt to distinguish the Sufi practice of cultivating divine love from indulgence in ordinary emotions, Nizami describes this practice as cultivating 'cosmic emotions.' As he says, these cosmic emotions were "to be experienced but never, ever talked about."[69]

Love for the Divine begins with longing, and the Sufi must progress through a long period of ever-increasing yearning. When visitors or disciples came to Sheikh Farid for a blessing, he often blessed them with the words: "May God grant you pain (*dard*)." *Dard* is defined as the 'pain of grieving' and as 'an eye full of tears and a heart full of emotions.' For some visitors, this must have seemed a strange blessing! He was speaking of the pain of love, the pain felt in separation from the Beloved.[70] As he indicated in Sloka 36, that pain is the very essence of life:

> Many talk of the pain and suffering of separation;
>> O pain, you are the ruler of all.
> Farid, that body, within which
>> love of the Lord does not well up –
>> look upon that body as a cremation ground.[71]

As this verse implies, talking about the pain of separation from the Beloved is easy, but experience is different from mere talk. Sheikh Farid says that one who does not experience this love might as well be dead.

The powerful imagery in Sheikh Farid's slokas in the Adi Granth conveys a hint of the intensity of his longing for a glimpse of his Beloved:

> The crows have searched my skeleton
>   and eaten up all flesh.
> O crows, touch not these two eyes,
>   as I hope to see my Beloved.[72]

Understandably, given his intensity of feeling, a Persian verse which he often recited almost challenges the Beloved for neglecting his suffering:

> Alas, You pay no heed to my suffering
> There will be remorse when You do![73]

Khwaja Chishti often compared divine love to a fire. It was a fire that burned away all traces of ego, annihilating the self. He said, "The lover's heart is a furnace of love. Whatever comes in it is burnt and becomes annihilated. There is no fire greater in its intensity than the fire of love."[74] Attempting to convey the intensity of this inner fire, he often referred to anecdotes about earlier Sufis, such as Rabia of Basra (early ninth century CE):

> Khwaja Sahib, describing the intensity of the love of Bibi Rabia of Basra says that one night, feeling distracted, she cried out, "I am burnt, I am burnt." The people of Basra, hearing this, ran up to her. They discussed among themselves, as to how the fire should be [put] out.
>
> Amongst them, there was a saintly man too. He said to the people, "O you people! You have not experienced such a sort of fire. This is the fire of love of [the] Friend, which is

kindled in the heart of Rabia of Basra. O you people! You cannot extinguish this fire. Such a fire is extinguished only when the lover is united with the Beloved. Now, in the heart of Rabia of Basra, the Friend is making His Own Abode. He is about to come. This pain and distraction are caused by the separation of the Friend. As soon as the Friend comes, all this pain will be removed out of itself."[75]

Sheikh Farid, attempting to convey the pain of yearning that only grew more and more intense the nearer one drew to the Friend, employed the same metaphor as Khwaja Chishti: The suffering he experiences in this love is like a fire that burns relentlessly within him:

> I yearn for my Beloved like a smouldering fire.[76]

In one of his Multani verses, he sang:

> Alone, the one Lord's love fills the mind with pain.
> Will fire affect the heart which love has set ablaze?*

In other words, love sets the heart on fire. Such a heart is so totally consumed in these flames of love that there is nothing more that physical fire can do to it.

Similarly, Sheikh Farid used an image familiar to his Punjabi listeners when he spoke of the Indian koel bird. This bird, who sings with a distinctive piercing voice, wears feathers of a black colour so intense that it looks as if they had been burned.

---

* This verse from Sheikh Farid was found in the fourteenth-century text, *Hidayat ul Qulub*, in a manuscript archived at the Chishti *khanqah* at Khuldabad. Translated by Christopher Shackle.

"O black koel, why have you turned black?"
(And she says) "I was burnt black
due to the separation from my spouse!"
Pray, how can one, without God, be at peace?[77]

Yet no matter how painful this longing, the spiritual state to which it leads is well worth it. A Persian poem attributed to Sheikh Farid makes a bold claim:

From the light of glory the Perfect One is born.
Behold what longing for God produces.[*78]

Therefore, although it may seem paradoxical given the intensity of Sufi expressions of the pain of longing, Khwaja Chishti said, "Love brings with it peace. It confers tranquillity."[79] He explained that ineffable peace comes with the actual vision of the Beloved:

The noise of the lover is only up to the time when he has not seen his Beloved. Once he sees the Beloved he becomes calm and quiet, just as the rivers are boisterous before they join the ocean, but, when they do so, they are becalmed forever.[80]

Love is then both an intense fire and utter tranquillity, both pain and joy. It is, in Khwaja Chishti's view, a divine mystery:

The mystery of love is strange. A dervish was seen dead, but he was smiling. Asked the reason of it, he replied, "Such is the mystery of love."[81]

---

*This verse was attributed to Farid by the modern scholars Mohan Singh Diwana, Mahmud Shirani, Miles Irving, and K.A. Nizami, but Dr S.A.H. Abidi is doubtful of its authenticity.

The bliss of love, Khwaja Chishti taught, was intoxicating. He related an anecdote about the ninth-century Sufi, Abu Yazid, to illustrate the bliss of love – a bliss so pure that one could not leave it even if one wished to do so. Once Abu Yazid went into the countryside and made an extended spiritual retreat:

> The love of God, in his heart, was so intense, that, enamoured of it, he said: "There is love, coming out from every branch, leaf and root of the tree, from fruit and from every stone – nay, from everything." He wished to come out of the kingdom of love, but he could not.[82]

According to Khwaja Chishti, love such as Abu Yazid experienced could not be acquired through personal effort. As Khwaja Chishti taught, "The springs of love are in God, not in us. Hence, love is divine."[83] Although the Sufi must struggle and make efforts in his spiritual discipline, ultimately, divine love comes as a gift from God. In Sufi terminology, saints are called friends of God. In other words, one becomes a saint when the gift of love is given by God. "When God makes someone His Friend, then He bestows upon him His love."[84] Khwaja Chishti taught:

> Love is not premeditated. It is spontaneous. It bursts up in extraordinary ways. There is nothing of mathematical certainty in love. Love is not thrust upon us from without. It is born within. Love is a rare commodity. It knows of no bargain, and is free from the limitations of Time, Space and Circumstances.[85]

These descriptions of love might sound as if the disciples of Sheikh Farid and other masters in the Chishti lineage were continually displaying uncontrolled frenzies of emotion and ecstasy. This was not the case. On the contrary, Sheikh Farid insisted that the path to God required discipline. In training one of his disciples, Badruddin Ishaq, Farid had to use stern measures to teach him the importance of remaining in control of oneself:

Maulana Badruddin Ishaq was a man of very intense mystic emotions. At times he was completely lost in his trances and tears flowed constantly from his eyes. One day Sheikh Farid asked him to lead the prayer. Maulana Ishaq, instead of reciting the Qur'an, chanted a Persian verse and fell down unconscious. When he recovered his senses, Baba Farid again ordered him to lead the prayer and to behave properly. One day the Sheikh called him, but he was so deeply lost in his mystic contemplation that he did not respond. Sheikh Farid became angry and, when the Maulana came to him, said, "All your previous prayers and devotion have been lost. Busy yourself in your work again."[86]

In the above incident, Sheikh Farid took away the ecstatic state that this disciple had attained because he had not developed the maturity to handle it. Badruddin Ishaq had to begin again with the work of spiritual practice. In taking away this ecstatic state, Sheikh Farid acted not in anger, but in the best interest of his disciple, who now would develop – slowly and steadily – into a vessel fit to contain the ecstasy of divine love. Badruddin Ishaq went on to become one of Sheikh Farid's closest disciples. He lived at the *khanqah* and served the sheikh and his visitors day and night. For years he was the chief steward of the *khanqah*. Eventually he also was given the *khilafat nama*, authorized as a representative or successor to grant initiation to disciples.

A fundamental part of Sufi discipline is that one must be able to carry on with normal, dutiful action, even while flooded with the bliss of divine love. This is part of observing 'the silence of the friends.'

By the silence of the friends they mean that the secrets of the heart should not be divulged. One should not disclose the manifestations of the Friend and all that one sees or hears from the invisible Source.[87]

When Khwaja Chishti said that intense, mysterious and divine love "ever lives in the heart of saints," he also conveyed that, "There is none who can carry the burden of love except the saints. They are the people given to devotion and contemplation."[88] By 'devotion and contemplation' he refers to the spiritual practices by which one cultivates the capacity to 'carry the burden of love.'

Remembering the Presence of the Divine

Sheikh Farid's successors have all stressed that practice, not talk, is the way to mystical realization. Khwaja Chishti once concluded a long teaching story with the words: "By this narration, you have come to know that much knowledge is not needed or required. What, in fact, is called for is purposeful practice."[89] Sheikh Bakhtiyar Kaki echoed the same sentiment: "Whosoever reached the place of reality, reached there by virtue of the beauty of his action."[90] And Baba Farid added, "If this [inner] knowledge could be attained merely by desiring, none in the world would remain ignorant. Therefore keep trying for it with perseverance; don't be lazy and don't forget."[91]

Sheikh Sharib puts it simply: "Spiritual life presupposes periods of preparation."[92] He writes:

The path of the Sufis is the path of self-development. They enter upon the path of mental, moral and spiritual evolution with all their main and might. This requires mastery of the mind. In order to get mastery of mind and development of

the will, they take to different practices. They meditate...
control their breath and do many other exercises.[93]

While there are different names for various spiritual practices,
the underlying principle of all is the remembrance of the presence of God. "Keeping the Lord always in one's mind is a sign
of love for Him and faith in His Omnipresence."[94] The practice
of remembrance leads to the experience of the nearness of God;
in the nearness of God is love, and this, for the Sufi, is life itself:

> To the Sufis death implies forgetfulness of Allah. The
> moments passed in the remembrance of Allah constitute
> the real life. The ideal to the Sufis consists in striving and
> struggling to achieve the nearness of Allah.[95]

Thus, the medieval Sufi text *Comfort of the Hearts* (*Rahat
ul-Qalub*) states: "Day or night, standing, sitting, waking, sleeping,
regardless whether the place is clean or filthy, one must always
keep the Lord in his thought and mind and never even for a
moment, be negligent in his commitment to Him."[96] Remembrance – the continual, vivid awareness of the Lord's presence – is
a sign of friendship with God. "When the Lord wishes to befriend
someone, He opens upon him the door of His remembrance."[97,]
It is said that Baba Farid lived continuously in this state of
'friendship' with God – always and everywhere intensely aware of
His presence. The following are among the well-known aphorisms
that are said to have come down to us from Baba Farid:

> *Strive to obtain fresh grace every day.*
>
> *Do not make the heart a plaything of the devil.*
>
> *Give up immediately that which your heart finds evil.*[98]

Hazrat Nizamuddin Auliya recalled having observed Baba Farid, outside of the regular time of prayer, in his cell prostrating himself again and again, often repeating with prayerful reverence:

> I wish to turn into dust
>> and find my abode under Your Feet;
>> I wish to live in Union with You.
> I am weary of both worlds
>> and my sole purpose here is You –
>> to live for You and die for You.[99]

As Nizami expresses it, "Baba Farid's prayer was not a lifeless or mechanical formality. It was a mature activity of a heart overflowing with cosmic emotion. When he prayed he linked himself with that inexhaustible power that spins the universe."[100]

The term 'prayer' is used in Chishti teachings in a very broad sense. According to Khwaja Chishti, prayer includes four different activities: petition, intercession, adoration, and contemplation:

> When we ask for anything for ourselves, it is an instance of petition. When we ask for anything for somebody other than ourselves, it is an instance of intercession. When we extol the Glory of God, and praise and cherish Him, directing our intellect, feeling, will and imagination in that behalf, it is an instance of adoration. When we achieve the state of alert passivity, and the soul lays itself open to the Divine ground, it is an instance of contemplation.[101]

Khwaja Chishti taught that the prayer of petition is a "plaintive, self-centered, morbid kind of prayer." According to Chishti teachings, "The object of prayer should be disinterested remembrance of God, to resign every kind of claim, and leave oneself entirely in His Hands. We should free ourselves from the morbid habit of thinking about ourselves."[102]

The higher types of prayer, adoration and contemplation, are "a great necessity for the development of soul." Such prayer is not a mere ritual performance. Rather, it "is a secret and a mystery, which man confides to God. Prayer furnishes an occasion to an individual to be close to God."[103] Sheikh Sharib writes:

> Prayer should not be the mere means of occasional feelings of the presence of God. It should be the means of real friendship with God. It is the discipline in the life of faith. Right relation with God means a life of freedom, and liberty and delight. In prayer, we should seek God's Will. The object of the prayer is to know God better.... We should think of prayer as the breath in our lungs and the blood from our hearts. The blood flows ceaselessly and breathing continues ceaselessly. We are not conscious of it, but it is always going on. Prayer is not an exercise. It is the life. Hence, "Pray without ceasing."[104]

Regularity and Discipline Supporting Spiritual Growth

Sheikh Farid encouraged his disciples to remain steadfast and unrelenting in their efforts at spiritual practice. All too often seekers get distracted from their spiritual goal. Poetically speaking, they turn away from attending at the Lord's doorstep, only to stand like a beggar at the doorstep of someone else. In Sloka 42, Farid begged to be saved from this calamity:

> Farid begs,
>   O Lord, do not make me sit at another's door.
> If this is the way you are going to keep me,
>   then go ahead and take the life out of my body.[105]

He recognized that one cannot become a true dervish (literally a beggar, a pauper; figuratively, a Sufi) attending at the Lord's doorstep so long as one craves the goods of this world. In Sloka 2 he said:

> Farid, it is so difficult to become a humble saint
>   at the Lord's door. I am so accustomed
>   to walking in the ways of the world.
> I have tied and picked up the bundle;
>   where can I go to throw it away?[106]

However, he assured his followers that if they only would keep knocking at that door, it would surely open one day. He often recited the following verse:

> It was not opened unto you
>   for you had not journeyed the distance.
> Otherwise, who has ever been denied
>   who has knocked on this door?[107]

To knock on the door where no one has ever been denied, the Sufis taught, one had to go beyond the ritual prayer which is obligatory for all Muslims five times a day at specified times. Khwaja Chishti taught that prayer serves two different objectives:

> The first is the prayer of the *ulema* [religious scholars], the jurists, and the pious, which is confined to precept and practice.... This does not secure union with Allah.... The second type of prayer is that of the Prophets, the saints and the caliphs [the Sufi sheikhs and their successors], which is performed with a receptive heart. Its reward is union with Allah.[108]

According to Khwaja Chishti, the obligatory ritual prayers (the first type, above) develops personal holiness within the individual. But, he said, "Personal holiness is not enough. It is self-consciousness. It focuses our eyes on our own self – our piety, our asceticism."[109]

Yet he laid great stress on following the rules of religious law, including performing all of the obligatory, ritual prayers. He even stressed punctuality in performing each of the five prayers at the appropriate time each day. Why this contradiction? As he pointed out, "The fact is that constancy, perseverance and regularity are great things in spiritual life."[110] He saw the discipline of following the religious laws as a foundation for the practice of the spiritual path. It established regularity and a well-ordered life. It trained the practitioner in self-control:

> According to the Sufis self-realization is impossible without self-discipline. Hence, they assert that control of the mind, control of the thoughts and control of the body is necessary and desirable for purification of the self, leading to spiritual advancement and progress.[111]

In the same vein, the dictum of 'eat little, talk little, sleep little' was a cardinal doctrine guiding the Chishti Sufis.[112] The purpose was not merely denying oneself for its own sake, or to display one's virtue to the world. Rather, as Khwaja Chishti explained the principle, the Sufi eats little so that he can give food to the poor and the hungry. The Sufi talks little so that he can listen, both in the sense of listening to the troubles and tribulations of others and in the sense of becoming silent deeply enough to listen within for God's will. The Sufi sleeps little so that he can pray, because the night-time should be given to prayers of adoration and contemplation.

Thus, the discipline of eating little, talking little, and sleeping little helps with overcoming the selfishness of a self-centred life driven by personal desires. This discipline serves as a foundation for the spiritual life. As Khwaja Chishti taught:

> The real conqueror is the one who has conquered his own self; this is a more difficult war. Self-conquest is, to the Sufis, the ladder to spiritual development, inner illumination and purification.[113]

For this self-conquest it is necessary to focus on one's higher purpose and rise above the demands of the body and senses. Sheikh Farid likens the body to a dog that is always barking and whining to get your attention. In Sloka 88 he says one must ignore these incessant demands:

> Farid, this body is ever barking;
>   who can stand this continuous suffering?
> I have put stoppers in my ears;
>   I care not how much the wind is blowing.[114]

The following are examples of Sheikh Farid's sayings that have been crystallized into aphorisms by being repeated through the generations:

> *Do not satisfy the demands of the carnal self, for its demands know no limit.*

> *Make wisdom and solitude your main provision.*

> *There is no compensation for the loss of time.*[115]

The Precious Opportunity of Human Life

In countless ways, Sheikh Farid reminded his disciples that the time to act is now. Sheikh Farid insisted that the very pleasures we waste our lives pursuing are not only short-lived, but also are a certain pathway to pain. They are like a kind of sugar that turns into poison as soon as it is eaten, making human life into one long tale of woe.

> See, O Farid, what has happened:
>   sugar has become poison.
> Without my Lord,
>   to whom should I tell my sorrow?[116]

Most people spend their entire lives toiling for desires and ambitions that entice them like a sugar-coated treat, only to find it laced with poison.

> Farid, these are poisonous sprouts
>   coated with sugar.
> Some die planting them, and some are ruined
>   harvesting and enjoying them.[117]

Sheikh Farid taught his followers to use the brief span of life for a higher purpose. If one wants God-realization, he stressed, one must strive for it now while alive, for no one knows when death will come. Farid sang of this in one of his Multani verses:*

> Today's the time for meeting,
>   however far the way.

---

* This verse from Sheikh Farid was found in the fourteenth-century text, *Hidayat ul Qulub*, in a manuscript archived at the Chishti *khanqah* at Khuldabad. This translation is by Professor Christopher Shackle.

These foolish folk know not,
     what will the morrow bring?[118]

What the morrow might bring is death. Farid urgently warned
his listeners that death comes suddenly and unannounced, when
we least expect it. In Sloka 99 he used an image, familiar to all in
the land of five rivers:

> Farid, the crane, perched on the riverbank,
>   enjoys (his hunt).
> But, lo, while enjoying this,
>   he is pounced upon by the hawks, unawares!
> Yea, when the hawks of God pounce upon him,
>   all his revelry goes,
>   and what was never in his mind came to pass:
>   Oh, such are the doings of God![119]

Since no one knows when death may come, Sheikh Farid
stressed that one must use the opportunity of life while it lasts.
While alive, it is possible to attend to spiritual practice and in
this way be fully prepared to meet death without fear. In Sloka
79, Farid reminds his listeners:

> Farid, the bird is a guest
>   in this beautiful world-garden.
> The morning drums are beating –
>   get ready to leave![120]

According to Sheikh Farid, devoting one's heart and mind to
prayer and remembrance of God is making proper use of the
brief and precious opportunity of life. To engage in these spiritual
practices, he said, was like building a raft that could carry one
across the waters to the 'distant shore' of union with the Divine.

In one of his hymns in the Adi Granth Farid stressed the urgency of building that 'raft':

> You were not able to make yourself a raft
>   when you should have.
> When the ocean is churning and overflowing,
>   then it is very difficult to cross over it.[121]

The five rivers that course through the Punjab flood seasonally. During much of the year they are easy to cross, but during the floods the turbulent waters swell to many times their normal volume. Those who need to get across must build a raft before the floods come. Similarly, the 'raft' of spirituality must be readied before death makes the crossing too hazardous to attempt. This sturdy raft can only be built through spiritual practice.

Extreme dedication was important to Sheikh Farid. He urged his followers to devote a portion of the night-time to prayer and spiritual practice. In Sufism the night is meant to be devoted to prayer and spiritual exercises. If the Sufi sleeps through the early part of the night, then he should at least get up and spend the latter part of the night in devotions. By dawn, the Sufi should certainly be among those attending at the door of the Lord.

> The first watch of the night brings flowers,
>   and the later watches of the night bring fruit.
> Those who remain awake and aware,
>   receive the gifts from the Lord.[122]

As he sang in one of his Persian verses:

> The more suffering you endure, the higher you rise.
> Nightly vigils produce elevated souls.[123]

In Sloka 80 he further stressed the importance of giving time to spiritual practice during the night, saying:

> Farid, musk is distributed at night.
>> Those who are asleep receive not a share.
> Those whose eyes are heavy with sleep –
>> how can they be blessed with it?[124]

Musk is a sweet fragrance. Being rare and expensive and considered very precious, it serves as an apt metaphor for the grace that comes to those who devote time and effort to spiritual practice. Sheikh Farid indicates that the night-time, when the rest of the world is sleeping, is particularly opportune for spiritual practice.

Sheikh Farid often counselled his listeners against being lazy and sleeping too long. Sometimes he used grim images of the grave to shock his listeners from the complacency of lying in bed too long:

> Farid, in the grave a stone is your pillow,
>> the earth your bed – worms will eat your flesh.
> For eons will you lie on one side, unchanging.[125]

However, Sheikh Farid also taught that there is a way to escape from the terrors of death. There is a way to make proper use of the brief span of life. If, during life, one has devoted himself to the spiritual discipline and has cultivated divine love, he may enter the 'lane of love.'

> In the lane of love
>> where lovers surrender their souls
>> no Angel of Death need appear.[126]

The Inner Path

Where is that 'lane of love' Sheikh Farid referred to? How do lovers 'surrender their souls?' To understand this we have to look to the teachings of Khwaja Chishti – Sheikh Farid's spiritual grandfather – and to the teachings of the Chishti lineage. The 'lane of love' where one loses oneself to love is where God resides, for God is love. The Chishti sheikhs teach that the heart of man is where God resides. According to Khwaja Chishti, however, this is not the physical heart:

> The heart is of two kinds, namely the unreal heart and the real heart. The real heart is neither on the right side nor on the left side, neither upward or downward and neither far nor near. But it is indeed difficult to recognize the real heart. Only those near to Allah know it. The heart of a perfect believer is in reality the throne of Allah.[127]

In other words, the 'unreal heart' is the physical organ that pumps blood. The 'real heart' is a placeless place at the core of the human being, and it is here that God is to be found. In the words of the Qur'an (Q 50:15): "We indeed created man; and We know what his soul whispers within him, and We are nearer to him than the jugular vein."

According to Chishti teachings, a human being is a great mystery. Although he goes through his mundane life as if he were nothing more than a thinking, talking animal, he actually hides within himself the 'Secret of God.'

> God says, "Man is My Secret." The first perfect man that God, in His Mercy, created was Adam.[128]

In Islam, as in Judaism and Christianity, Adam was the first human being God created, the prototype for human beings.

The 'Secret of God' is that He has hidden Himself in the heart of man. His very purpose in creating human beings was so that humans would know Him and, finding Him within their own body, would love Him:

> Describing the purpose of bringing Adam into existence, Khwaja Sahib says that God said to him, "Pray and remember Me in thy heart. Know me to be present in the body. Give place to My love in thy head. I have created thee for this purpose, that thou may'st know Me, glorify Me and love Me."[129]

How does one reach this placeless place in the heart of one's own being? Where is the path which leads there? The practising Sufi's gradual transformation of consciousness is often described with the metaphor of a journey; that is, a journey into oneself, a journey to the 'heart of man' where God resides. As Khwaja Chishti taught, "Man is a kingdom in himself."*[130] The meditative states experienced in spiritual practice are likened to travelling through that kingdom deep into the interior of oneself.

This inner journey, according to Khwaja Chishti, is the true pilgrimage. He compared it to the *hajj* – the pilgrimage to Mecca where the pilgrim circumambulates the Ka'bah. The *hajj* is a sacred duty for every Muslim male at least once in his lifetime.† Year after year, hundreds of thousands of pious Muslims make the long and arduous trek. Khwaja Chishti himself had performed the *hajj* before settling in the Indian subcontinent. However, he taught this to his disciples:

---

*The specific spiritual practices taught by the Chishti lineage of Sufi sheikhs to traverse the inner path are discussed in the Appendix.

†Exceptions are made in particular circumstances, such as extreme poverty.

The heart of man is Ka'bah.... The existence of man is akin to four walls. If the curtain of doubts and diffidence and non-godly objects is removed therefrom, then, in the courtyard of the heart, the Vision of God-Almighty will be seen. This is the real Pilgrimage to Ka'bah.[131]

This 'real pilgrimage' is not traversed on foot or by horse, car, plane or train; it is a pilgrimage traversed by the consciousness.

Khwaja Muinuddin has said: *Hajjis* perform *twaaf* (walking with great reverence) around the mosque of Ka'bah with their bodies, but *arifs* (mystics) do *twaaf* around the heavens with their heart. Their only longing is to see God.[132]

Sheikh Bakhtiyar Kaki never made the outward pilgrimage to Mecca, nor did Sheikh Farid. One time Farid had set out to perform *hajj* and he went as far as the city of Uch, the birthplace of Sheikh Bakhtiyar Kaki. Here, it suddenly came into his mind that his pir had never made the *hajj*. Thinking it would not be proper to depart from the tradition established by his pir, Farid returned home.[133] Following his example, Nizamuddin never performed the *hajj*, nor did his successor, Nasiruddin Chiragh. What happened? Did each of these celebrated Sufis (who actually taught the importance of following religious law as a foundation for the spiritual life) fail in this sacred obligation?

Carl Ernst says this of Sheikh Farid and the early Chishti sheikhs: "They internalized the imagery of the pilgrimage, as did Sufis elsewhere, speaking of the true pilgrimage as a journey into the depths of the heart in search of God."[134]

Just as the *hajj* across land to Mecca involves crossing the boundary from one kingdom to another, so also the mystical pilgrimage takes the disciple across boundaries between physical and spiritual realms. Sufis have described this journey and the boundaries crossed in terms of various spiritual 'states,' 'stations,' and 'stages.'

One great boundary crossing – intimidating even to the most adventurous – is stepping beyond the limitations of the physical body. Khwaja Chishti says: "If you are desirous of beholding the splendour of the Lord, go beyond the shell of your physical covering."[135] Thus, he likens this transition to breaking out of a confining shell; one breaks out of the physical covering of the body and enters a non-physical realm of reality. In this vein, Khwaja Chishti declared: "The Sufis pursue, follow and obey the command of the Prophet, which lays down: 'Die before you die!'"[136]

For the Sufi disciple, this mystical pilgrimage could be made only with the help and guidance of his pir. Sharafuddin Maneri (1263–1381 CE) likens the inner 'path' to an unmarked route through the desert, where constantly shifting sands leave a track discernible only to those who have travelled it many times. He writes,

> Imagine what it must be like on that Road along which 124,000 prophets have travelled, and yet no trace of their journey remains! Without a guide who knows the way, it is impossible to travel along this Road.[137]

In other words, all the prophets since the beginning of time had travelled this exact same 'Road,' but left no trace or footstep in the shifting sands. Maneri points out that dangers and deceptions lurk:

> Also various types of mystical experiences might occur; some might be satanic, others might be produced by his own ego, still others could come from the merciful One Himself. This is all entirely new to the novice and he cannot discern the source of these spiritual experiences. He needs the assistance of one well versed in discerning these

various spirits, in the same way as cocks alone understand the crowing of their peers.[138]

Thus, the inner pilgrimage is impossible for anyone without a spiritual guide. But the disciple of a Sufi sheikh has an ever-present friend to help and guide him. As Abu Sa'id Abul-Khayr said, "If there is a dangerous place somewhere, he will tell him to be on his guard, and will give him kindly encouragement, so that travelling that path with a strengthened heart, he may reach the goal."[139] In the words of Abu al-Qasim al-Qushayri (d. 1072), "each 'wayfarer' on this inner pilgrimage needs a master from whom he can learn his path, one breath at a time."[140]

One time Nizamuddin was sitting with his disciple, Amir Hasan Sijzi. Amir Hasan remarked that perhaps the *hajj* to Mecca was only for those who have no pir. Nizamuddin smiled and quietly confirmed this sentiment by reciting the line, "That way to Ka'bah leads, this one to the Friend."[141]

Annihilation of the Self

According to Chishti teachings, the ego is a formidable obstacle on the spiritual path. It is seemingly impossible to overcome. Yet, as Khwaja Chishti taught, God can make anything possible:

> The greatest obstacle to the unitive knowledge of God is the insistence of man on a separate self. This God-eclipsing and anti-spiritual selfness is the greatest enemy of man eager to be united with God. Apparently, it looks difficult, but nothing is difficult or impossible for God.[142]

After all the personal effort of the disciple, ultimately the dissolution of this 'God-eclipsing and anti-spiritual self' is accomplished by the only power capable of such a feat: love. Khwaja Chishti said,

"The path of love is such that the one who treads on it loses his name and identity."[143] What is this 'trade' that one makes along the path of love? One gives up the self and receives the Beloved. To the Sufi, it is a fabulous bargain, and it leads to the supreme state of enlightenment.

> The perfection of the Enlightened depends upon the loss of his self. He is said to be perfect only when all else is removed from in between him and the Friend. Either he must live or the Friend.[144]

For Khwaja Chishti, this annihilation of the ego was like shedding a skin in the same way as a snake does. Leaving behind this old and useless snakeskin – the ego – the Sufi goes on to a freer, more expansive life. He is now in tune with reality, and he experiences oneness with the Divine.

> Khwaja Muinuddin has said: When I came out of my covering, the way a snake comes out of its covering, and saw around me, I found that the Lover, the Beloved, and the Love were one. That means, in the state of *Aalam-i-Tauhid* (the mystical state of oneness) they are all one.[145]

The ego is not only the single greatest obstacle to the experience of oneness with God. From the Chishti point of view, this same ego is also the cause of all disharmony, suffering, and strife in the creation. For the individual, and for humanity at large, all pain and grief can be traced to this one source, the egocentric self.

> The fact is, that selfishness cannot be controlled, regulated and curbed, so long as there is emphasis upon 'Self.' So it is advisable in the interest of harmonious working of the

society and in the larger interest of humanity at large, to merge 'self' in the ocean of Divine Reality.[146]

For the Chishtis, then, there is no discontinuity between the inward development of mystical consciousness and its outward manifestation in the way one treats one's fellow human beings. Both are part and parcel of the same thing: love. When the mystic loses himself in the divine love – annihilating his ego and experiencing God as ever present – his attitude towards humanity also undergoes a radical change:

> The first noticeable effect of the love of God is the destruction and effacement of prejudices and passions, parochial notions, caste considerations, social distinctions, pride of birth, etc. The whole world then appears to be one love-knit family, where there are no ignoble jealousies, social animosities, mutual feuds, recriminations and quarrels. It appears then that the whole human race has been created to glorify God and to be a witness to His Glory.[147]

Transformation of the Inner Life

Khwaja Chishti taught: "It is the inner life, which marks out one as a mystic. It is the possession of certain qualities which give the mystic the mystic vision and lead him on safely to the mystic way of life."[148]

The 'inner life' here refers to the quality of the devotees' thoughts, attitudes, and inner nature as they go through their daily lives. Outward actions can try to hide this inner life, but generally, sooner or later, the daily behaviour will belie the true state of the practitioner's inner life. Certain attitudes, whether spoken out loud or not, support the development of mystical consciousness. Paradoxically, these same attitudes also come as the result of the development of mystical consciousness. The experience of divine love leaves an indelible mark on the character of the individual.

> The power of love is such that it makes one unmindful of the external circumstances. Poverty, troubles, hunger, or privation cannot move him. They have no meaning for him. A true lover is like a rock whom nothing can shake. Love is eternal. Water cannot quench it. Flood cannot drown it. Fire cannot burn it. Famine cannot starve it. Time cannot efface it. Circumstances cannot wipe it out.[149]

Everyone talks of love, but to Khwaja Chishti, "he alone is constant and firm in love who voluntarily, with delight and without any grudge, accepts all troubles and pain received from the Friend."[150] When the mystic discovers the 'Secret of God' in his own heart – the secret that God has hidden Himself within man – love of such a high order is awakened that:

> There is nothing which can wedge in between the love of God and the Enlightened. The Enlightened feels the unmerited, fathomless marvel of the love of God. The distress, persecutions, hardships, troubles, trials and tribulations produce in the Enlightened super-joy. They are not the things to fight with. He is happy in the midst of them. He is more than a conqueror.[151]

For the disciple who is yet some distance removed from enlightenment, he strives to cultivate an attitude of surrender. Outwardly, this attitude of surrender manifests as contentment and gratitude in all circumstances and as forgiveness in the face of all enmity and opposition. Inwardly, it requires giving over all wishes, desires, and hopes – including the hope of paradise – to the sweet will of the Beloved. As Khwaja Chishti taught, "Those who have surrendered their will to God, they have undoubtedly nothing to do with paradise and its comforts. Their only object is nothing but the Friend."[152]

Sheikh Farid's state of loving surrender to the will of the Lord was so complete that it guided his every action. There is a legend associated with one of his verses in the Adi Granth:

> Mighty river, erode not your banks;
>   you, too, are answerable to your maker.
> What power has the river to flow this way or that?
>   God's will guides its course.[153]

The story is that a nearby river had begun to change its course, causing widespread devastation. Knowing that a holy man like Sheikh Farid had the power to perform miracles, the villagers went to him to beg for his help. Farid assented to their request and followed them to the riverbank. There he stood a long while as the villagers gathered close around him to see how he would save them, their homes, and their crops.

Suddenly, to their surprise, he picked up a shovel and started shovelling dirt from the riverbank into the swift current. The people were aghast. Sheikh Farid explained: "Friends, the river says that it is only doing God's will. When the river is flowing according to God's will, to find fault with its actions will amount to questioning divine wisdom. Therefore, I am helping the river." After a moment he concluded, "Take my advice and move to a safer location."[154]

Who was this saint who delivered his message in such direct actions? Although he became known as the Treasure of Sweetness, clearly he never sugar-coated the truth. To understand the spirituality he taught, we must look not only to his words, but also to his actions, his responses to the challenges of life, his way of living. Here we find the outward signs of an inner life that was utterly shaped by divine love, in which no conflicting self-interest remains.

Sheikh Farid's Way of Life

S HEIKH FARID'S WAY OF LIFE seems to have been a perfect reflection of the principles he taught. His actions and words, as recalled in various anecdotes and incidents, show the outward, visible expression of his inner life and mystical awareness.

Badruddin Ishaq lived in close proximity to his pir for decades. Serving in the *khanqah*, being with Sheikh Farid day and night, in public and in private, he was awestruck by the utter harmony between his pir's thoughts, words, and actions:

> The greatest attribute of Sheikh Farid in the eyes of his nearest disciple, Sheikh Badruddin Ishaq, was his absolute sincerity and complete absence of hypocrisy. His private life was a perfect mirror of his public life and he never said or did different things in public and in private. There was complete harmony between his thought, words and action. This was, as Maulana Ishaq correctly said, a unique and wonderful thing.[155]

Sheikh Farid's aphorism, "Keep your internal self better than the external one,"[156] gives eloquent expression to the importance of utter sincerity. In his slokas he cries out against all hypocrisy and pretence:

> Says Farid: Those who carry the prayer mat
> on their shoulder and wear rough wool,

but bear daggers in their heart
and with glib tongue utter falsehood –
These are bright outside,
but have the dark night in their hearts.[157]

To Sheikh Farid, integrity meant that the outward actions of charity and the inward actions of prayer must also be accompanied by the development of human virtues. Without these positive qualities of character, all pretence at being spiritual and charitable is worthless. In one of his Persian poems he said:

You may attend to the sick all day
and pray all night long;
but if your heart is not empty of anger and desire,
to a single thorn
you sacrifice a hundred heaps of roses.[158]

The idea that one's outward actions must reflect the inner state is central to Sufi teachings. As Abu Hamid al-Ghazali expresses it:

To be a Sufi means to abide continuously in God and to live at peace with men: whoever abides and deals rightly with men, treating them with unfailing kindness, is a Sufi. The right attitude towards your fellow men is that you should not lay burdens upon them according to your own desire, but rather burden yourself according to their desire. In your dealings with others, treat them as you would wish them to treat you, for the faith of God's servant is not made perfect unless he desires for others what he desires for himself.[159]

This principle runs deep in the Sufi tradition. The Sufi saint, Abu al-Qasim Qushayri, describes the qualities of a saint (*wali*), when he writes:

The *wali*, in his normal conscious state, tries in all sincerity to acquit himself of all his obligations to God. Further, in whatever state he may be, he treats the people with unfailing kindness and affection. He spreads his graciousness on all creatures; and he bears with good cheer their malevolence. And without their requesting it, he prays to God to take good care of them, and tries his very best for their salvation. He never takes vengeance on others, and he does his best to keep his heart free from malice against them. With all this he never tries to extend his hands on what belongs to others, and he does everything to keep away from greed. He keeps his tongue under control so that it does not speak ill of them. And he keeps his soul from seeing the failings of others, and he never quarrels with any one either in this world or the other.[160]

Sheikh Farid had great respect for scholarship, believing that those who studied the scriptures and deeply pondered their meaning brought light into the darkness of ignorance that envelops this world. Yet, he said, "A dervish among the *ulema* is like a full moon among the stars."[161] That is, one who pursues the mystical path, making the inner pilgrimage within the heart of man, shines a light into the darkness of this world to which the flickering starlight of the learned cannot be compared. As he explained, "What the learned people (*ulema*) have to offer in their speech, the *arifs* (mystics) offer in their action."[162]

Trust in God

In his actions, more than in his speech, Sheikh Farid demonstrated his unmitigated trust in the one God. The principle of trusting in God (*tawakkul*) has always been central to Sufi practice. The earliest Sufis living in the barren deserts near Basra, Iraq, laid their lives trustingly in the hands of God. *Tawakkul* implies gratefully and gladly accepting whatever God sends; it means neither expecting nor wishing for anything more or less than whatever He provides. It is a principle easier to profess than to live by.

Life in Sheikh Farid's *khanqah* transformed 'trust in God' from an idealized concept into a very concrete reality. Farid's *khanqah* was a simple, stark structure adjacent to his small hut built of unbaked bricks. One large hall with mud-daubed walls and a thatched roof offered no separate rooms or individual meditation cells for moments of privacy. Here in this single room his disciples and visitors ate, slept, discussed, recited poetry, listened to discourses, and prayed together. There was no furniture or decoration; all sat, stood or slept on the bare dirt floor. Sheikh Farid's *khanqah* came to be called *jama'at khanah* (congregational or gathering place) because of the emphasis on communal life that was enforced by the simplicity of the structure. It set a pattern that was followed by subsequent generations of Chishti masters.

The *jama'at khanah* was supported in all its needs by the practice of unsolicited donations (*futuh*). The principles of *futuh* were that whatever was freely given should be accepted as a gift from God, but the thought of wishing for something more should not even cross the mind. Moreover, whatever was received in a day must be used or given away in the same day. Nothing whatsoever should be kept for the next day. For the Sufi, each new day was a new opportunity to place his trust in God.

As Khwaja Muinuddin Chishti taught, "It is of utmost importance for the mystic, that he should surrender his will to the Will of God. He should ask for nothing. He should wish for nothing. Whatever God wills, that is best for him."[163] Khwaja Chishti says that genuine trust in God goes beyond relying on God for daily necessities; it is applied to all circumstances of life:

He should repose his trust in God. 'Tawakkul,' or trust in God, is the sign of a mature soul. As regards trust in God,

Khwaja Sahib says that "Really speaking, he alone can be said to repose his trust in God who on receiving injury from the people, does not complain of it to anyone."[164]

For Sheikh Farid, *tawakkul* was a matter of maintaining 'independence of spirit,' which meant placing no reliance on anything or anyone other than God.[165] A tale has been passed down the generations about Sheikh Farid and his single-minded trust in God. The event may never have happened, but as a mystical teaching story it illustrates how much his name has been associated with the principle of *tawakkul*:

> One day he was walking a little distance with the aid of a stick. All of a sudden he threw away the stick and became restless. When the reason was asked he replied that he was reprimanded because he was depending on something other than God. God for Baba Farid was omnipotent. It was his firm belief that He was the only bestower.[166]

The discipline of not keeping anything of one day's donations till the next day meant that periods of plenty were followed by periods of hunger, sometimes to the point of near starvation. Sheikh Farid and his disciples had to cultivate contentment and gratitude through these shifting circumstances. Even on days when extraordinary wealth poured into the *jama'at khanah*, the next might be one with empty stomachs for all.

Ulugh Khan, minister to the Sultan Nasiruddin, once came to visit Sheikh Farid, bringing as a gift from the sultan not only a large amount of money but also a grant of four villages. This grant conferred the rights to receive regular revenues from these four villages: in essence, an annuity that could be counted on year after year. The sheikh accepted the money to distribute among the needy right away. But he refused the grant of the four villages, diplomatically giving as his reason that "there might be several other aspirants desirous to possess them."[167]

To accept this type of land grant, with its regular revenue stream, did not suit the principle of trusting in God. And to entangle oneself with royalty, whose political manoeuvrings and shifting fortunes always bring misfortune sooner or later, was against the principles of the Chishti lineage. As Ulugh Khan stood anxiously waiting to see whether his visit and his gifts had made a positive impression on the sheikh, Baba Farid extemporaneously spoke the following couplets to him:

> King Fereydoon was not an angelic being,
>   neither was he made of amber and incense.
> He gained his fame by being just and generous.
> Through justice and generosity,
>   you too may become a Fereydoon.[168]

However, the ambitious Ulugh Khan was eager to make a connection with Sheikh Farid, whose growing popularity must have seemed to him to be a power base. Another time he again sent a gift of regal dimensions, a huge amount of money in the form of coins, causing some discomfort for Farid.

A seventeenth century biographer of Sheikh Farid writes that once Balban*sent a dish full of *tankahs* [coins] to the saint who accepted it after considerable reluctance and ordered Maulana Badruddin Ishaq to distribute it among the poor and the needy. The sun had already set and it was getting dark but the Sheikh would not wait for the day. His *khanqah*, he used to say, was not a storehouse for royal gifts.

---

* In this story, Ulugh Khan is called Balban. When Ulugh Khan, through craftiness and an assassination, became the Sultan he changed his name to Balban.

In obedience to his instructions, the Maulana doled out all the money. He then brought a candle to see whether anything was still left. He found just one coin and put it in his cap to hand over to a needy person the next morning. When Baba Farid went to the mosque to lead the 'ishā' (night) prayer, he realized that something was disturbing his mind. Three times he began his prayer but could not finish it.

In great excitement he asked Maulana Badruddin if he had distributed the royal gift. The Maulana replied that he had given away all excepting one coin. Baba Farid angrily took back that coin and threw it away, and then peacefully led the prayer. 'Ali Asghar Chishti further informs us that throughout the whole of that night Baba Farid deeply regretted having touched that coin.[169]

Baba Farid's way of life could be summed up as 'radical simplicity.' Khwaja Chishti had recommended eating one meal a day. Sheikh Farid treated every day as though it was the time of Ramaḍan and, each day, before the evening prayer he broke his fast with 'sharbat,' a drink made with dairy, dried fruits (raisins and apricots or other fruit) and nuts. Once Hazrat Nizamuddin Auliya chatted with his disciples about Sheikh Farid's daily routine:

He told the assembly that the Sheikh usually broke his fast with sherbet, which was brought to him in a bowl with some raisins in it. Mixing it with water in a large cup, he distributed half or two-thirds of it among those present in his assembly. He reserved the one-third or so that was left over for himself, but even of that he would give some to select persons, and it was considered auspicious for those thus favoured.... Then he performed the evening prayer and remained totally absorbed in God till dinner. For dinner

87

they laid a table, setting out every kind of food. After dinner the Sheikh did not eat again till the moment of breaking fast the next evening.[170]

The principle of eating lightly is one of the most basic disciplines in the life of a Sufi. As the twentieth-century Chishti Sheikh Sharib explains:

> To eat less is one of the qualities of the Sufis. The Sufi only eats to live and does not live to eat! To them, to remain hungry is to follow the *sunnat* [tradition] of the prophet, who never ate to his heart's content. At times, he could not get a handful of barley to eat. Jalaluddin Rumi (d. 1273 CE) was once asked as to when a Sufi commits a sin. He replied: 'When he eats without hunger.'[171]

Like most mystics of his day, however, Sheikh Farid went beyond eating lightly. According to Nizamuddin, Sheikh Farid sometimes broke his fast only on alternate days, so that he would have one meal every two days. But the Chishti lineage does not recommend fasting for its own sake. As Sheikh Sharib says:

> The people who keep fast abstain from eating and drinking. But this is not the real fast. It is the unreal fast. Such a fast does not imply the renunciation of things other than God. The idea of Self continues to dominate. Such a fast has this much utility, that an individual comes to realize the pang of hunger and thirst of other people, thus enabling him to extend his sympathy to the sufferers.[172]

Thus, the purpose of fasting lies in developing compassion and the ability to give to others. For Sheikh Farid, eating lightly and fasting did enable him to give to others, even when he had almost nothing. Of course, not every guest had the spiritual maturity to see past the rough conditions in the *khanqah* and accept the sheikh's rudimentary offering with gratitude. Nizamuddin related an incident:

> Once there was a man named Muhammad. He came and sat down in the presence of Sheikh al-Islam Fariduddin – may God bless his lofty secret. When they brought in a loaf of bread, they couldn't find a tablecloth or linen on which to set it. Sheikh Fariduddin instructed them to put it on the ground. That Muhammad thought to himself, 'How good it would be were there a cloth.' The Sheikh, with his index finger, drew a design on the ground and declared to that man: "O Muhammad, know that this is a tablecloth!" "That Muhammad," added the master, "He was still a spiritual novice."[173]

Normally, the disciples relied on *futuh*. The challenge of actually living the principle of *tawakkul* can scarcely be imagined. Sometimes in lean periods the disciples had to go out into the forest and gather wild fruits (called *pilu* and *dele*) which, apparently, were inedible until boiled – and, once boiled, were quite unappetizing. The sheikh and his family would weave baskets, which earned enough for two loaves of bread a day. In general, one loaf was divided among his disciples and visitors; the second loaf among his large family. This was coarse millet bread and, on the days when little or no *futuh* was received, it was unbuttered. Yet in Sloka 29, Sheikh Farid sings of his contentment with this simple fare:

> Farid, eat your dry crust of bread;
> > take simple cold water.
> Envy not the delicacies another is enjoying.[174]

However, the sheikh, his family, and all those in the *khanqah* also faced periods when even this minimal food was not forthcoming, and near starvation seemed to be the will of God – certainly a stern test of their extreme trust in God. Among Sheikh Farid's aphorisms that have been preserved through the oral tradition in the lineage are:

If you wish to avoid disgrace, do not beg.

Accept affliction as a gift.

Do not flee from the calamity sent to you by God.

Do not rely on your own strength.

Pray to God alone, for everyone else takes away, but He gives.

Whatever He gives cannot be taken away by anyone else.[175]

Sheikh Gesu Daraz, a sheikh in the Chishti lineage three generations after him, records that Sheikh Farid always kept four sets of clothes, one on his body, one due for washing, one for an emergency change, and one to give away to someone needing clothes.[176] This description relates to periods when *futuh* flowed like a river into the *khanqah* ... and when an equal river of gifts flowed immediately out to the needy. His attitude towards clothing illustrates his clear intention to be always at the ready to give whatever was needed to the people he met.

But there were also lean periods when Sheikh Farid's only set of clothes was grimy and tattered. Even then his principle of giving away whatever he had continued unabated. One time he went to Delhi and attended a discourse by Sheikh Badruddin Ghaznavi. As the head of the Chishti Order, Sheikh Farid would have been shown some respect, but he was in such dirty, ragged clothes that no one recognized him. After that evening a man, embarrassed by the neglect shown to Sheikh Farid, gave him a new set of clothes, which he accepted. But his younger brother, Sheikh Najibuddin Mutawakkil, who also lived in Delhi, was extremely poor. Sheikh Farid took off the clothes and presented them to his brother. Perhaps his brother may have objected, but he graciously replied, "The pleasure that I have in my grimy and tattered garments is not to be found in these new clothes."[177]

The Virtues of a True Human Being

According to Chishti teachings the development of mystical consciousness is, and must always be, paired with a life of the highest human virtues. This way of life includes selfless service, helping the needy, and loving kindness for all, regardless of religious or caste distinctions. For the Chishtis, these outward actions are a form of prayer. Sheikh Sharib says prayer means the continual remembrance of God's presence with a receptive heart, and it also implies kindness to His creatures as a natural outcome of this awareness. He writes:

> Instead of limiting prayer in its implication, expression and meaning, Khwaja Sahib [Chishti] gives a wide connotation to the word 'prayer.' Prayer consists in selfless service, sympathy and fellow-feeling. Thus, hearing the complaints of the aggrieved is itself a type of prayer. Likewise, helping the weak and the aggrieved constitutes prayer. To help the needy and oppressed is also prayer. To feed the hungry and the poor is an efficacious type of prayer. To set free the captives from captivity is itself a type of prayer.[178]

For the mystic, such acts of service and kindness are neither self-conscious nor calculated. They are the natural consequence of the experience of divine love. As Sheikh Sharib expresses the teachings that have been passed down the Chishti lineage:

> The true love knows of no consideration. It is not carried away to do something for God, not as a duty, nor as being useful, nor for the simple fact that there was anything in it at all beyond the fact of loving Him.... Genuine love rules out the idea of serving the Friend with a reserve.[179]

Khwaja Chishti's often-repeated description of the qualities of a saint was: "A generosity like the ocean, a beneficence like the sun, a humility like the earth."[180] There could not be a more fitting description of Baba Farid.

A Generosity Like the Ocean

Sheikh Farid's generosity was, indeed, boundless like the ocean. An ocean is so vast that it remains itself, unchanged by changing circumstances, unlike a smaller body of water like a river or a lake. In a period of extreme drought, a river may shrink to a muddy trickle. In a period of extreme cold, a lake may freeze over. But the ocean neither shrinks in a dry period, nor freezes in the cold. And Sheikh Farid, through the wide swings of fortune he faced in his life, remained ever the same.

In his generosity, he instituted a free kitchen. Anyone who came to him was fed, free of charge, regardless of whether they were Hindu or Muslim, rich or poor, spiritual seeker or simply someone who was hungry. The idea of a free kitchen (*langar*) was subsequently to become a hallmark of the culture of the Punjab. In the generation after Sheikh Farid, the idea was further developed by Nizamuddin, whose *khanqah* in the teeming city of Delhi fed masses of poor people with a kitchen that ran twenty-four hours a day. Chishti *khanqah*s through the centuries have continued the tradition of running a free community kitchen . Thus, spiritual teachers' providing free food for all became deeply rooted in Punjabi culture. The *langar* tradition assures that all are fed, free of charge, and eat side by side, regardless of caste, wealth or status.

One might wonder how Sheikh Farid, whose poverty was such that he had absolutely no resources, could possibly provide free food to all the residents and visitors. The answer can only be that his generosity was unrelated to his own resources. Whatever came to him, he understood it to have come from the Lord. And, having no claim on it himself, he gave it away to God's beloved creatures. Through periods of scarcity and periods of plenty, his generosity was unchanged. What changed was only the amount and types of food and gifts given. Nizamuddin recalled how "Silver and food and blessings due to the kindness of the Almighty Creator, all were distributed from there to all comers."[181] It was a generosity only possible for one who has lost himself in the love of his Beloved – the generosity of the selfless.

Helping the poor, feeding the hungry, and caring for the distressed are deeply rooted in the Chishti tradition. Khwaja Chishti himself is called Gharib Nawaz, 'Helper of the Poor.' And throughout the centuries since his time, Chishti *khanqah*s have been especially known for their unstinting aid to the destitute. In this, the Chishtis follow the example and precept of the Prophet Muhammad:

> In the Qur'an *infaq* (giving away, that is, in charity) is a recurring theme. It is a moral and religious imperative.... The Prophet expressed his preference for the poor over the rich in no uncertain manner. "The people before you," he warned his followers, "were destroyed because they used to inflict punishments on the poor and forgive the rich." The majority of the dwellers of the Paradise, declared the Prophet, would

be poor people.... The Prophet undoubtedly visualized a society wherein the state, society and the well-to-do would all help the poor and the indigent and in general favour the weak against the strong. It is an altogether different matter how long the Prophet's followers took to forget his message; within a century after his demise, observes a modern Arab historian, the system of poor aid had been turned upside down and become a 'gigantic system of relief for the ruling class.'[182]

Under *shariah*, the rule of required alms (*zakat*) is that each person must give two and a half percent of his wealth in charity to the poor. But Sheikh Farid made a striking distinction between the alms required by law and the alms of those who are following the Sufi path. And the alms required from those who have realized the Truth are still more all-encompassing:

He used to say that alms are of three kinds: alms of the Law, of the Path, and of Truth. Alms of the Law means that one gives 5 *dirams* of every 200. Alms of the Path means that one keeps but 5 *dirams* of every 200, while alms of Truth means that you expend all that you have and keep nothing![183]

Sheikh Farid taught his followers the principle of generosity both through his actions and through his words. A disciple came to Sheikh Farid, telling him that he had once thrown some grain to feed the sparrows and the next day he had unexpectedly received a maund* of wheat as well as some coins. Sheikh Farid was quick to roll out the following couplet extempore:

---

*A traditional unit of weight that ranged from 25 pounds (11 kg) to 160 pounds (72.5 kg). The modern standard for India and Pakistan is about 37 kg.

Feed birds small and large
  so mayhap someday
  you snare the Humā.*[184]

Some of the aphorisms derived from Sheikh Farid's sayings relate
to the importance he attached to a generous spirit:

While doing good to others, think that you are helping yourself.

Do not eat everyone's bread, but give bread to everyone.

Be grateful, but do not compel others to be grateful to you.

Be magnanimous during a period of personal affluence.[185]

Sheikh Farid's generosity was not only in giving food, clothing, and shelter; nor was it only in8 giving away everything that
came in *futuh*. He was also unstintingly generous with his time,
his attention, and his blessings. One time the soldiers of Sultan
Nasiruddin were passing through Ajodhan. This was at a time
when Sheikh Farid's fame had spread far and wide. His shirt was
hanging outside the window to dry and the soldiers, frantic for the
blessings of the Sheikh, crowded around it to kiss the cloth. Soon,
in their eagerness to grab a talisman from the holy sheikh, they
had shredded the shirt. In the midst of this chaos, Sheikh Farid
had to walk to the mosque, and he instructed his disciples to form
a circle around him, as a protection from the frenzied soldiers.
However, a day labourer broke through the circle and implored
Sheikh Farid to allow his devotees access to him. Accordingly,

---

*The Humā is a mythical bird believed to raise to the throne anyone coming
under the shadow of its wings.

Sheikh Farid stepped out of the circle and, notwithstanding the danger, walked through the crowd.[186]

Every morning the door to Sheikh Farid's hut remained closed until he had finished his prayers and spiritual exercises. During that sacred time no one was allowed to disturb him, but always, as soon as he emerged, there was a constant line of people wanting his attention. Baba Farid saw each one and listened attentively to their concerns.

> Tales of human sufferings racked his heart and seared his soul. He suffered for others and shared their grief. His kind words of sympathy and advice were like balm to the afflicted who came to him. How correct is Barani's [a well-known thirteenth-century historian] estimate of the Sheikh when he says: 'He had taken the inhabitants of this region under his wings!'[187]

Once his door was opened in the morning, it remained so until midnight, as a welcome to all who sought his help. He said that his meditation didn't feel complete unless he had also responded to all who needed his attention. Nizamuddin described Sheikh Farid's way of life at the *jama'at khanah*:

> Despite his longing for solitude, there was no limit to the number of people who were forever visiting him. The door to his hospice was never closed except for half of the night, more or less; that is to say, it was continuously open.... What a marvelous power! What a splendid life. To none of the sons of Adam had such grace previously been available. If someone came into his presence for the first time and someone else who had been an acquaintance for some years also came, he would pay equal attention to each, and of kindness and concern he would give them equal measure.[188]

A Beneficence Like the Sun

The sun does not discriminate as to where its life-giving rays should fall. It does not shine on one person's field and withhold its rays from his neighbour's field, even if the two happen to be fighting with each other, nor if they happen to be of different religions or castes. The visitors who thronged to Sheikh Farid's *khanqah* were Sufis or yogis, merchants, soldiers, or scholars. They arrived from "Khurasan, Jurjan, Delhi, Uch, Nagaur, Multan, Ajmer, Buhar and Lakmawti."[189] The *khanqah* had a stable for the horses, and travellers were welcomed to stay in the *jama'at khanah*.[190] Local tribesmen, herdsmen, and farmers, and the destitute struggling in grinding poverty also came. In short, his visitors came from all classes of society. Sheikh Farid's kindness and welcoming hospitality were for all.

> Though within the political confines of the Sultanate of Delhi, the *jama'at khanah* of Sheikh Farid was not a part of the Delhi Empire. It was at that time, the only place under the Indian sun where the Emperor of Hindustan and a penniless pauper were received in the same way. The contamination of court life had not touched its spiritual serenity and classless atmosphere. It was an oasis of love in a world of strifes and conflicts. The Sheikh who presided over this *jama'at khanah* was a tower of strength for the low-born, the downtrodden, the humble and the despised people whom he inspired and cheered in their struggle for existence.[191]

At the time, the Mamluk Turkish ruling class discriminated between Turks and non-Turks, Muslims and non-Muslims, high-placed officials and destitute labourers. The original Islamic ideals of equality and fraternity were lost in the struggle for power. Meanwhile, the caste system in medieval India placed individuals in a rigidly defined social order.[192]

> The Hadis, Domas, Chandulas and Badhatus were given
> sub-human status in the social hierarchy of medieval India...
> and treated as outcasts.... All amenities of civic life were
> denied to them.... They had no access to the temples....
> The unassuming ways of the mystics, their broad human
> sympathies, the classless atmosphere of the *khanqahs*
> attracted these despised sections of Indian society to their
> fold. Here they found an entirely different social order; all
> discriminations and distinctions which Hindu society had
> imposed upon them were meaningless in the *khanqahs*. All
> lived, slept and ate together.[193]

In this milieu, we might guess that some of Sheikh Farid's
disciples may have struggled within themselves to overcome
long-standing prejudices; in the *khanqah*, they sat side by side
with people they had been taught to hate. Someone once brought
Sheikh Farid a pair of scissors. He commented, "Don't bring me
scissors; bring me a needle. I don't cut apart; I sew together."[194]
This statement has become one of Sheikh Farid's best-known sayings, emblematic of his consistent efforts to bridge the divisions
that create hatred among people.

It is ironic – and unfortunate – that Sheikh Farid has often
been personally credited with 'the Islamization of India.' In fact,
based on the recorded evidence, Sheikh Farid never converted
a single Hindu to Islam.[195] The *khilafat namas* – the documents
by which Sheikh Farid appointed his *khalifas*, authorizing them
to initiate disciples – give incredibly detailed instructions. These
documents say nothing about bringing Hindus to Islam. [196] One
of Sheikh Farid's aphorisms, preserved in the lineage, may be
related to his approach to non-Muslims:

Do not sell what people do not wish to buy.[197]

As we have seen, Sheikh Farid did initiate non-Muslims into the spiritual path, giving them words to use for repetition that came from their own language and religious background. Even yogis – teachers and practitioners of a spiritual tradition distinctly different from Sufism – were among the visitors who came to Sheikh Farid's *khanqah*. As seen in Nizamuddin's recollections, these visitors were warmly welcomed. In fact, the sheikh and his disciples listened respectfully to their ideas and teachings:

> Yogis seem to have been attracted to the hospice of Fariduddin Ganj-i Shakar, where Nizamuddin met one of them and was impressed by his classification of the human body in two parts, the upper the seat of the spiritual, and the lower, that of the profane aspect of human nature; and by the yogic principle that one was required to develop truth, benevolence and kindness in the upper part and preserve chastity and purity in the lower.[198]

All in all, Sheikh Farid stands out as a striking example of the broad-mindedness of saints. As a Muslim, he faithfully observed the commands of *shariah* – as the Sufi path he followed and taught had deep roots in Islam – and also understood that mystical realization involved a reality that was universal and could be expressed through other languages, other metaphors, and other cultural forms.

Following in his footsteps, Nizamuddin never converted Hindus to Islam, nor did his successor, Nasiruddin Chiragh.[199] Once, Nizamuddin watched a procession of Hindus chanting with drums and bells making their way towards the Jamuna River. He commented, "Every [group of] people has its own path of righteousness, beliefs, and their own focus of adoration."[200] He understood that it was the adoration more than the form of worship that really mattered. This idea would have shocked a magistrate in his time. Amir Khusrau, the well-known poet who was a disciple of Nizamuddin, put it poetically: "O you who sneer at the idolatry of the Hindu, learn also from him how worship is done."[201]

How, then, are we to understand the widespread belief that Sheikh Farid personally converted masses of Hindus to Islam? "The tribes claim and have been claiming for centuries that their ancestors were converted to Islam by the great saint."[202] The most plausible explanation comes from Richard Eaton who has charted the "gradual conversion to Islam by a process of intergenerational accretion among tribal groups in the Punjab"[203] during the centuries since Sheikh Farid's time. The tomb of Sheikh Farid became a shrine and a prominent place of pilgrimage. Over the centuries after his death, as the city of Pakpattan attracted a stream of visitors to the shrine of Sheikh Farid, it grew in wealth and influence.

Studying the local records, Richard Eaton found a slow, steady increase in the percentage of Islamic names among the population. His theory is that in the nomadic and tribal lifestyles of western Punjab the Brahmanical culture was not as deeply ingrained as in other parts of India. The gradual shift to a settled agricultural lifestyle took place under the influence of the political system and literate traditions of Islam, and therefore was accompanied by a gradual conversion to Islam.[204]

This sociological explanation of the Islamization of these parts of the Punjab seems valid, yet has little bearing on the Sufi experience. Not only Sheikh Farid and his successors, but also Sufis throughout the Indian subcontinent, have repeatedly stressed that mysticism transcends the boundaries of religion. As Mir Dard (1721–1785 CE) wrote:

> In monastery, at Ka'bah or in temple
> We all are guests; only You are the Master of the house.[205]

And in the words of Bulleh Shah (1680–1757 CE):

> We are neither Hindus nor Muslims
> We sit and spin leaving pride of creed
> We are neither Sunnis nor Shias
> We are non-violent towards everyone.[206]

Sultan Bahu (1628–1691 CE) agrees, writing of the Sufis:

> They are neither Hindus nor Muslims,
> Nor do they bow down to pray in mosque.
> In every breath they see God
> And never miss the mystic cry of Hoo!*[207]

The Sindhi mystic, Sachal Sarmast (1739–1829 CE), adds his voice to this chorus:

> Those hearts have drunk the cup of the wine of love.
> Their heart remains ever intoxicated,
> Religion, creeds do not remain intact –
> Nor do paganism nor Islam.[208]

Throughout the centuries – not only during Sheikh Farid's time, but also before and after – the Chishti Sufi Order has continued to work to eliminate prejudice and discrimination among people. Sheikh Sharib states that the Sufis' "guiding principle is universal love, kindness, and regard."[209]

The Sufis hold that the outward enemies are not so dangerous as the inward enemies. The Sufis pay respect to all the religions, whether it be Hinduism, Buddhism, Judaism,

---

*Hoo (literally meaning He) refers to God. It is often spelled Hu.

Zoroastrianism, Christianity or Sikhism. They see Allah in everything and in every object. According to them Allah is not in a temple, a mosque or church alone, but He is in everything. He is everywhere! Allah is free from all forms and names. Call Him by whatever name you like, He is still Allah. All things come from Allah and, hence, should be accepted without murmur.[210]

The stated mission of the Chishti Sufi Order today is to:

> ...shatter the barriers which stand between man and man for diverse reasons and knit them together in [a] common bond of fraternity, love, regardless of religion, caste or creed affiliations. We also believe and practise that God is symbolic of love and the entire humanity in its diverse form constitutes a single family. It is indeed almost akin and similar to the Vedanta principle '*vasu dheva kutumbakam*' (meaning, the world is one family).[211]

A Humility Like the Earth

The earth is trampled underfoot, yet it also provides the nourishment that sustains all life. We take the earth for granted, yet it is what supports us. Sheikh Farid's humility was as enduring and as unshakeable as the earth.

And so, to the *khanqah* of this humble giver came disciples and sincere seekers after truth. To his *khanqah* came the poor and the distressed in need of help. However, it also seemed to attract some visitors who were rude, demanding, and offensive. In all these cases, Sheikh Farid remained a model of the "Chishtiyya principles of peaceable meekness and boundless forbearance for human foibles."[212]

One typical example was an old man, accompanied by his son who was insolent and began arguing with Sheikh Farid. When a disciple heard the boy shouting loudly at the sheikh, he slapped the boy. Sheikh Farid intervened and quietly asked his disciple to "please the visitors." Both father and son were given some money, with apologies, and they left the *jama'at khanah* happy and satisfied.[213] It was from incidents like this one that Nizamuddin learned a lesson that he later applied when he was sheikh in his *khanqah* in Delhi: no one should leave the *khanqah* unhappy.

Sheikh Farid was a living example of the advice he gave in his slokas:

> Farid, answer evil with goodness;
>> do not fill your mind with anger.[214]

His way was not to judge others, even when their behaviour was by any standards unacceptable. He said:

> Farid, if you have a keen understanding,
>> then do not write
>> black remarks against anyone else.
> Look underneath your own collar instead.[215]

This was illustrated in a particularly vivid way by an incident involving a *qalandar* (a type of wandering Sufi who deliberately flouts all social norms). When the *qalandar* arrived at the *khanqah*, he was treated graciously. Sheikh Farid was in his room at the time, engaged in devotion, but his prayer mat was in front of his door. The *qalandar*, without asking, sat down on it. Badruddin Ishaq restrained himself from objecting and offered the guest some food. The *qalandar* made himself at home, ate the food, and then began to prepare hemp, making a paste of it. When pieces of the intoxicating hemp fell on the carpet, it was too much for Badruddin Ishaq. He tried to restrain the *qalandar*, who raised his hand to strike him. At that moment, Sheikh Farid came out of his room and begged the *qalandar* to forgive his disciple. But the *qalandar* declared that once he raised his hand, he never brought it down without accomplishing something. Sheikh Farid suggested that he take out his vengeance on the wall, instead of on Badruddin Ishaq. The *qalandar* struck the wall, and the entire wall collapsed.[216]

Yet another incident, related by Nizamuddin, illustrates the sheikh's boundless patience and his good will even to those who were antagonistic to him:

> Once, five dervishes came into the presence of the Sheikh. They were harsh in temperament and stood defiantly before the Sheikh. 'Though we have travelled far and wide,' they declared, 'we have yet to find a true dervish.' 'Please be seated,' said Sheikh Fariduddin, 'and I will show you a dervish.' They had been standing up and they continued to stand up. 'When you leave,' advised the Sheikh, 'do not take the road through the jungle. Go by another road.' Disregarding the Sheikh's advice, they took the jungle road. Now the Sheikh had sent someone to trail them and to note which road they took. Word came back to him that they had taken the jungle road. On hearing this report, he cried out, 'Oh! Oh!' as if someone had just died. In short, after the defiant dervishes took the jungle road, a violent dust storm blew up. It killed four of them on the spot. The fifth dervish struggled to a well and, after drinking too much water, died there.[217]

Modelling restraint and forbearance himself, Sheikh Farid also taught his disciples the importance of sweet speech and gentle, polite manners. One time he instructed Nizamuddin and Badruddin Ishaq to sit with a group of dervishes who were particularly kind and self-effacing in their manner of talking with one another. Nizamuddin recalled marvelling over the way these dervishes continually expressed such respect for each other:

In short, they continued to speak things like this in the same manner until I and Badruddin Ishaq were reduced to tears by their humility and restraint. I said to myself, these are divine messengers sent to teach us how discourse (between dervishes) should take place! Afterward, on the master's blessed tongue came this pronouncement: "You must control the jugular vein, that is, you must not show the effect of anger or intemperance (in discourse)."

After this there was much discussion of patience and forbearance. He said: "Everyone who bears injury is better than he who can scarcely repress anger, for one must not be bent on retaliation." These two lines of poetry came on his blessed tongue:

May God befriend all those who are my foes,
May all who hurt me gain increased repose.

After that he added another couplet:

May all who in my path place thorns from spite
Lead lives that flower like a thornless rose.

Then he remarked, "If someone puts a thorn [in your path] and you put a thorn [in his], there are thorns everywhere!" And he concluded: "It is like this among men, that you are straight with those who are straight with you, and crooked to those who are crooked. But among dervishes, it is like this, that you are straight with those who are straight with you, and with the crooked, you are also straight."[218]

However, it is one thing to be patient and gentle with guests who are rude, and it is quite another thing to deal with outright malevolent opposition. As Sheikh Farid's popularity grew, the local magistrate in Ajodhan grew jealous. After trying unsuccessfully to undermine Sheikh Farid's position in various ways, he went to Multan to try to get an official decree against him. His pretext was Sheikh Farid's fondness for *sama*, always a controversial practice. He went before the judges in Multan and said, "Where is it permitted that someone may sit in a mosque, listen to musical performances, and from time to time even begin to dance?" They asked: "Of whom do you speak? Be specific. Tell us who does such things." But when he told them it was Sheikh Farid, they demurred, "Oh. About him we can say nothing."[219]

Infuriated by his failure, the magistrate's next attempt was to hire an assassin and try to have Sheikh Farid killed. Nizamuddin was at the *khanqah* at the time, and he recalled the incident. Sheikh Farid had just finished his morning prayer, and he was still on his knees with his head on the ground.

> Still engrossed in God, his head remained prostrate on the ground. For a long time, as often happened, he remained like that, absorbed in God, his head prostrate on the ground. But because it was winter they had brought a garment and spread it over his blessed body. No attendants remained. Just I and he and no one else.

> Suddenly someone entered and in a loud voice shouted 'Peace!' The Sheikh was jolted from his meditative mood. But with his head still prostrate on the ground and the

garment covering him, he asked: 'Who is here?' I spoke up and said: 'I am!'

'The man who just entered,' said the Sheikh, 'is a Turk of medium stature with a sallow complexion.' I looked at the man. He was exactly as the Sheikh described him. I said: 'Yes, he is.' 'Does he have a chain around his waist?' I looked at him, and saw that he did. 'Yes, he has,' I replied. 'And does he also have something in his ears?' I looked and saw that he did. 'Yes, he has an earring,' I replied. And every time I looked at him and then responded to the Sheikh, the man became more and more uneasy.

After I had said 'Yes, he has an earring,' the Sheikh replied: 'Tell him to go away lest he become disgraced.' When I looked back toward the man, he had already taken to his heels and disappeared.[220]

What could be more humble, or more forgiving, than to help the would-be assassin to escape before he took on the sin of killing a saint? According to Chishti teachings, such peaceable forbearance is the sign of a developed soul:

The Sufis look at good and evil as emanating from Allah. They are guided in this respect by the principle underlying the law of forgiveness, which is that of returning good for evil. This law is a fundamental plank in the spiritual life.... It is a law for individual conduct; it raises man, the brute, to the position of a saint.... The Sufis believe that forgiveness is a divine quality. It should be inculcated, practised and preached. Human nature is weak. Man is liable to make mistakes. Retribution does not reform a man, it does not lead to introspection. Forgiveness not only wins over a person, but also makes him realize his mistakes. Forgiveness is the sign of the developed soul. It is a signal of illumination and inner purification.[221]

Among Sheikh Farid's sayings are the following gems of wisdom:

Always keep the doors of peace open in war.

If you wish to be great, be humble.

If you want to make the whole world your enemy, be arrogant.[222]

Another face of Sheikh Farid's humility – and of his deep wisdom – was his scrupulous avoidance of accepting favours from high-placed government officials or ruling princes. It was one of the fundamental teachings of Khwaja Chishti that Sufis should avoid all dealings with royalty. In those days governing sultans and ministers often sought to establish a connection with a popular Sufi sheikh. Perhaps it enhanced the image of a rising military chieftain to be seen associated with a Sufi sheikh. However, in a world where one dynasty overthrew another, with intrigue and assassination as routes to power, a Sufi sheikh who allowed himself to be connected to any ruler was likely to be drawn into the political intrigues of the powerful. According to Chishti teachings, the Sufi must maintain his spiritual independence from the ups and downs of worldly powers.

Of course, the offers of wealth and power might be tempting to a lesser mind. Only a deeply ingrained humility, paired with contentment in a state of poverty, could keep a Sufi sheikh safe. Sheikh Farid's advice to disciples tempted to become embroiled in politics is captured in several of his aphorisms:

Do not worry about position and wealth.

Do not lower yourself in order to secure a position.

Do not forget religion in the company of state dignitaries.[223]

But this is the best known and most often repeated of these aphorisms:

If you desire elevation in your spiritual ranks, keep away from hereditary princes.[224]

This advice is so indelibly associated with Sheikh Farid that several well-known modern scholars attribute the following Persian verse to him even though no early source has been found to confirm his authorship:

> Keep your distance from kings and rulers;
> 　　avoid them so they do not appear at your door.
> Your desire to attract their sort
> 　　will block you from reaching your self.[225]

For his disciples and for the common people he had many pearls of advice, but for royalty he had only one thing to say: "The reins of administration in the kingdom should be given into the hands of a God-fearing minister."[226]

When Sayyidi Maula came to him to ask permission to leave Ajodhan and settle in Delhi, Sheikh Farid warned him sternly: "But keep in mind my one advice. Do not associate with kings and nobles. Regard their visits to your house as calamities. Every dervish who opens the door of association with kings and nobles is doomed."[227] It was advice that fell on deaf ears. Sayyidi Maula went on to dabble in politics, lavishly entertaining high-placed officials. In the end, his was a grim fate. When his patron's fortunes turned, he himself was imprisoned and then tortured to death.

Badruddin Ghaznavi's case was not as extreme as Sayyidi Maula's, but it illustrates just how hard it was to be the *khalifa* of Sheikh Bakhtiyar Kaki in Delhi and to remain fully independent of all political intrigues. Badruddin Ghaznavi allowed a high government official to build a new *khanqah* for him and to pay for its ongoing maintenance. Then before long, an investigation proved that this government official had been embezzling. Soon Badruddin Ghaznavi was also suspect. He wrote to Sheikh Farid, expressing his anxiety over the situation.

Sheikh Farid's response was stern: "Whoever does not follow the conduct and custom of our spiritual masters will end up like this."[228] In other words, Khwaja Chishti and Sheikh Bakhtiyar Kaki had never allowed any government official to endow the building of a *khanqah*. Farid's point was that any sheikh who does not follow their example will face the troubles that now threatened Badruddin Ghaznavi. Happily, Badruddin survived the incident, escaping the fate of Sayyidi Maula. But his reputation was tarnished and, due to this incident, the Chishti Sufi Order lost both its following and its respect in Delhi.*

Even in Ajodhan, remote as it was from the capital, maintaining a strict independence from all connections with government was not easy. Sheikh Farid was repeatedly requested to write to Ulugh Khan, the future Sultan Balban, to recommend a certain person for a position. Finally, he gave in and wrote. His wording of the letter demonstrates his extreme care to remain independent of any obligation to the crafty soon-to-be sultan. He wrote:

> I put his case first before God and then before you. If you award him something, you will be thanked for it because you are the agent for this award, but God, in the real sense,

---

* Still, Badruddin Ghaznavi himself lived to a ripe old age. Like his master, Sheikh Bakhtiyar Kaki, he was devoted to *sama*, and it is said that in his eighties he still danced like a boy of ten!

is the only bestower; if you refuse it, then you are helpless in this matter, because God is the only refuser.[229]

Still, for all his scrupulous care, his own case proved the truth of his warning: 'Regard the visits of kings or nobles to your house as a calamity.' Although he had not invited Ulugh Khan to Ajodhan and although he refused the grant of four villages and instantly gave away the gifts of money, nonetheless his seeming association with Sultan Balban brought misfortune in its wake. Sher Khan became antagonistic to Sheikh Farid due to his perceived association with Balban. It was due to Sher Khan's influence that merchants and wealthy patrons stopped sending any donations to the *khanqah* in Ajodhan. The last few years of Sheikh Farid's life were spent in the most extreme poverty.

Undoubtedly, Sheikh Farid himself would have viewed the situation as having nothing to do with Sher Khan. God, in His bounty, sent the *futuh*; God, in His grace, withheld the *futuh*. Still, for those last few years, Sheikh Farid and his family and near disciples faced near starvation. In his final year, Sheikh Farid had an 'affliction of the bowels' which, ultimately, was the cause of death. Nizamuddin's description of the ancient sheikh is poignant: his frail ninety-three-year-old body stretched out on a cot with the small carpet he sat on during the day laid over him, a carpet too small to cover his legs. Sick as he was, he kept to his routine of prayers, and he died with the names of God, "O the Living! O the Eternal," on his lips.[230]

The evening of the fifth of the month of Muharram he became very ill. In the company of others he said the final evening prayer, then fell unconscious. After a while he regained consciousness, asking: 'Did I say the final evening prayer?' 'Yes, you did,' they all replied. 'I better say it once again,' he murmured, 'for who knows what will happen?'

Then he became unconscious for still longer, but once again regained consciousness. 'Did I say the final evening prayer?' he asked. 'You have already said it twice,' they replied. 'Then I better say it once again,' he murmured 'for who knows what will happen?' Then, saying the evening prayer a third time, he became joined to the mercy of God [i.e., he died].[231]

At the time of his death, Sheikh Farid was so poor that there was not even a piece of cloth to use for a burial sheet. There were no bricks for his grave. They had to take down a wall of his hut to make the grave for the great Sheikh Farid.[232]

Multan and Ajodhan: A Study in Contrasts

Sheikh Farid modelled an approach to Sufism in which the virtues of humility, generosity, and unstinting hospitality were paramount. However, Sufism in India in this period was diverse, and other Sufi sheikhs modelled different approaches. Although the fundamental mystical teachings were the same, different Sufi Orders presented quite different faces of the Sufi path.

A comparison between Sheikh Farid and Sheikh Bahauddin Zakariya may provide a broader context of Sufism in the Punjab during this period. The differences between the Chishti *khanqah* in Ajodhan and the Suhrawardi *khanqah* in nearby Multan are striking. Interestingly, in spite of these differences, the sheikhs of the two lineages maintained deep respect for each other.

Sheikh Zakariya's *khanqah* in Multan was spacious and well built, with separate rooms for the disciples staying there. The furnishings and arrangements were very comfortable, unlike the rough conditions in Sheikh Farid's *khanqah* where everyone sat and slept on the mud-plastered floor in one big room. The Suhrawardi approach to *futuh* – or, one might say, their understanding of 'trusting in God' – was also different. They had no rule of giving away everything that was received the same day, and they also accepted land grants with the right to the annual revenues from a particular village or area. Consequently, the *khanqah* of Sheikh Zakariya in Multan eventually became quite wealthy.[233]

While Sheikh Farid had to face periods of severe deprivation, and while he also fasted as a part of his discipline, Sheikh Zakariya was well fed. In fact, the meals in Multan were sumptuous by comparison with the meagre fare in Ajodhan. Sheikh Farid's successor, Nizamuddin, followed in his pir's footsteps. *Futuh* flowed so profusely into his *khanqah* in Delhi that, in the words of one commentator, it seemed the River Yamuna had been diverted into the *khanqah*. And his *langar* operated around the clock, feeding thousands of poor people each day. In the midst of this bounty, however, Nizamuddin himself hardly ate anything and fasted often. He said he simply could not eat when he thought of the suffering of so many destitute people.

In such a circumstance of contrasts – at least if these were ordinary, worldly people – one might expect Nizamuddin to express a negative judgment of Sheikh Zakariya's easy enjoyment of tasty food. On the contrary, when he spoke to his own disciples about Sheikh Zakariya he said, "He would seldom fast, yet he performed numerous acts of obedience and devotion." He quoted from the Qur'an: "Eat of good things and do righteous deeds (Q 51)." And then he added, "This verse was fulfilled in the case of Sheikh Bahauddin!"[234]

The Suhrawardi sheikh also took an entirely different approach to hospitality to that of Sheikh Farid and his successors. While every kind of visitor was welcomed to the *jama'at khanah* of Sheikh Farid, Sheikh Zakariya was much more particular about who was allowed to come into his *khanqah*. The atmosphere was more formal, with care given to rules of conduct and manners. Random travellers, visitors, and the common people were not welcome.[235] The rude *qalandar* who had imposed himself on

Sheikh Farid, mixing hemp paste on his prayer carpet, would certainly not have found kindly treatment.

One time a group of *juwaliqs* (a type of itinerant, wild, and unruly dervish, like the *qalandars*) came to Sheikh Zakariya. As Nizamuddin related:

> The Sheikh had a very low regard for this group. Upon their arrival the juwaliqs expected the Sheikh to give them something. He did not. They went outside and began to quarrel. As they made an uproar, they also began picking up bricks. The Sheikh ordered the door to be closed. After it was closed, the juwaliqs began to heave bricks against it. A little while later Sheikh Bahauddin Zakariya declared, 'I am occupying this place at the command of Sheikh Shihabuddin Suhrawardi. I did not come here of my own accord. It was a man of God who bade me come here.' He then ordered them to open the door of his hospice. When they did, the juwaliqs fell on the ground, prostrating themselves before the Sheikh. Then they got up and left.[236]

Nizamuddin, commenting on this incident, explained: "The first time that Sheikh Bahauddin ordered the door closed, it was out of human instinct, but he also was not sure of the spiritual quality of that moment. But after a little while [when his mind had become clear] he ordered the door to be opened."[237] In this explanation, we see not only Nizamuddin's understanding of the difference between acting on human instinct versus as an agent of the Divine, we also see his clear respect for Sheikh Zakariya's authority as vested in him by Sheikh Shihabuddin Suhrawardi.

When Sheikh Suhrawardi appointed Sheikh Zakariya as his successor, he had sent him to Multan to establish his *khanqah* there and begin initiating disciples. Sheikh Zakariya's statement to the *juwaliqs* that he did not come to Multan of his own accord was true. Apparently, in his early years at Multan he so longed to spend time with his pir, Sheikh Suhrawardi, that he even set out on a return trip to Baghdad. Evidently Sheikh Suhrawardi was aware of his intention and sent Sheikh Tabrizi to intercept Sheikh Zakariya and tell him, "It is the command of the Sheikh of Sheikhs that you return."[238] And so, once again in obedience, Sheikh Zakariya turned back and returned to Multan.

Among Sufis of this period, the concept of *wilayat* supported the mutual respect among the several different Sufi Orders being established throughout the region. *Wilayat* means the grace, blessing or power of a sheikh. In this period in Indian Sufism, however, the term *wilayat* also connoted governorship, the responsibility of a particular geographic area. A sheikh would bestow on his successor the *wilayat* to serve as spiritual guide within a specific location.

It is in this sense that Khwaja Chishti said to Sheikh Bakhtiyar Kaki, "I have placed this city [Delhi] under your protection."[239], Khwaja Chishti had sent Sheikh Bakhtiyar Kaki to Delhi, but on his way there Sheikh Bakhtiyar Kaki stopped in Multan. According to Jamali, the ruler of Multan requested him to settle there permanently and establish his *khanqah* there. He refused, saying, "This region has been placed under the spiritual protection of Sheikh Zakariya and it will remain under him forever."[240]

An illustrative incident that is often repeated concerns a time when Sheikh Bakhtiyar Kaki was staying in the mosque in Multan. Sheikh Zakariya arrived, perhaps returning from a trip.

The Suhrawardi saint did not like the stay of Khwaja Qutbuddin in Multan and considered it an undesirable intrusion into his own spiritual jurisdiction. The polite way of asking a saint to leave one's jurisdiction (*wilayat*) was to place his shoes in the direction one would like him to go. Sheikh Bahauddin Zakariya did so and Khwaja Qutbuddin Bakhtiyar, taking the hint, left for Delhi.[241]

This idea of a particular territory being placed under the protection of a given sheikh is vividly illustrated in Sheikh Farid's attitude towards Multan. Apparently, he considered that his own *wilayat* extended only a certain distance towards Multan and not past that point. If a traveller, passing through, asked for his protection as he travelled on, he said he could only give protection up to that boundary, and that after that it was for Sheikh Zakariya to extend his hand of protection.[242]

The mutual respect and deference for territorial boundaries notwithstanding, a Suhrawardi sheikh might well be used in a teaching story by a Chishti sheikh. Once Nizamuddin was teaching his disciples not to dismiss or disregard any particular group of people. He was discussing the Sufi concept that in the midst of every group of people there is – hidden and perhaps unrecognizable – one of God's own Friends. In making this point he related an incident involving Sheikh Zakariya. The story may not be factual, but Sheikh Zakariya, known as he was for disliking and avoiding various groups, made a suitable character for the teaching story:

The Sheikh travelled much. Once he came upon a group of *juwaliqs*, and sat down among them. A light appeared in that group. As his eyes focused on it, he saw that the light emanated from a member of that group. Slowly he approached the man. 'What are you doing in the midst of this group?' he asked. 'Zakariya!' retorted the man. '[I am here] that you may know that in the midst of every group of people there is one of God's elect!'[243]

Guiding His Disciples

SHEIKH FARID was attentive to the task of guiding disciples on the spiritual path. In the stories that have been preserved, we can catch glimpses of his sensitivity to his disciples' needs and fears. During the thirty years in Ajodhan, through all the changing circumstances – whether food was plentiful or scarce, whether unruly *qalandars* knocked down walls or assassins sneaked in, then sneaked back out again – this fact was a constant.

A disciple who was a teacher in the congregational mosque in Delhi went to Ajodhan to visit his pir. All the way to Ajodhan he was trembling with fear that Sheikh Farid might bring up a subject that he knew nothing about, because his own knowledge of the Arabic classics was very limited. But Sheikh Farid took one look at him and brought up the exact subject that this disciple taught:

> I went to visit Sheikh Fariduddin – may God bless his lofty secret – and I knew nothing about jurisprudence or grammar or other sciences. I had learned only the science of disputation. It came to my mind: "If the Sheikh asks me about jurisprudence or grammar or other sciences, what will I say?" I had no sooner greeted the Sheikh and sat down than he looked at me and asked, "What is the meaning of the technical term 'examination of the object of dispute' (*tanqih-i manat*)?" I was relieved. I began to clarify that term, explaining both the negative and the positive connotations of its meaning.[244]

Hazrat Nizamuddin Auliya commented on this incident: "What perfect intuition had the Sheikh that he asked him not only about his profession but also about his particular discipline. Praise be to God the Lord of the universe!"[245]

Sheikh Farid lived in a time when slavery was a common and well-accepted practice. But he, like other sheikhs in the Chishti lineage, believed that a human being should not be kept in slavery. To set a slave free was the ideal course of action, though he recognized that it might not always be a practical choice for some of his disciples. At the least, he taught, "do not retain a slave who wishes to be sold."[246] In this way, he conveyed to his disciples the idea that the wishes of a slave, in fact, do matter and should be attended to. This, in itself, was a revolutionary idea at the time.

An incident with the grandson of Sheikh Hamiduddin Nagauri who travelled to Ajodhan to ask for initiation illustrates Sheikh Farid's delicate and subtle way of getting his point across. The young man's name was Sharafuddin:

> Sharafuddin wished to become a disciple of Sheikh al-Islam.... With this intention he departed Nagaur. Now it happened that he had an expensive female slave, worth loo tankas [a valuable coin at the time], more or less. That slave asked her master: 'When you go to the Sheikh and become his disciple, also indicate my indenture to him, and take this turban wrapped around my head and give it to him as a token of my submission.' In short, after Maulana Sharafuddin met with the Sheikh and had obtained the honour of becoming his disciple, he said: 'I have a household slave. Bowing her head to the ground, she asked me: "Please take this turban that I am giving you and present it to the Sheikh."' [247]

On hearing this, Sheikh Farid simply said, "May God Almighty set her free!" [248] The newly initiated Sharafuddin's response illustrates the slippery nature of the mind still caught in egocentric thinking. Yet it also illustrates the effectiveness of Sheikh Farid's simple statement:

> When Maulana Sharafuddin heard this pronouncement, he got up, thinking to himself: 'Since these words come from the blessed Sheikh, they must be true; she will be set free. But this is an expensive slave, and I can't afford to set her free. I will sell her, and it may be that the buyer will set her free.' No sooner had he entertained this thought than a further thought crossed his mind: 'If this slave is set free in another house, that person will obtain the reward, so why don't I set her free.' Resolving to free her, he came before the Sheikh and announced: 'I have set her free!'[249]

Sheikh Farid's awareness of the foibles and weaknesses of his disciples – and his gentle humour in dealing with them – are also apparent in his dealings with another disciple named 'Arif. Sheikh Farid had made this disciple a *khalifa*, giving him permission to initiate disciples, and had sent him to Siwistan. 'Arif settled in Siwistan and was hired as the prayer leader in a mosque. The ruler in that area wanted to send a gift of 100 tankas to Sheikh Farid, and asked 'Arif to carry it to his pir.

> Keeping fifty tankas for himself, 'Arif gave the other fifty to the Sheikh. Smiling, Sheikh Fariduddin remarked: 'You have made this division on a brotherly basis [i.e., each receives half of the whole]!' That 'Arif became embarrassed. Immediately he handed over his fifty tankas to the Sheikh and, pleading for forgiveness, asked to renew his oath of loyalty as a disciple. The Sheikh gave him the hand of allegiance. He also had his head shaven. After that he remained so fully committed to serving the Sheikh that

eventually the Sheikh once again gave him permission to enrol disciples and sent him toward Siwistan.[250]

The disciples of Sheikh Farid were naturally awed by the spiritual atmosphere that surrounded him. Rumours evidently flew among the circle of disciples as they wished to understand his spiritual station, so far beyond their comprehension. One time Sheikh Najibuddin Mutawakkil, Sheikh Farid's younger brother and disciple, was deputed by the other disciples to find out what exactly Sheikh Farid experienced in his prayers. In this delightful exchange, we catch a glimpse of Sheikh Farid's sense of the insufficiency of words and his playful sense of humour:

> Once Sheikh Najibuddin asked... "It is rumoured that when you are praying, after you say 'O Lord!' you hear the reply: 'I am present, my creature!'" "No, that is not true," replied the Sheikh. "'Rumours are the midwives of facts' [i.e., what they produce are fictions, not facts]." Again Sheikh Najibuddin asked: "It is also rumoured that the esteemed Khidr* visits you." "No, that too is untrue," replied the Sheikh. Sheikh Najibuddin persisted: "Some say that men of the Unseen call on you." The Sheikh did not deny this statement but instead quipped: "You, too, Najibuddin, may be one of God's special deputies."†[251]

---

*al-Khidr is not a living, physical spiritual guide, but a spiritual being who gives guidance. al-Khidr figures in many Sufi teaching stories. It is a rare and elevated Sufi who is graced by a visit from al-Khidr.

†According to Sufi teachings, there are certain people whose highly elevated spiritual status is hidden, but on whom the continued existence of the world is dependent. These are God's deputies on earth and, though they are so close to God, no one knows who they are. Some Sufis describe a detailed hierarchy of such deputies operating like a hidden government, keeping the world in balance.

Disciples turned to Sheikh Farid, both for spiritual teaching and for solace in worldly troubles. Sometimes they needed clarity about the right course of action. Sheikh Farid's younger brother, Najibuddin, once went through a situation he found confusing. He wasn't sure whether he had acted rightly. A wealthy Turk in Delhi had built a mosque and had hired Najibuddin as the prayer leader, thus providing an ample income for him and his family. Najibuddin made a comment, based on a verse from the Qur'an, which this wealthy benefactor took as a criticism.

> The Turk took umbrage at this remark. He withdrew Sheikh Najibuddin's appointment as imam, and also evicted him from his house. Sheikh Najibuddin left Delhi and returned to Ajodhan. Coming before Sheikh al-Islam Farid...he related to him what had happened. The Sheikh replied, "God the Almighty the Exalted has promised us, 'We do not abrogate a verse of Ours or cause it to be forgotten, unless we bring another like it or better' (Q2:106). That is to say, we do not abrogate any verse of the Qur'an without sending a better in its stead. And so we should not concern ourselves with this matter."[252]

In other words, he reassured him that he had acted rightly, and that he need not concern himself in any way about it.

Some of his disciples were palpably aware of Sheikh Farid's presence near them at all times, whether they were near him or far away. One disciple who was an army officer, and therefore was stationed at a distance from Ajodhan much of the time, reported that whenever he wanted to see the sheikh, he would visualize him. This vision, he was convinced, was not mere imagination; rather it was a living reality. When he had to make a decision regarding which way he should go, the vision of Sheikh Farid would appear before him, and he would proceed in whatever direction the vision of Sheikh Farid appeared from. And then, he said, "along the way he experienced much comfort and ease of mind."[253]

Even when at a distance, disciples experienced an unmistakable awareness of Sheikh Farid's protection. There was one disciple who was living in Delhi. He may not have been living up to the standards of conduct of a true Sufi, because he set out for Ajodhan with the intention of repenting before the sheikh. He joined a caravan for the journey. Among the travellers was a woman singer. It seemed to him that she might be trying to tempt him, but he held firm to his intention to go to the sheikh and repent. That is, he held firm until:

> They reached a way-station on the road where it happened that they both had to proceed riding on one camel. That woman sat so close to that man that every barrier and obstacle between them was removed. In such a circumstance there appeared a bit of lust in the man's heart. He was on the verge of wanting to say something to her or to extend his hand toward her. At that moment he saw a man come and slap him on the face. 'You are going to such-and-such a saint,' he exclaimed, 'with the intention of repenting, so what is this?' That man immediately got the message and no longer looked toward his woman companion. When at last he came before Sheikh al-Islam Fariduddin, the first words the Sheikh uttered to him were: "That day God the Exalted kept a firm vigil over you!"[254]

But times spent at a distance from the sheikh – his protecting hand notwithstanding – could not be compared with the joy of being in his company. Sheikh Farid enjoyed poetry,

and so did his circle of disciples. Sheikh Farid's disciples sometimes marvelled over his deep appreciation of mystical poetry.
Nizamuddin recalled:

Once the following verse came on his blessed lips:

> O Nizami, what secrets are these,
>   revealed from your heart?
> His secret no one knows; bridle your tongue!
>   Bridle your tongue!

Throughout most of the day, right up till the time of evening
prayer, he kept reciting this couplet. At the breaking of fast
the same couplet remained on his blessed lips. It is reported
that at dawn the following day he was still repeating this couplet, and each time he uttered it his countenance changed.[255]

Nizamuddin, speaking with his own disciples about this incident,
commented that each person had to discern the mystical connotations of a verse for himself; one had to go deep into oneself
to find the meaning.

We read of gatherings where they all recited poetry together,
sometimes sharing their own compositions, sometimes simply
revelling in the inspiring beauty of well-known Persian mystical
verses. Sometimes the sheikh commented on a poem one of the
disciples had written, or added something, improving it. In these
gatherings the pleasure of being together and with Sheikh Farid,
along with the exquisite pleasure of beautiful poetry on mystical
subjects, was overwhelming.

Once when Sheikh Farid was with his disciples and in the
mood for *sama*, there was no *qawwal* available. For Sheikh Farid,
music was not essential for the mood of the moment; it was

sufficient to simply hear the words from a God-intoxicated saint. He asked Badruddin Ishaq to bring out a letter from Hamiduddin Nagauri, which began, "This humble, weak and worthless beggar Muhammad Ata, who is the servant of the dervishes and from head to toe is but dust under their feet." Hearing just this much read aloud, "a spiritual state and a taste for God became manifest in him [Sheikh Farid]." In that spiritualized atmosphere, Badruddin Ishaq went on reading the letter, which included the quatrain:

> Where's the mind to grasp Your sovereignty?
> Where's the soul to mirror Your majesty?
> Beauty's face, I know, You could unveil
> But where are eyes to behold Your beauty?[256]

Another time, a disciple named Shams Dabir brought a long poem he had composed in praise of the sheikh and asked for permission to recite it. After he had finished, Sheikh Farid asked him to recite it again. Then the sheikh "began to explain every line in that poem, and in some places he improved it, and in others he noted his appreciation. At this Shams became very happy."

> In short, when he had finished listening to Dabir, he asked: "What do you want?" "I am indigent," pleaded Dabir, "and I must provide for my aged mother." "Go fetch the alms of gratitude (*shukrana*)," ordered the Sheikh. Shams went and returned with some *jitals*. Now in those days *jitals* were a favoured currency (equivalent in value to about ten *dirams*). Shams brought back five *jitals*, more or less.[257]

Then Sheikh Farid asked that the *jitals* be distributed among the party; everyone, including Shams Dabir, received some.

Years later, Nizamuddin commented on this incident. "In every instance," he observed, "where Sheikh al-Islam asked someone to fetch alms of gratitude, his affairs proceeded favourably."[258] The poet, Shams Dabir, received something more than a few *dirams* to provide for his aged mother. His affairs went well from that time on; he was installed in a prestigious post and became wealthy.

This incident, however, offers a mixed message. How differently might things have turned out for Shams Dabir if – when Sheikh Farid in his extreme pleasure asked what he would like – he had asked for spiritual uplift, rather than money? He did receive money but, it seems, he gradually lost his spiritual compass. Nizamuddin discussed the case of Shams Dabir with his own disciples, explaining how over time he became more insensitive and self-centred. During the final years of Sheikh Farid's life, when he and his family were starving, Shams Dabir, who was now quite wealthy, did not send any donations. After Sheikh Farid's death, Nizamuddin took responsibility for raising and educating several of his dependants. Shams Dabir did nothing for them. But, as Nizamuddin graciously suggested, "Perhaps he did not know, nor did anyone inform him about their condition."[259]

Several of Sheikh Farid's aphorisms might have guided Shams Dabir, had he been receptive:

Consider the dervish who seeks riches as covetous.

Treat a calamity as the consequence of greed.

Be magnanimous during a period of personal affluence.

Consider worldliness an unforeseen calamity.[260]

Evidently, several of Sheikh Farid's disciples were unreceptive. In fact, he had some complainers. One of these was a disciple named Yusuf.

> One time Yusuf came before the Sheikh and began to complain: "I have been in your service for many years. Everyone but me has received something from the Sheikh's beneficence. It ought to be that I am honoured before all the others." This and similar things he said.

> "There has been no shortcoming on my part," replied Sheikh al-Islam Fariduddin. "There must be preparedness and capability on your part. I do all that I can, but if God Almighty does not give the capacity, what can anyone else do?"[261]

Nizamuddin struggled to understand how anyone could fail to appreciate the magnitude of the blessing of receiving initiation from Sheikh Farid. Yet, there were some who were slow to realize what 'grasping the hand of the sheikh' really meant, such as the scholar named Nasir, who came to Ajodhan to make an oath of allegiance to Sheikh Farid. As Nizamuddin points out:

> He was still attached to commercial pursuits. In short, after meeting the Sheikh, he was admitted as a disciple and, having professed the oath of allegiance, had his head shaved. One day a yogin came to the hospice. That scholar-turned-disciple queried the yogin. He sought to learn from him how one could make hair grow long![262]

This troubled and annoyed the young Nizamuddin.

> When I heard that a stranger who had been granted the honour of professing allegiance to the Sheikh had asked

a yogin how to make the hair of his head grow long, there arose a suspicion within me: 'Why would one who has made a profession of allegiance need to ask about growing long hair? Moreover, since the whole purpose of having one's hair cut is to remove pride, what would be the point of wanting long hair?'[263]

Much as it annoyed Nizamuddin, however, Sheikh Farid didn't seem troubled at all by the wavering nature of his new disciple's commitment. Time went by and, soon enough, Nasir came forward and begged to have his head shaved again. Now – through the mysterious ways a sheikh works with a disciple – he had a sense of what he had been given, and he eagerly wanted the shaved head that indicated his discipleship.

Sheikh Farid taught that some Sufis did not make spiritual allegiance in the proper manner. It was essential, in his view, to swear allegiance to one sheikh, and to remain loyal to him. Joining oneself to one pir, then to another, was not right; nor was the practice of going to the tomb of a dead sheikh, shaving your head, and claiming to be a disciple. He said, "Discipleship and allegiance require that you grasp the hand of a sheikh."[264] 'Grasping the hand' implied both that the sheikh must be alive and that life-long loyalty must be firm.

One time he discussed the importance of loyalty. He said that remaining in the company of the sheikh can help a disciple who otherwise might waver. Being away from his company for long periods of time can undermine his loyalty. But whether near or far, continual remembrance of the sheikh can support the wavering disciple in his loyalty. He told of a disciple who, after going away from the sheikh, remained firm on the principles, steady in the spiritual practice, and loyal to his sheikh...for some time. But then, eventually, "his disposition changed."[265]

Then Sheikh Farid motioned to Nizamuddin, who was sitting nearby. Nizamuddin was in his early twenties, a young disciple of the venerable ninety-year-old sheikh. He lived in Delhi and came once each year to stay with his sheikh in Ajodhan. "This man who has remained attached to me," Sheikh Farid announced, "has the same disposition and has not changed one whit." Decades later, when Nizamuddin was sitting with his own disciples, he recalled this conversation. His disciple Amir Hasan Sijzi relates that he "began to cry. With tears in his eyes, he made this blessed declaration: 'Till today I remain constant in my love for the Sheikh. Nay, my love for him increases more and more!'"[266]

For Sheikh Farid's disciples, the moment of initiation was the turning point in their lives. They believed that whatever bad deeds they may have done in the past, before initiation, all were forgiven as of the time of initiation. They were now in the hands of Sheikh Farid.

Sirajuddin and his wife were both initiated. One time some of the people in their town became annoyed with the family of Sirajuddin's wife.

> There was an unpleasant exchange of harsh words. The relatives of Sirajuddin were accused of having committed some grave offences. His wife spoke up for herself. "Those things of which you accuse me," she observed, "please reflect on them: Did they occur before or after we pledged allegiance to Sheikh Fariduddin? [For if they occurred before, which she clearly felt they did, then she was forgiven by Sheikh Fariduddin and exempt from being punished for them]."[267]

The wife might seem unduly carefree, wholeheartedly believing that whatever "grave offences" had been committed before initiation, they were all forgiven. And we cannot say whether Sheikh

Farid himself taught this principle. Yet Nizamuddin commented on this incident, simply saying, "How nice she spoke, this wife of Sirajuddin!"[268]

It is worth noting that Sheikh Farid initiated women. When he died and there was no cloth to use as a burial sheet, it was a female disciple who provided one. This was the grandmother of Amir Khurd. In the all-male world of so many schools of yogis, sadhus, and Sufis at this time, the Chishtis were unusual in initiating women. Sheikh Farid's three daughters were notable for their dedication to spiritual practice. Sheikh Farid used to say about one of them, Bibi Sharifa, that if it had been permissible for him to pass on the *khilafat nama* and *sajjada* [prayer mat] to a woman (i.e., making her his primary successor), he would have conferred them on her without any hesitation.[269]

Baba Farid appointed seven *khalifa* during his lifetime. (Some accounts name a larger number, but seven are definite.) These were: Sheikh Nizamuddin Auliya, who received Baba Farid's staff, robe and sandals as his recognized successor, Sheikh Najibuddin Mutawakkil, Maulana Badruddin Ishaq, Sheikh Jamaluddin Hansawi, Sheikh 'Arif, Sheikh Ali Sabir and Maulana Fakharuddin Safhani.[270]

In selecting *khalifa*, Sheikh Farid said he followed inner guidance: the assignment came from God. No amount of pressure could force him to grant the *khilafat nama* to anyone. He said:

> This is an assignment of God.
> A Caliph [khalifa] cannot be confirmed merely
> Because it is being asked for.
> Whoever is worthy of it, gets it unasked.[271]

In the *khilafat nama* he gave to Nizamuddin, he wrote, "God alone deserves all praise. He is the first and the last, the Manifest and the Hidden. Whomsoever He elevates, none can bring him down and whomsoever He throws down, none can elevate him. None can bring to light what He has concealed and none can conceal whatever He has revealed."[272]

To Nizamuddin he said, "God has blessed you with knowledge, wisdom, and devotion – the three essential prerequisites for a disciple to qualify himself for nomination as a representative of the master."[273]

Sheikh Farid as Seen
by One Disciple

CLASSIC PORTRAITURE IS AN ART that makes no attempt to view the subject from all angles. The subject of the portrait is seen from a particular angle, illuminated by particular lighting that brings out highlights and casts shadows. In this singular view it attempts to capture something essential about the subject. Similarly, viewing Sheikh Farid through the lens of one disciple's experience presents us with something like a portrait. Through one disciple's perspective, we may see the sheikh's spiritual power and his gentleness, his insight into the disciple's real needs and, above all, his love. That disciple is Hazrat Nizamuddin Auliya.

We are fortunate today to have many of Nizamuddin's reminiscences about Sheikh Farid, preserved by Nizamuddin's disciple Amir Hasan Sijzi. The close circle of disciples who attended Nizamuddin's informal gatherings often posed questions designed to encourage their master to reminisce about Sheikh Farid, because the spiritual atmosphere became so elevated whenever he spoke of his pir. Amir Hasan recalled one such conversation: "On that particular evening he [Nizamuddin] continued to speak only about Sheikh Fariduddin and, in listening to his discourse, those present experienced an indescribable taste of the divine presence."[274]

With Nizamuddin's words serving as the brush and paint, we find a portrait of Sheikh Farid.

The Sheikh's Power of Attraction

Nizamuddin marvelled at Sheikh Farid's spiritual power, a power of attraction that could reach across the distances and pull the child who was later to become his disciple and successor. Nizamuddin was twelve years old at the time, a skinny, half-starved boy in rags, but a stellar student and the pride of his teachers. One day a *qawwal* stopped by just as Nizamuddin was reciting a poem before his teacher. The *qawwal* stayed and chatted with the teacher about the various sheikhs and *khanqahs* he had visited.

Nizamuddin recalled later that when the *qawwal* began to speak about Sheikh Farid, instantly and inexplicably, "a love and sincere desire took root in my heart." Young Nizamuddin started repeating the name of Sheikh Farid ten times after every prayer. Even his friends and playmates recognized that "if they asked me something and they wanted me to swear by it, they would say 'Swear by the name of Sheikh Fariduddin.'"[275] Swearing in this way, they knew they could count on his complete and unflinching truthfulness.

Over the next few years Nizamuddin was aware of Sheikh Farid's unseen hand of guidance and protection, though he had never yet met the sheikh. For example, when Nizamuddin had to travel from his village to Delhi but was too young to travel alone, he found a 'dear old man' who was going that way and could take him along:

> In short, when I resolved to go to Delhi, a dear old man named 'Awad accompanied me. Along the way, if we came to a place where he feared that lions or robbers might be lurking, he would cry out 'O master, be present!' or 'O our master, we are proceeding under your protection!' 'Who is the master to whom you are calling out?' I asked. 'His Eminence Sheikh Fariduddin.'[276]

Then, when they reached the outskirts of Delhi, they stopped at the house of Sheikh Najibuddin Mutawakkil, the younger brother of Sheikh Farid. Coincidence? Perhaps. Nizamuddin, however, interpreted these events as signs of Sheikh Farid pulling him into the orbit of his love. As Nizamuddin commented, "When God Almighty decides to reveal that benefit of discipleship, the means appropriate to its attainment will appear."[277]

Later, even long after Nizamuddin had been initiated, Sheikh Farid's power of attraction never diminished. Just as Nizamuddin had felt powerfully pulled to the sheikh from a distance when he was a child, so also he was drawn as if by a magnet into close proximity, pulled into the atmosphere of Sheikh Farid's presence. Nizamuddin recalled that often, whenever Sheikh Farid was alone, he would recite mystical verses. At these times, Nizamuddin was unable to stay away.

Standing just outside the door, waiting and listening, scarcely able to move, he found that the spiritual atmosphere became intoxicatingly elevated. Sometimes, after Baba Farid had finished reciting a particularly moving verse, he would prostrate himself in prayer. Nizamuddin recalled, "Only then would I enter and lay my head at his feet. 'Khwaja,' he would ask, 'what do you wish?' I would then ask for some spiritual gift, which he would grant. But many times since I have regretted that I did not ask to die in *sama*."[278]

Sheikh Farid's Recognition of His Disciple

The first time Nizamuddin went to Ajodhan he was barely in his twenties. The aged Sheikh Farid, a truly venerable figure, was now spiritual master to an extensive community of disciples spread throughout the Punjab and northern India. The young Nizamuddin trembled as he was conducted into Sheikh Farid's august presence. In fact, he was shaking so much he was unable to speak. But Sheikh Farid took one look at him and said:

What is absence from You? A fire, heart upon heart burning!
And yearning for You? A tide, soul after soul upturning!

With these words, Sheikh Farid gave voice to the mysterious fact that the spiritual master longs for his destined disciple as much as the disciple does for his pir. He then tried to soothe the young man's nervousness by saying gently that every newcomer is nervous: "To everyone who enters, there is a sense of awe."[279] Only then was Nizamuddin able to stammer out that he had an intense desire to kiss the sheikh's hand.

Sheikh Farid's tender and solicitous attention to this new-comer was immediately apparent. He instructed Badruddin Ishaq to provide a bed for him. This was extremely unusual, as everyone slept on the bare dirt floor. Nizamuddin was so flustered he forgot even the most basic etiquette. Unable to bear the idea of being given a bed to sleep on when so many disciples – who were older and clearly more advanced than he was – were sleeping on the ground, he declined the bed. It was only when Badruddin Ishaq sent him a message: "Will you do as you wish or will you obey the orders of the Sheikh?" that Nizamuddin pulled himself together and submitted to lying down on the bed.[280]

The Sheikh's Awareness of His Disciple's Unspoken Feelings

At the time of initiation, the usual practice was to have the disciple's head shaved. The hair was allowed to grow back – Sufis did not keep their heads shaven for life – but the shaved head was a visible symbol of having sworn allegiance to a sheikh. It was a symbol of humility, and a mark of being a beginner who has just entered the spiritual path.

However, at the time of his initiation, Nizamuddin had a fine head of long curly hair and deep inside he was resisting the idea of having it shaved. He knew that when he returned to Delhi he would be teaching classes and he feared what his students would think of him if he appeared before them with a shaved head. In this situation, Sheikh Farid demonstrated his delicate sensitivity to the inner feelings of his disciple. At initiation he simply did not say anything about shaving Nizamuddin's head, and the new disciple was glad to let it pass. A few days later, the enormity of the grace he had received began to dawn on him.

> When he saw others with shaven heads, he felt something attractive in them and approached his Master for permission to get his own head shaved. The permission was readily granted.[281]

Sheikh Farid again demonstrated his awareness of his disciple's inner feelings when Nizamuddin asked about whether he should continue his studies. In reality, he was strongly drawn to the pursuit of scholarship, in which he excelled. He asked: "What is your command? I will abandon scholarship and pursue my devotions and supererogatory prayers (prayers and spiritual exercises which go beyond the obligatory prayers required of every Muslim)."

Sheikh Farid replied: "I do not restrict anyone from learning. Do both till one predominates. A dervish should have some measure of learning."[282] In this instance he showed that he understood the inner conflict his disciple felt but did not express in words. He understood also the organic process by which this disciple would progress through a gradual transformation until the spiritual aim would predominate over all other aims.

The Channel for Disclosing the World of Secrets

During Nizamuddin's first stay in Ajodhan, Sheikh Farid repeated several times that, "One should be reconciled with one's enemies."

Similarly, he stressed, "One must make restitution to those who have a claim on you."[283] Those words haunted Nizamuddin after he returned to Delhi. It came into his mind that he owed twenty *jitals* to someone. He also had borrowed a book from someone else and had lost it. In those days a book, copied by hand, was a rare and precious thing. Nizamuddin had not said anything to his pir about these debts, but when he remembered the repeated instructions about settling all claims, he realized that Sheikh Farid "was indeed the channel for disclosing the world of secrets."[284]

In Delhi, Nizamuddin struggled to earn enough money to pay back the twenty *jitals*, but just couldn't scrape together this amount. When finally he had saved up ten *jitals*, he went to the man to give him the money, promising to bring the rest as soon as he could.

> When he had heard me out, the man remarked: 'Fine. You have come from the Sheikh.' Then taking the ten *jitals*, he told me: 'I forgive you the ten remaining *jitals*!' Next I went to see the man whose book I had borrowed. When I met him, he did not recognize me. 'Who are you?' he asked. 'O sir,' I replied, 'I am the person who took a book on loan from you and lost it. Now I will see to making another copy of the book like the one you lent me, and I will bring it to you.' When he had heard my pledge, this man replied: 'Fine. You show the influence of the place from which you came. I forgive you that book!'[285]

Nizamuddin then composed a poem and sent it to Baba Farid from Delhi:

> People love me
>   because I am known to be
>   a slave of yours.

Your love for all
  has blessed me with a kind favour.
Otherwise, what am I
  that people should know me?

The next time he went to Ajodhan, Baba Farid greeted him and recited this quatrain, saying that he had committed it to memory.[286]

Dissolving the Fear of Public Opinion

During the three years that Sheikh Farid was alive after Nizamuddin's initiation, Nizamuddin taught in Delhi and visited his sheikh in Ajodhan once a year, staying for several months each time. These visits were full of lessons for him, lessons that were taught not through texts but through action. For example, one day in Ajodhan he met an old classmate who was staying at an inn. Well dressed, with a servant attending to his needs, the classmate was appalled to see Nizamuddin in his grimy and tattered clothes. He exclaimed: "Maulana Nizamuddin! What misfortune has befallen you? Had you adopted teaching work at Delhi, you would have become a leading scholar of this age, enjoying affluent circumstances."[287] Nizamuddin did not know what to say. He went to Sheikh Farid in some consternation and told him about the incident.

"What would be your answer to such a question?" asked the Sheikh. "As the Sheikh directs," replied Nizamuddin. "When you meet him next," replied Baba Farid, "recite the couplet, meaning

You are not my travelling companion. Go, take your own path.
May prosperity be your portion in life and misfortune mine."[288]

Then Sheikh Farid told him to take a tray of food from the kitchen of the *jama'at khanah* and, carrying it on his head, to bring it to his friend. The classmate's curiosity was piqued so he went to see Sheikh Farid. In the end, he begged to swear allegiance and become a disciple.[289]

Modelling the Ideal of Trust in God

Nizamuddin's life, after giving up the prospect of a prestigious teaching post in favour of following the spiritual path, was not easy. He lived in abject poverty, hardly managing to get even the bare necessities. Sheikh Farid was well aware of the conditions he lived in, and when Nizamuddin was to leave Ajodhan to return to Delhi, Baba Farid gave him a gold coin for his expenses.

> Later Nizamuddin came to know that this was the last coin in Sheikh Farid's house. At the *iftar* [time of breaking the fast] Baba Farid had nothing to break his fast with. Nizamuddin placed his master's gift at his feet. It was accepted with the remark: "I have prayed to God to grant you a portion of earthly goods." Nizamuddin was worried at this, lest worldly comforts destroy his spiritual personality. The Sheikh removed his anxiety by observing: "Don't be afraid. This will not entangle you in any trouble or calamity."[290]

Years later, Nizamuddin explained to his own disciples that Sheikh Farid's example of "total, unconditional renunciation" and having "no regard for either this world or the next" had made a deep impression on him.[291] From his pir's example, he had learned that, "The real purpose of amassing gold and silver is to use it for the benefit of others." Before he became Sheikh Farid's disciple, he said, his poverty was a great struggle for him and "contentment was not my lot." The change that was brought about within him through the influence of Sheikh Farid is evident in an incident he recalled:

> Then one day in the evening a passerby gave me half a *tanka*. I said to myself: "Evening has already arrived, and whatever I needed was taken care of earlier. I will keep this and spend it in the morning." When night came, I busied myself in prayer and meditation, but that half *tanka* clung to the skirt of my heart and disrupted my concentration. When I saw what had happened to my spiritual state, I exclaimed: "O God, when will morning come so that I may dispense with that coin!"[292]

Crushing the Last Remnants of Intellectual Pride

Still, there was one great hurdle Nizamuddin had to overcome. Although seemingly he had given his all to pursuing the spiritual path, and although his love for his pir seemed to know no bounds, Sheikh Farid detected in him some subtle intellectual pride. This pride in his scholarship had to be crushed if he was to reach perfection. One day Sheikh Farid was giving a discourse, using a text by Sheikh Shihabuddin Suhrawardi (*Awarif al-Ma'arif*), to explain the spiritual teachings to his disciples. In the copy of the text he was using, the script was faint and the copyist had made errors that Sheikh Farid had to correct as he read.

Nizamuddin blurted out that Najibuddin (Sheikh Farid's younger brother) had a clean, accurate copy of the text. Over the next hour, Nizamuddin began to realize that Sheikh Farid was annoyed, as he repeated several times, "Has the dervish no power to correct a defective manuscript?"

> I did not know to whom he was speaking. If I had realized that he was referring to me, I would have immediately

implored his forgiveness, but I remained oblivious to the fact that I was the one whom he had in mind. After my Master had repeated this question several times, Maulana Badruddin Ishaq...turned toward me: 'The Sheikh is addressing this remark to you,' he said. I rose, bared my head and threw myself at the Sheikh's feet. 'As God is my witness,' I pleaded, 'I had not realized that the esteemed Master was referring to me in this question. I had seen another manuscript and was reporting that fact; I had absolutely nothing else in mind.' But however much I apologized, I saw that it did not diminish the Sheikh's rage.

When at last I arose from there, I did not know what I was doing. May it never happen that anyone else experiences the anguish that befell me that day! Tears overwhelmed me. Distraught and bewildered, I walked around till I arrived at the edge of a well. I thought to myself, 'Better to be a dead beggar than to go on living with the bad name that this indiscretion has given me!' In this state of anxiety and confusion, I wandered toward the desert, weeping and lamenting. Only God Almighty knows what state had overcome me at that moment.

Fortunately, the Sheikh had a son named Shihabuddin. He and I were very close friends. On hearing what had happened to me, he approached Sheikh Fariduddin and interceded on my behalf. The Sheikh relented; he sent his servant Muhammad to fetch me. I came and placed my head at his blessed feet. He was pleased. The next day, summoning me to his presence, he showered me with words of compassion and comfort. 'I have done all this for the perfection of your spiritual state,' he explained.[293]

Sheikh Farid then remarked, "A spiritual master is a dresser of brides."[294] That is, the pir works to bring out the true beauty of his disciple. He perfects every facet of the disciple's potential.

After this, Sheikh Farid returned to discoursing from the *Awarif al-Ma'arif*, covering five chapters of the text. Nizamuddin recalled years later how the depth of insight came, not from the brilliance of the text, but from the experience of hearing Sheikh Farid's discourse.

> How can I reiterate what he explained from those five chapters? No one other could have offered such insights. How many times, due to the taste for God which his commentary evoked, did those present wish to expire then and there! They would have welcomed such a death as propitious.[295]

He went on to speak about how the sheikh's delivery:

> ...evokes a pleasure that none other can match. For when you hear the same discourse from someone else it does not evoke the taste for God. Who can match the person who speaks from a station in which he has been touched by the light of divine intuition?[296]

A Portrait of Divine Perfection

If we view Sheikh Farid through the eyes of Nizamuddin, we can see only divine perfection. Even Sheikh Farid's pronunciation of Arabic seemed, to Nizamuddin, to embody a perfection unimaginable to ordinary mortals. In the Arabic language, the sound expressed by the letter *ḍād* is extremely difficult for any non-native speaker to achieve. Nizamuddin tried, while reciting passages from the Qur'an, to pronounce the *ḍād* as Sheikh Farid did. "I tried and tried, but however much I wanted to say it as he said it, I could not. So articulate, so eloquent was the Sheikh," remarked the master [Nizamuddin], "that no one could succeed in pronouncing the ḍād as he did."[297]

As far as Nizamuddin was concerned, everything about Sheikh Farid was perfection itself. Mystical verses sung in *sama* often praise the beauty and grace of the Divine, but to Nizamuddin, they all seemed to refer to Sheikh Farid. Years later, talking with his own disciples, he wept as he recalled:

> Every time that I heard a musical performance, each attribute that I heard the reciter depict – I swear by the cloak of my Sheikh – I attributed all of them, all those virtues and all those attributes, to the Sheikh. Once, while he was still alive, I was in an assembly where the reciter delivered the following couplet:
>
> *Stroll not so gracefully as this, lest*
> *From the evil eye you're made distressed.*
>
> I was at once reminded of the pleasing virtues and laudable qualities of the Sheikh. His perfect saintliness, his extraordinary piety, his surpassing grace, all overwhelmed me to such an extent that I cannot describe the mood they evoked. The reciter wanted to move on and recite other verses, but I had him repeat again and again these two lines.[298]

A Promise Only a True Sheikh Could Keep

When Sheikh Farid conferred his *khilafat nama* on Nizamuddin, granting him permission to initiate disciples, Nizamuddin tried to refuse, saying:

"You have bestowed great honour on me.... This position is very high and beyond my capacity to shoulder.... For me your kindness and favour is enough." However, Sheikh Farid was not to be dissuaded.

"This task will be efficiently performed by you," rejoined the Sheikh. But when he found Nizamuddin still hesitant, Baba Farid had to insist, and in great excitement declared: "Nizam! Take it from me; though I do not know if I will be honoured before the Almighty or not, I promise not to enter paradise without your disciples in my company."[299]

Once that promise was spoken, there was nothing more Nizamuddin could say. In obedience to his pir's instruction, he left for Delhi. It was not long afterward that Sheikh Farid died.

Once, one of Nizamuddin's disciples asked him if he had been present at the time of Sheikh Farid's death.

His eyes teemed with tears as he replied: "No, he sent me to Delhi in the month of Shawwal! He died on the fifth of the month of Muharram. But he did remember me at the time of his death and sent this message: 'I, too, was not present at the death of Sheikh Qutbuddin Bakhtiyar Kaki.'"[300]

One evening, Nizamuddin and his disciples were discussing the death of saints. Someone spoke of a saint who had died with the name of God, the Exalted, on his lips. Nizamuddin became tearful and recited a quatrain:

I have come to Your street in a rush, in a rush.
My cheeks with my tears are all awash, all awash.
To be at one with you, how I try, how I try.
As I invoke Your name, let me die, let me die.[301]

He could only have been thinking of Sheikh Farid, who died while repeating names of God: "O the Living! O the Eternal!"

Taken together, Nizamuddin's reminiscences offer us an intimate glimpse of Sheikh Farid, as seen by a very loving disciple. Like a portrait, these recollections highlight certain features: his spiritual power to reach across the distance and pull his destined disciple to him; his deep insight into the inner feelings and real needs of his disciple; and his perfect timing in using seemingly harsh measures to bring his disciple past an obstacle the disciple was not even aware of. It is a portrait illuminated by Sheikh Farid's ever-present love.

Poetry

Overview

SHEIKH FARID'S IMMENSE POPULARITY as a poet derives overwhelmingly from his Punjabi slokas, although his primary language was Persian. Seven centuries have increased rather than diminished the popularity of this beloved poet-saint. Prof. Rakshat Puri suggests why his slokas are so dear to the hearts of so many Punjabis:

> The primary reason for the popularity of Farid's Punjabi poetry may be that it expresses the genius of the Punjabi language and – with its dry and laconic wit, with its quaint mixture of irony and romantic imagination – the wily ruggedness of the Punjabi mind, which of course gave the language its historical and literary direction.[1]

Composing verses in a time when Persian, Arabic and Turkish were the languages of the educated elite among Muslims, and Sanskrit was likewise the language of the elite among Hindus, Baba Farid sang these rhyming couplets in the language of the common people. This dialect was formerly known as Multani: that is, the dialect spoken in the region around the city of Multan. Today in Pakistan, Multani is commonly referred to as Sarieki. As Puri points out, "Farid spoke to communicate not only with the scholarly and intellectual.... This necessitated a kind of stretchable ambiguity in symbolization."[2]

Sheikh Farid's Language and Imagery

Using imagery from everyday life, Farid's slokas are remarkably spare, the diction precise. Their powerful impact derives from their brevity and compactness. Najm Hosain Syed writes that the 'austerity' of Sheikh Farid's speech rhythm "borders on abstemiousness. The evenness of movement is assured by balancing the stresses in each line. The austerity of rhythm is supported by a strikingly plain vocabulary. Farid…aims at a deliberate ordinariness in his words."[3]

On first reading, these slokas may appear simple; yet upon further study and contemplation they reveal profound depths of meaning. Prof. Christopher Shackle, a noted scholar of linguistics and the literature of this period, points out that each line is divided into two parts containing not more than three or four words each. This two-line form, he says, "has room only for the most condensed images and the most succinct message."[4] That Sheikh Farid could manage to express so exquisitely the full import of his message in such a brief form is the genius of his poetic works.

Stretching for the right word to express his meaning, Baba Farid freely mixed Arabic or Persian words into the local Punjabi dialect of his slokas. These words, which were not a part of Punjabi speech before he used them, have become part of the Punjabi language, understood by all. It is widely believed that he also coined new words and that he used words in new and flexible ways. Given that there are no written texts in the dialect before his slokas, it is impossible to prove this claim.

However, we can see that he added a shade of meaning to words by the way in which he added a suffix to them. For example, he sings in Sloka 103 of the coarse woollen blanket he wears, calling it *kambalrree*, instead of the usual word for blanket, *kamblee*. The added 'rree' colours the word with a sense of endearment and sweetness. Sheikh Farid speaks here in the language one might use with a small child, the gentle language of a loving mother who can hardly express her fondness without making up her own pet names for the child. Similarly, in Sloka 20 the earthen pot that holds his water is called *koojarraa*, rather than simply *kooja*, thus carrying a note of fondness and familiarity. Again, the two lamps burning in Sloka 48 are called *deevrre*, rather than simply *deeve*. They are sweet lamps, beloved lamps.

This sweetness in his language extends also to those slokas that ostensibly admonish and warn. In Sloka 59 he tells his listener to give up those deeds that bring no merit. *Kamm*, translated here as 'deeds,' can mean work or chores or actions. He calls these useless deeds, which will cause the doer to lose face in the court of the Lord, *kammarre*; the simple addition of the suffix *arre* acknowledges that these are the much-loved deeds to which his listener is so attached! Even in Sloka 56, in which he admonishes the listener for being asleep to her Husband, the Lord, he softens the word *need* (pronounced *neend*) – which can mean sleep, neglect, apathy or indifference – to *needarree* (pronounced *neendarree*).

In so many subtle ways he shows a tender understanding of the weaknesses that hold spiritual seekers back from reaching their goal. Even when speaking in Sloka 2 of the 'bundle' of worldly attachments that keep the seeker from remaining steadfast at the Lord's door, he uses the word *potalee* to mean a small bundle one holds very close to the heart so that no harm can come to it.

It may be impossible for these subtleties in Sheikh Farid's language to come through in an English translation. Some of his slokas, rendered into English and lacking these softening touches, may even seem harsh. In the original language, there is a sweetness in his manner of expressing himself, as if his abounding love overflows – perhaps almost in spite of himself – into his words. Surely, the affectionate tone that resonates in his word choice is one of the reasons that Sheikh Farid became known as the 'Treasure of Sweetness.'

Several of Sheikh Farid's verses have made their way into colloquial language in the Punjab. The common expression, *'chaar gavaa'iaa,'* literally meaning 'four lost,' might seem mysterious without understanding that it comes from Sloka 38.

> Farid, men lose four watches of the day in wandering,
>> and the four of the night in sleep.
> God will call for your account and ask you
>> the purpose for which you came into the world.[5]

A watch is three hours. The four watches of the day and the four of the night comprise the full twenty-four hours. In Punjabi everyday speech in abbreviated form as *'chaar gavaa'iaa'* would be understood to mean something like, 'Don't waste your time!' or 'Get to work on what you're really supposed to be doing.'

Another saying that has become an integral part of colloquial speech, not only in the Punjab, but also throughout northern India, is *'rukhee sukhee.'* In an Indian household this saying is as common as lentils and bread, standard fare in northern India; *rukhee sukhee* implies something less than a full meal – food with no embellishment, no seasoning, no butter. The saying comes from Sloka 29:

> *rukhee sukhee khaa'e kai thandhaa paanee pee'o.*

The literal meaning is 'eat basics, drink water.' *Rukhee sukhee* has become a proverb in the Indian culture among people speaking Hindi or Punjabi that means 'live within your means,' 'don't overdo things,' 'be contented,' or 'control your desires.'

Similarly, the saying, 'Don't slander dust' (*khaak na nindee'ai khaakoo jed na ko'e*) comes from the first line of Sloka 17:

> Farid, do not slander the dust; nothing is as great as dust.[6]

Today in the Punjab, one might use this expression to mean don't criticize anything; even something as insignificant as dust is not to be criticized, because you don't know its true value. This expression is used often and can be applied to anything, at any time. Sheikh Farid uses dust which, he reminds us, supports every step we take today and will one day cover our grave.

Another often-repeated verse that has become an adage is Sloka 6:

> *fareedaa je too akal lateef kaale likh na lekh.*
> *aapnare gireevaan mah sir neevaa kar dekh.*

This could be translated as: 'Farid, if you had good sense you wouldn't think ill of others; before you do, look within.' This verse is frequently invoked in everyday speech in the same sense as the adages: 'If you point one finger, three fingers point back at you' or 'those who live in glass houses shouldn't throw stones.'

Our Translation Approach

In both his Persian and Multani verses, Sheikh Farid composed poems with a strict metre and rhyming pattern. However, in the translations we have chosen for this book, the verses in English do not attempt to capture the rhyming scheme or the rhythm of the original. To strive for the rhyme in English in every sloka would inevitably lead to twisting the meaning beyond recognition. The translations by the Radha Soami Satsang Beas (RSSB) multi-lingual translation team presented here, as well as the approved English-language translations that we have chosen for the Adi Granth, attempt to convey Sheikh Farid's message as closely as possible, while keeping to his extremely brief form.

To understand how these verses could have been sung, remembered, and passed down the generations, however, we may need to hear something approximating the sound of the poetry with its lilting rhythm and catchy rhymes. Therefore, it may be helpful to look at a few slokas that Shackle translated with something like the rhythm and rhyme of the original. The following are Slokas 9, 68, and 107:

> See, Farid, what's happened, your beard is now quite grey
> As what was far approaches, the past slips far away.

> The lovely pot is broken, its rope has frayed away.
> In whose house is Azrael* a guest today?

> Night ends, but still you sleep; you die while living yet.
> Though you forget the Lord, still He does not forget.

Reading these skilful renderings in English, one can easily see how the slokas of Sheikh Farid would have been learned by heart. The words seem simple enough to understand, the images clear. If we imagine hearing such slokas sung, it is easy to see how they would lodge in the mind. And, perhaps, while the words and the tune turn over and over in one's mind, deeper levels of meaning might gradually become clear.

In some cases, Sheikh Farid presents a particularly vivid, striking image whose meaning is, at first glance, mysterious. He offers no elaboration, no explanation. He invites his listeners to ponder his words, allowing the imagery to settle deep into the mind to find the depth of his meaning. Again, in Shackle's rhyming translation, we can see this quality in Slokas 85 and 64:

> In pain the day is spent, in grief the night is passed.
> 'Upon the shoals,' he cries, 'the ferry is stuck fast.'

---

* Azrael ('izrā'il) is the Angel of Death.

Upon the brackish pond, the geese came to alight.
They dip their beaks but drink not, burning to take flight.

Sheikh Farid's use of the sloka is reminiscent of the Persian *ruba'i*. Collections of *rubaiyat*, rhyming four-line verses, were popular with the classic Persian poets for much the same reason: it was so easy to memorize and to recite. The sloka, as Farid uses it, might best be described as a *doha*, the two-lined verse that Shackle refers to as "the classic teaching couplet of medieval India."[7]

Najm Hosain Syed calls the verse form of Sheikh Farid's poetry *dohra*, as distinguished from *doha*. In a *dohra*, each line of the rhymed couplet has a division in the middle of the line. But, as distinguished from the *doha*, each couplet stands alone, self-sufficient, a complete unit; it is not meant to be read as a part of a sequence of verses to glean its meaning. The *dohra* is like a Persian miniature, all by itself, full of compressed meaning. This description however could also be applied to the traditional Indian poetic form called *dupad* or *ducharan*. Puri sums up his discussion of the poetic form of Baba Farid's Punjabi verse:

> Farid's couplets, then, being flexible in relation to con-
> ventional rhyme and metre, though taut in form and terse
> in their import, might most accurately be described as
> *dupad* or *ducharan*. But since they have been traditionally
> called slokas it seems convenient to continue employing
> this description.[8]

Two Collections of Poetry

We have included two collections of Sheikh Farid's verses: First and foremost, verses from the Adi Granth. These 130 slokas and 4 hymns are by far the best-known and best-loved of Farid's poetry. It is upon this body of work that his reputation as the great poet-saint of the Punjab rests.

The second collection is comprised of poems that were not among those given to Guru Nanak and preserved in the Adi Granth. These poems were composed orally – some in Persian, some in Multani – and only a few of these were recorded in writing within one or two generations after the death of Sheikh Farid. The rest have been passed down through a rich and vibrant oral tradition, each one appearing in writing for the first time anywhere from 200 to 600 years later.

The Persian and the Multani verses presented here have been translated into English by a multi-lingual team on behalf of the RSSB Publications Department. These translations strive to capture the layered meanings of Sheikh Farid's words and images as accurately as possible, without attempting to reproduce his rhyming scheme. To the best of our knowledge, these verses have never before been published in English. We are particularly honoured to present the little-known Persian and Multani verses for the English-speaking reader.

We invite readers to enjoy these two diverse collections of poetry. Taken together, these poems offer intriguing glimpses into the many-faceted character and the spiritual teachings of the great Sufi mystic, Sheikh Farid.

Sheikh Farid's Slokas
in the Adi Granth

THE ADI GRANTH is a voluminous anthology of hymns compiled and edited by Guru Arjun Dev (1563–1606 CE), the fifth
Guru in the line of Guru Nanak.* In addition to his own hymns
and those of his predecessors, Guru Arjun took great effort and
care to collect the works of exemplary mystics and devotees
from various parts of India, regardless of their religious, social
or cultural backgrounds. He included in the Adi Granth the
hymns of thirty of these saints and devotees, one of whom was
Sheikh Farid.

Guru Arjun Dev, who was himself above the pettiness of
sectarian constraints, showed unprecedented leadership by
incorporating the writings of such a famous Sufi sheikh into the
Adi Granth. When one considers that Guru Arjun Dev lived
during the time of the Mughal Empire, a time of oppression of
Sikhs and forced conversions of Hindus at the hands of Muslim
rulers, one can begin to appreciate the level of moral courage and
clear insight it took to incorporate Sheikh Farid's slokas into the
Sikh's primal scripture. But such were the spiritual teachings of
Guru Nanak Dev – to look past the distinctions of religion and

---

*The first four Gurus were Guru Nanak Dev, Guru Angad Dev, Guru Amar Das
and Guru Ram Das, in chronological order. Hymns of the first five Gurus were
included in the original Adi Granth; those of Guru Tegh Bahadur, the ninth
Guru, were later added by Guru Gobind Singh, the tenth Guru.

culture, and focus on the oneness of the message of the great saints and mystics.

To understand how Sheikh Farid's writings came into Guru Arjun's possession we must begin with the stories of the life of Guru Nanak Dev that have been passed down through the Sikh tradition. It is said that Guru Nanak, together with his disciple and ever-loyal travelling companion, Bhai Mardana, went to Pakpattan. This was roughly two-and-a-half centuries after the lifetime of Sheikh Farid; Emperor Akbar had recently renamed Ajodhan to Pakpattan in Farid's honour. The current Chishti sheikh at Pakpattan, renamed as Sheikh Ibrahim, was the twelfth descendant in the lineage from Sheikh Farid.

By this time the Sufi Chishti sheikhs who traced their heritage back to Sheikh Farid had spread far and wide. In towns and cities all across northern India and as far south as the Deccan, there were Chishti *khanqahs* modelled after Sheikh Farid's gathering place. In each one of these places the Sufis followed Sheikh Farid's example in feeding the poor and helping the needy, while also attending to the prayers and spiritual exercises of the Sufi path. Therefore, by the time of Guru Nanak, the fame of the beloved Baba Farid *Ganj-i shakar* was already deeply rooted in the culture of the Punjab.

According to traditional biographical stories, Guru Nanak and Sheikh Ibrahim met and discussed several of Sheikh Farid's verses. These stories record various exchanges between the two of them and, in the end, Sheikh Ibrahim requested Guru Nanak to compose a prayer praising the one God. In response, Guru Nanak is said to have composed the *Asa ki Var* and given it to Sheikh Ibrahim. In return, Sheikh Ibrahim gave Guru Nanak some verses composed by Sheikh Farid.

The idea that these slokas were indeed composed by Sheikh Farid was universally accepted by Sikhs and non-Sikhs alike, until the Irish scholar of Sikhism, M.A. Macauliffe, published *The Sikh*

Religion in 1909. Macauliffe claimed that this was impossible and that Sheikh Ibrahim, who was sometimes known as the Second Farid (*Farid Thani*), must have given Guru Nanak verses that he himself had composed. Macauliffe's claim opened up an extended scholarly debate about the authenticity of this work.

Prof. Shackle writes that the content of this collection of slokas in the Adi Granth "is broadly compatible with what is known of the Chishti Sheikh Farid from the early Persian sources."[9] But can we know for sure that they were composed by him? Macauliffe had cited the fact that there was no written record of this collection of verses in the local language existing before Guru Nanak's time. Although this absence in the written record may be surprising, Shackle notes that it "may be accounted for by the almost exclusively Persian focus of the early Sufi records."[10] The profusion of writings from the Chishti sheikhs of the fourteenth to sixteenth centuries was exclusively in Persian. Verses in the local language may have been seen as less important, or as belonging to an oral, not a written tradition – and left unmentioned.

The standard methods used by linguistics scholars are not effective for dating Sheikh Farid's slokas to the thirteenth century. These scholars would normally place them side by side with other examples of writing from the thirteenth to sixteenth centuries and determine in which time period the language belonged. However, as Shackle points out, "we lack reliable comparators in the form of thirteenth-century vernacular texts." Sheikh Farid stands in stark isolation as a thirteenth-century poet composing in the local language.[11]

In any case, it is well known that Guru Arjun edited the language in Sheikh Farid's slokas, making the antiquated language readable for his contemporary Sikhs. Sayyed Nazeer Ahmad points out that the verses from Farid would have been written in Persian script at the time they were handed to Guru Nanak, who was fluent in the Persian language. Ahmad, renowned compiler and editor of Sufi poetry, suggests that it was Guru Arjun who finally transcribed the slokas into Punjabi in the Gurmukhi script.[12]

Still, written in a slightly different dialect from the rest of the scripture, Sheikh Farid's material does stand out in the Adi Granth. Farid's slokas are in the dialect of southwestern Punjab, the area around Multan, while other writings of the Adi Granth are in a dialect Shackle labels western Hindi-based *sant bhasha*.[13] Traditional sources portray two of Guru Nanak's hymns in the Adi Granth as direct responses to hymns by Sheikh Farid. Guru Nanak responds to Sheikh Farid's hymn in *Raag Soohi* that begins with *berraa bandh na sakio* (you did not build your boat when you had the opportunity) with his own closely similar hymn in *Raag Soohi* beginning with *jap tap kaa bandh berrulaa* (build the raft of meditation and self-discipline). Again, Guru Nanak responds to Sheikh Farid's hymn that begins *dilonh muhabbat jinh* (true devotees are those who love the Lord from the depths of their hearts) with the hymn called *Suchajji* (noble and graceful bride). Guru Nanak's deliberate use of the southwestern dialect in *Suchajji* illustrates his familiarity with the poetry of Sheikh Farid. Shackle writes:

> While Guru Nanak uses the style to express his own ideas, it is quite clear that he must have had an existing poetic model in mind for it, and even if we assume there was once much more poetry in this style in circulation, it is hardly to be imagined – given Farid's great spiritual prestige – that Guru Nanak was unaware of the verses attributed to him.[14]

The first clear textual evidence of Sheikh Farid's work existing before the time of Guru Nanak came to light in 1992 with the publication of Carl Ernst's *Eternal Garden*. He found a manuscript of

Hidayat ul-Qulub in the archives of the Chishti Sufis at Khuldabad. This text, originally written between 1344 and 1367, included seven verses in an early dialect of Punjabi. Shackle was able to translate and identify one of these as being the same as Sloka 7 in the Adi Granth.[15] While this discovery cannot confirm that all the slokas date back to Sheikh Farid himself, it does confirm that the Multani slokas believed to be by Sheikh Farid were in circulation among the Chishti Sufis within a century of Sheikh Farid's lifetime – including one sloka that was later included in the Adi Granth.

Hymns and Slokas

Four short hymns and 112 slokas comprise Sheikh Farid's portion of the Adi Granth. An additional 18 slokas composed by the Gurus are interspersed with these verses.* Sheikh Farid's first sloka is lengthy, being eight lines long. After this, his slokas are nearly all in the extremely concise form of two rhyming lines. He breaks from this very brief poetic form only in two cases: once with a three-line verse and once with a six-line verse.

Occasionally two slokas appear in a natural pairing. For example, consider Slokas 129 and 130:

> Do not utter even a single harsh word;
> > your true Lord and Master abides in all.
> Do not break anyone's heart;
> > these are all priceless jewels.

---

*Slokas 32, 113, 120, and 124 were added by Guru Nanak Dev; Slokas 13, 52, 104, 122 were added by Guru Amar Das; Sloka 121 was added by Guru Ram Das; and Slokas 75, 82, 83, 105, 108, 109, 110, and 111 were added by Guru Arjun Dev. We have reproduced the material as it is in the Adi Granth, where an attribution is shown on some, but not all, of the slokas by the Gurus.

> The minds of all are like precious jewels;
>> to harm them is not good at all.
> If you desire your Beloved,
>> then do not break anyone's heart.

Most slokas stand alone as miniatures of condensed meaning requiring neither the sloka before, nor the one after it, to complete its message. All efforts at rearranging the slokas thematically or forcing them into a logical order remain unsatisfactory. So we present them here, simply, in the order in which Guru Arjun Dev placed them.

In the midst of Sheikh Farid's work the occasional interjection by the Gurus forms a kind of conversation. It is a brilliant spiritual conversation across the distances both of time and of religion: between the thirteenth-century Sufi sheikh and the Gurus in the line of Guru Nanak of the fifteenth and sixteenth centuries. The Gurus' words often serve to soften Sheikh Farid's message, providing a comforting reminder of the Lord's grace. For example, in Sloka 12 Sheikh Farid urges his listener to act now, before it is too late:

> Farid, those who did not enjoy their spouse
>> when their hair was black –
>> hardly any of them enjoy him
>> when their hair turns grey.
> So be in love with the Lord,
>> so that your colour may ever be new.

To which, Guru Amar Das responds in Sloka 13, reminding the reader that the Lord can do anything and at any time. His gift of love and mercy will come when He wishes, even in old age:

Farid, whether one's hair is black or grey,
    our Lord and Master is always here
    if one remembers Him.
This loving devotion to the Lord
    does not come by one's own efforts,
    even though all may long for it.
This cup of loving devotion
    belongs to our Lord and Master;
    He gives it to whomever He likes.

Virtually unique in the spiritual literature of the world, Sheikh Farid's verses are incorporated into the scripture of a tradition different from his own and woven into a dialogue that resonates with the mutual respect shared by those lovers of the Lord who can see beyond cultural and religious distinctions.

aasaa sekh Farid jee'o kee baanee

ik oankaar satgur prasaad.
diloh muhabat jinnh se'ee sachiaa.
jinh man hor mukh hor
se kaandhe kachiaa.
rate isak khudaa'e rang deedaar ke.
visariaa jinh naam
te bhu'e bhaar thee'e. rahaa'o.
aap lee'e larr laa'e
dar darves se.
tin dhann janedee maa'o
aa'e saphal se.
parvadgaar apaar
agam be'ant too.
jinaa pachhaataa sach
chummaa pair moon.
teree panah khudaa'e
too bakhsandagee.
sekh fareedai
khair deejai bandagee. AG:488

Hymn by Sheikh Farid in Raag Aasa

There is but one God; He is realized
    through the true Guru's grace.
They alone are true,
    whose love for God is deep and heartfelt.
Those who have one thing in their heart
    and something else in their mouth
    are judged to be false.
Those who are imbued with love for the Lord
    are delighted by His vision.
Those who forget Nam, the Name of the Lord,
    are a burden on the earth.
Those whom the Lord attaches
    to the hem of His robe
    are the true dervishes at His door.
Blessed are the mothers who gave birth to them,
    and fruitful is their coming into the world.
O Lord, sustainer and cherisher,
    You are infinite, unfathomable and endless.
Those who recognize the true Lord –
    I kiss their feet.
I seek Your protection –
    You are the forgiving Lord.
Please, bless Sheikh Farid with the bounty
    of Your meditative worship.

aasaa

bolai sekh Farid piaare alah lage.
eh tan hosee khaak
nimaanee gor ghare.
aaj milaavaa sekh Farid
taakim koonjarree'aa
manoh machindarree'aa. rahaa'o.
je jaanaa mar jaa'ee'ai
ghum na aa'ee'ai.
jhoothee dunee'aa lag
na aap vanjaa'ee'ai.
bolee'ai sach dharam
jhooth na bolee'ai.
jo gur dasai vaat
mureedaa jolee'ai.
chhail langhande paar
goree man dheeriaa.
kanchan vanne paase
kalvat cheeriaa.
sekh hai'yaatee jag
na ko'ee thir rahiaa.
jis aasan ham baithe
kete bais ga'iaa.
katik koonjaan chet dau
saavan bijulee'aan.
see'aale sohandee'aan
pir gal baahrree'aan.
chale chalan-haar
vichaaraa le' mano.

Hymn by Sheikh Farid in Raag Aasa

Says Sheikh Farid, O my dear friend,
   attach yourself to the Lord;
   this body shall turn to dust,
   and its home shall be a neglected graveyard.
You can meet the Lord today, O Sheikh Farid,
   if you restrain your bird-like desires
   which keep your mind in turmoil.
If I had known that I was to die and not return again,
   I would not have ruined myself
   by clinging to the world of falsehood.
So speak the truth, in righteousness,
   and do not speak falsehood;
   the disciple ought to travel the route
   pointed out by the Guru.
Seeing the youths being carried across, the hearts
   of the beautiful young soul-brides are encouraged;
   those who side with the glitter of gold
   are cut down with a saw.
O Sheikh, no one's life is permanent in this world.
   That seat, upon which we now sit –
   many others sat on it and have since departed.
As the swallows appear in the month of Kattak,
   forest fires in the month of Chet, and lightning
   in Sawan, and as the bride's arms adorn
   her husband's neck in winter; just so,
   the transitory human bodies pass away.

gandhediaan chhe' maah
turrandiaa hik khino.
jimee puchhai asmaan
fareedaa khevat kinn ga'e.
jaalan goraan naal
ulaame jee' sahe. AG:488

Reflect upon this in your mind:
 It takes six months* to form the body,
 but it breaks in an instant.
O Farid, the earth asks the sky,
 "Where have the boatmen gone?"
Some have been cremated,
 and some lie in their graves;
 their souls are suffering rebukes.

---

*Sheikh Farid is referring to the time a baby takes to mature in the womb. Although commonly understood to take nine months, it is stated to be six in this poem. The idea may reflect an understanding of the in-womb development of the child from Farid's esoteric understanding.

raag soohee baanee sekh Farid jee kee

tap tap lohe lohe haath marorau.
baaval ho'ee so sauh loraun.
tai sah man mah kee'aa ros.
mujh avgan sah naahee dos.
tai saahib kee mai saar na jaanee.
joban kho'e paachhai pachhutaanee.
rahaa'o.
kaalee koil too kit gun kaalee.
apne preetam ke hau birahai jaalee.
pirah bihoon katah sukh paa'e.
jaa ho'e kripaal
taa prabhoo milaa'e.
vidhan khoohee mundh ikelee.
naa ko saathee naa ko belee.
kar kirpaa prabh
saadh-sang melee.
jaa phir dekhaa
taa meraa alah belee.
vaat hamaaree kharee udeenee.
khannioh tikhee bahut pieenee.
us oopar hai maarag meraa.
sekh fareedaa
panth samhaar saveraa. AG:794

Hymn by Sheikh Farid in Raag Soohi

I writhe in pain, in utter remorse;
    like mad, I seek out my God.
My Lord has become cross with me;
    but the evil is within me –
    my God is not to blame.
I knew not the Glory of my Lord, and now
    when my youth has become a waste, I grieve.
"O black koel, why have you turned black?"
    (And she says) "I was burnt black
    due to the separation from my spouse!"
Pray, how can one, without God, be at peace?
    (But), when the Lord is merciful,
    He unites one with Himself.
In the lone well (of the world)
    writhes the soul alone,
    where she neither has a friend nor a guide.
In His mercy, the Lord leads her on
    to the society of the Saints;
    and, now, wherever she sees,
    she sees the one God, her only Friend.
The (treacherous) path (in the yond) saddens me,
    for, it is sharper than a dagger's edge
    and finer than a hair.
I have to walk on this path, alone. Says Farid:
    "O God, be with me, that I come (back)
    to Your path as soon as may be."

soohee lalit

berraa bandh na sakio
bandhan kee velaa.
bhar sarvar jab oochalai
tab taran duhelaa.
hath na laa'e kasumbharrai
jal jaasee dholaa. rahaa'o.
ik aapeenhai patlee sah kere bolaa.
dudhaa thanee na aava'ee
phir ho'e na melaa.
kahai Farid saheleeho sauh
alaa'esee.
hans chalsee dummanaa
ah tan dheree theesee. AG:794

Hymn by Sheikh Farid in Raag Soohi Lalit

When I could build my boat, I didn't.
   And now, when the sea-waves lash,
   how shall I be ferried across?
Love not the safflower, O life;
   its colour will fade away.
My soul is weak,
   the command of the Lord is hard to bear;
   and life's milk, once spilt,
   will be gathered no more.
Says Farid, "O my mates, the Lord will call you all.
   And this swan-soul will fly away, sad at heart,
   and dust return to dust."

slok sekh Farid ke

ik oankaar satgur prasaad.
jit dihaarrai dhan varee
saahe la'e likhaa'e.
malak je kannee suneedaa
muh dekhaale aa'e.
jind nimaanee kadhee'ai
hadaa koo karrkaa'e.
saahe likhe na chalnee
jindoo koon samjhaa'e.
jind vahutee maran var
lai jaasee parnaa'e.
aapan hathee jol kai
kai gal lagai dhaa'e.
vaaloh nikee purslaat
kannee na sunee aa'e.
fareedaa kirree pavandee'ee
kharraa na aap muhaa'e. [1] AG:1377

fareedaa dar darvesee gaakharree
chalaan dunee'aa bhat.
bannh uthaa'ee potalee
kithai vanjaa ghat. [2]AG:1377–8

kijh na bujhai kijh na sujhai
dunee'aa gujhee bhaah.
saa'een merai changaa keetaa
naahee ta ham bhee dajhaan aah. [3] AG:1378

Sheikh Farid's slokas

**There is but one God; He is realized
through the true Guru's grace.**
The day of the bride's wedding is pre-ordained.
On that day, the Messenger of Death,
of whom she had only heard,
comes and shows its face.
It breaks the bones of the body
and pulls the helpless soul out.
That pre-ordained time of marriage
cannot be avoided.
Explain this to your soul.
The soul is the bride, and death is the groom.
He will marry her and take her away.
After the body sends her away with its own hands,
whose neck will it embrace?
The bridge to hell is narrower than a hair;
haven't you heard of it with your ears?
Farid, the call has come; be careful now –
don't let yourself be robbed. [1]

Farid, it is so difficult to become a humble saint
at the Lord's door. I am so accustomed
to walking in the ways of the world.
I have tied and picked up the bundle;
where can I go to throw it away? [2]

I know nothing; I understand nothing.
The world is a smouldering fire.
My Lord did well to warn me about it;
otherwise, I would have been burnt as well. [3]

173

fareedaa je jaanaa til thorrarre
sammal buk bharee.
je jaanaa sahu nandharraa
taan thorraa maan karee. [4] AG:1378

je jaanaa larr chhijanaa
peedee paa'een gandh.
tai jevad mai naahe ko
sabh jag dithaa handh. [5] AG:1378

fareedaa je too akal lateef
kaale likh na lekh.
aapnarre gireevaan mah
sir neevaan kar dekh. [6] AG:1378

fareedaa jo tai maaran mukee'aan
tinhaa na maare ghumm.
aapnarrai ghar jaa'ee'ai
pair tinhaa de chumm. [7] AG:1378

Farid, if I had known that I had so few sesame seeds,
   I would have been more careful with them in my hands.*
If I had known that my Husband Lord
   was so young and innocent,
   I would not have been so arrogant. [4]

Had I known my ties [with You] would be broken loose,
   I would have tightened the knots.†
For, like You, O love, there is not another;
   I have searched the whole world through. [5]

Farid, if you have a keen understanding,
   then do not write
   black remarks against anyone else.
Look underneath your own collar instead. [6]

Farid, those who beat you with fists,
   turning around do not beat them;
kiss their feet and go to your own home. [7]

---

*Farid likens the sesame seeds to our breaths, which serve as units of measurement for our life-span – we use up our breaths at the rate of twenty-four thousand a day. He advises us to value this gift from God and use every breath in devotion to Him, lest this precious capital of life is wasted through indiscriminate use and we fail to attain union with the Beloved.

†Marriages in India are usually solemnized by tying a knot between the bridegroom's and the bride's scarfs before they circle the sacred fire or the holy texts in the course of the wedding ceremony. If the knot, which is symbolic of the bond of love being created through marriage, gets loosened or untied, it is an ill omen for the relationship.

fareedaa jaan tau khatan vel
taan too rataa dunee sio.
marag savaa'ee neeh
jaan bhariaa taan ladiaa. [8] AG:1378

dekh fareedaa ju thee'aa
daarree ho'ee bhoor.
agoh nerraa aa'iaa
pichhaa rahiaa door. [9] AG:1378

dekh fareedaa je thee'aa
sakar ho'ee vis.
saa'een baajhoh aapne
vedan kahee'ai kis. [10] AG:1378

fareedaa akhee dekh pateenee'aan
sun sun reene kann.
saakh pakandee aa'ee'aa
hor karendee vann. [11] AG:1378

fareedaa kaaleen jinee na raaviaa
dhaulee raavai ko'e.
kar saa'een sio piraharree
rang navelaa ho'e. [12] AG:1378

Farid, when there was time for you to earn (God),
    you involved yourself with the world;
    now that death has overpowered you,
    your carriage must trundle along! [8]

Look Farid! what has befallen you:
    Your beard turned grey,
    your end approaching,
    the past far behind. [9]

See, O Farid, what has happened:
    sugar has become poison.
Without my Lord,
    to whom should I tell my sorrow? [10]

Farid, your eyes have turned feeble,
    your ears lost power to listen;
The body is now like a ripening stalk,
    changing colour. [11]

Farid, those who thought not of God
    when their hair was black,
    rarely turn to Him while gone grey:
Love the Lord while the hue of youth
    is still on you. [12]

mahlaa 3.
fareedaa kaalee dhaulee sahib sadaa
hai je ko chit kare.
aapnaa laa'iaa piram na laga'ee
je lochai sabh ko'e.
eh piram piaalaa khasam kaa
jai bhaavai tai de'e. [13] AG:1378

fareedaa jinh lo'in jag mohiaa
se lo'in mai dith.
kajal rekh na sahadiaa
se pankhee soo'e bahith. [14] AG:1378

fareedaa kookediaa chaangediaa
matee dediaa nit.
jo saitaan vanjaa'iaa
se kit pherah chit. [15] AG:1378

fareedaa thee'o pavaahee dabh.
je saa'een lorrah sabh.
ik chhijah biaa lataarree'ah.
taan saa'een dai dar vaarree'ah. [16] AG:1378

Third Guru
Farid, whether one's hair be black or grey,
    the Lord is ever there,
    if anyone remembers Him.
This devotion comes not of man's own effort
    or desire, even though all may long for it.
This cup of love belongs to the Lord.
    He gives it to whom He likes. [13]

Farid, those eyes which have enticed the world -
    I have seen those eyes.
Once, they could not endure even a bit of mascara;
    now, the birds hatch their young in them!* [14]

O Farid, despite the saints' shouts,
    shrieks and ever giving good advice,
those whom the devil has spoiled,
    how can they turn their mind towards God? [15]

Farid, become the grass on the path,
    if you long for the Lord of all.
One will cut you down
    and another will trample you underfoot;
    then, you shall enter the court of the Lord. [16]

---

*It is believed that Sheikh Farid once saw a prostitute punish her maid for not grinding the collyrium fine enough for her because the gritty substance had hurt her delicate eyes. During one of his subsequent rounds of the place years later, Farid found the prostitute's house empty and deserted – she had died. Once during his wanderings, Farid saw a pair of small birds nesting in the eye-sockets of a human skull and reminisced about the above incident.

fareedaa khaak na nindee'ai
khaakoo jed na ko'e.
jeevadiaa pairaa talai
mo'iaa upar ho'e. [17] AG:1378

fareedaa jaa lab taa neh kiaa
lab ta koorraa neh.
kichar jhat laghaa'ee'ai
chhapar tutai meh. [18] AG:1378

fareedaa jangal jangal kiaa bhavah
van kandaa morreh.
vasee rab hiaalee'ai
jangal kiaa dhoodheh. [19] AG:1378

fareedaa inee nikee janghee'ai
thal doongar bhaviom.
aj fareedai koojarraa
sai kohaan thee'om. [20] AG:1378

Do not speak ill of the dust, O Farid,
  for there is nothing to equal the dust:
In life it is beneath your feet and,
  after death, you are beneath it! [17]

Farid, love of God and greed go not together.
  With greed is love rendered impure.*
Such love is frail as a leaking straw roof against rain. [18]

Why wander through the woods, O Farid,
  crushing the thorns under your feet?
The Lord abides within you;
  why search for Him in the woods? [19]

Farid, with these small legs,
  I crossed deserts and mountains.
But today, Farid, my water jug seems
  hundreds of miles away.† [20]

---

*Love demands submission and self-sacrifice for the sake of the object of one's love whereas greed means a selfish approach to relationships. Approaching the Lord with a selfish love is as ineffective as expecting a leaky thatched roof to keep one dry in a downpour.

†Sheikh Farid compares the present state of his health, when he is old and helplessly frail, with the drive and vitality of his younger days. He wants us to learn from his experience and devote ourselves to God before it is too late.

fareedaa raatee vadee'aan
dhukh dhukh uthan paas.
dhig tinhaa daa jeeviaa
jinaa vidaanee aas. [21] AG:1378–9

fareedaa je mai hodaa vaariaa
mitaa aa'irriaan.
herraa jalai majeeth jio
upar angaaraa. [22] AG:1379

fareedaa lorrai daakh bijauree'aan
kikar beejai jat.
handhai unn kataa'idaa
paidhaa lorrai pat. [23] AG:1379

fareedaa galee'e chikarr door ghar
naal piaare neh.
chalaa ta bhijai kamblee
rahaan ta tutai neh. [24] AG:1379

bhijau sijau kamblee
alah varsau meh.
jaa'e milaa tinaa sajnaa
tutau naahee neh. [25] AG:1379

Farid, the nights are long
    and my sides are aching in pain.
Cursed are the lives of those
    who place their hopes in others. [21]

Farid, if I had been there when my Friend came,
    I would have made myself a sacrifice to Him.
Now my flesh is burning red on the hot coals. [22]

Farid, the farmer plants the tree of *Acacia arabica*
    and desires the grapes of Bajaur.
He goes about spinning wool,
    but wishes to wear silk. [23]

Farid, the path is muddy
    and the house of my Beloved is so far away.
If I go out, my blanket will get soaked,
    but if I remain at home, my heart will be broken. [24]

My blanket is soaked, drenched
    with the downpour of the Lord's rain.
I am going out to meet my Friend,
    so that my heart will not be broken. [25]

fareedaa mai bholaavaa pag daa
mat mailee ho'e jaa'e.
gahilaa rooh na jaana'ee
sir bhee mitee khaa'e. [26] AG:1379

fareedaa sakar khand nivaat gurr
maakhio maanjhaa dudh.
sabhe vastoo mithee'aan
rab na pujan tudh. [27] AG:1379

fareedaa rotee meree kaath kee
laavan meree bhukh.
jinaa khaadhee choprree
ghane sahanige dukh. [28] AG:1379

rukhee sukhee khaa'e kai
thandhaa paanee pee'o.
fareedaa dekh paraa'ee choparree
naa tarsaa'e jee'o. [29] AG:1379

aj na sutee kant sio
ang murre murr jaa'e.
jaa'e puchhoh dohaagnee
tum kio rain vihaa'e. [30] AG:1379

Farid, I was worried
    that my turban might become dirty.
My thoughtless self did not realize that, one day,
    dust will consume my head as well. [26]

Sweet are sugar and candy
    and honey and buffalo's milk.*
Yea, sweet are all of these,
    but sweeter by far is God! [27]

Farid, my bread is made of wood
    and hunger is my cooked vegetable.
Those who eat buttered bread
    shall suffer great pain. [28]

Farid, eat your dry crust of bread;
    take simple cold water:
Envy not the delicacies another is enjoying. [29]

This night, I did not sleep with my Husband Lord
    and now my body is suffering in pain.
Go and ask the deserted bride
    how she passes her night. [30]

---

*Water buffaloes are domesticated as dairy cattle in India and their milk is highly
prized for its rich quality.

saahurai dho'ee na lahai
pe'ee'ai naahee thaa'o.
pir vaatarree na puchha'ee
dhan sohaagan naa'o. [31] AG:1379

saahurai pe'ee'ai kant kee
kant agamm athaah.
Nanak so sohaagnee
ju bhaavai beparvaah. [32] AG:1379

naatee dhotee sambahee
sutee aa'e nachind.
fareedaa rahee su berree hing dee
ga'ee kathooree gandh. [33] AG:1379

joban jaande na daraan
je sah preet na jaa'e.
fareedaa kiteen joban preet bin
suk ga'e kumlaa'e. [34] AG:1379

She who finds comfort
  neither in the husband's home
  nor in the parents',
Neglected by her love –
  what kind of wedded wife would she be? [31]

Here and hereafter,
  the bride belongs to her Groom, the Groom,
  who is inaccessible and unfathomable.*
Nanak says, she alone is the happily wedded bride
  who is pleasing to the carefree Lord. [32]

She bathed and perfumed herself;
  and decking herself, she slept without care.
But, [being abandoned], the bad odour of the
  asafoetida remained in her; and gone was the
  fragrance of musk!† [33]

I do not fear the departure of youth,
  if my Bridegroom's love does not depart.
O Farid, many of the young have withered
  and dried up without the Lord's love. [34]

---

* In the writings of the Gurus in the lineage of Guru Nanak, inaccessible and
unfathomable are descriptions of the Lord.

† A woman bathes and adorns herself to make herself attractive to win the heart
of her spouse. But in this sloka, Farid depicts a woman who falls asleep when it
is the time to meet the spouse. That the fragrance of musk turns into the foul
smell of the asafoetida plant means that all her preparations for union have
gone sour.

fareedaa chint khatolaa vaan dukh
birah vichhaavan lef.
eh hamaaraa jeevnaa
too saahib sache vekh. [35] AG:1379

birahaa birahaa aakhee'ai
birhaa too sultaan.
fareedaa jit tan biraho na oopjai
so tan jaan masaan. [36] AG:1379

fareedaa e' vis gandlaan
dharee'aan khand livaarr.
ik raahede rah ga'e
ik raadhee ga'e ujaarr. [37] AG:1379

fareedaa chaar gavaa'iaa handh kai
chaar gavaa'iaa samm.
lekhaa rab mangesee'aa
too aanho kehre kamm. [38] AG:1379

fareedaa dar darvaajai jaa'e kai
kio ditho gharree'aal.
eh nidosaan maaree'ai
ham dosaan daa kiaa haal. [39] AG:1379

Farid, anxiety is my bed, pain is my mattress,
    and the pain of separation is my blanket and quilt.
Behold, this is my life, O my true Lord and Master. [35]

Many talk of the pain and suffering of separation;
    O pain, you are the ruler of all.
Farid, that body within which
    love of the Lord does not well up –
    look upon that body as a cremation ground. [36]

Farid, these are poisonous sprouts
    coated with sugar.
Some die planting them, and some are ruined
    harvesting and enjoying them. [37]

Farid, men lose four watches of the day in wandering
    and the four of the night in sleep.
God will call for your account and ask
    for what purpose you hade come into the world. [38]

Farid, while going to the Lord's gate,
    have you not noticed the gong?
The sinless is being beaten, what shall be
    the condition of us, the sinners? [39]

gharree'e gharree'e maaree'ai
pahreen lahai sajaa'e.
so herraa gharree'aal jio
dukhee rain vihaa'e. [40] AG:1379

budhaa ho'aa sekh Fareed
kamban lagee deh.
je sau varhiaa jeevnaa
bhee tan hosee kheh. [41] AG:1380

fareedaa baar paraa'iai baisnaa
saa'een mujhai na deh.
je too evai rakhsee
jee'o sareeroh leh. [42] AG:1380

kandh kuhaarraa sir gharraa
van kai sar lohaar.
fareedaa hau lorree sauh aapnaa
too lorrah angiaar. [43] AG:1380

fareedaa iknaa aataa agalaa
iknaa naahee lon.
agai ga'e sinjaapsan
chotaan khaasee kaun. [44] AG:1380

The gong is beaten every hour
    and every quarter hour, it receives punishment.
The beautiful body is like the gong
    and passes the night in pain. [40]

Sheikh Farid has grown old
    and his body has begun to tremble.
Even if he lives for hundreds of years,
    his body shall ultimately become dust. [41]

Farid begs,
    O Lord, do not make me sit at another's door.
If this is the way you are going to keep me,
    then go ahead and take the life out of my body. [42]

With the axe on his shoulder
    and a bucket on his head,
    the blacksmith is ready to cut down the tree.
Farid, I long for my Lord;
    you long only for the charcoal. [43]

Farid, some have lots of flour
    while others do not even have salt.
When they go beyond this world
    it shall be seen who will be punished. [44]

paas damaame chhat sir
bheree sado rad.
jaa'e sute jeeraan mah
thee'e ateemaa gad. [45] AG:1380

fareedaa kothe mandap maarree'aa
usaarede bhee ga'e.
koorraa saudaa kar ga'e
goree aa'e pa'e. [46] AG:1380

fareedaa khintharr mekhaa aglee'aa
jind na kaa'ee mekh.
vaaree aapo aapnee
chale masaa'ik sekh. [47] AG:1380

fareedaa dohu deevee balandiaa
malak bahithaa aa'e.
garr leetaa ghat lutiaa
deevrre ga'iaa bujhaa'e. [48] AG:1380

fareedaa vekh kapaahai je thee'aa
je sir thee'aa tilaah.
kamaadai ar kaagdai
kunne ko'iliaah.
mande amal karediaa
eh sajaa'e tinaah. [49] AG:1380

Drums were beaten in their honour,
    there were canopies above their heads,
    and bugles announced their coming.
They have gone to sleep in the cemetery,
    buried like poor orphans. [45]

Farid, those who built houses, mansions
    and lofty buildings, oh, they have also departed.
They transacted false business
    and dropped into graves. [46]

Farid says, your patched coat has many stitches
    but there is no stitch on your life frame [soul].
The sheikhs and their disciples have all departed,
    each in his own turn. [47]

While the two lamps of the eyes* are alight,
    death's courier comes and seats himself, O Farid.
He captures the fortress, robs it of the souls
    and having put out the lamps, departs. [48]

Farid, see how cotton and sesame
    are crushed in the press, so also sugarcane;
    how paper and the pot are put into flames –
    such will be the punishment of evil-doers. [49]

---

*The two eyes watching.

fareedaa kann musalaa soof gal
dil kaatee gurr vaat.
baahar disai chaananaa
dil andhiaaree raat. [50] AG:1380

fareedaa ratee rat na niklai
je tan cheerai ko'e.
jo tan rate rab sio
tin tan rat na ho'e. [51] AG:1380

mahlaa 3.
eh tan sabho rat hai
rat bin tann na ho'e.
jo sah rate aapne
tit tan lobh rat na ho'e.
bhai pa'iai tan kheen ho'e
lobh rat vichoh jaa'e.
jio baisantar dhaat sudh ho'e
tio har kaa bhau durmat mail gavaa'e.
Nanak te jan sohne
je rate har rang laa'e. [52] AG:1380

fareedaa so'ee sarvar dhoodh laho
jithoh labhee vath.
chhaparr dhoodhai kiaa hovai
chikarr dubai hath. [53] AG:1380

Says Farid: Those who carry the prayer mat
    on their shoulders and wear rough wool,
    but bear daggers in their hearts
    and with glib tongue utter falsehood –
    these are bright outside,
    but have the dark night in their hearts. [50]

Farid, if anyone cuts my body,
    not even a bit of blood would issue forth from it.
The bodies which are imbued with God;
    those bodies contain no blood. [51]

Third Guru
This body is all blood;
    without blood, this body could not exist.
Those who are imbued with their Lord
    do not have the blood of greed in their bodies.
When the fear of God fills the body,
    it becomes thin;
    the blood of greed departs from within.
Just as metal is purified by fire,
    the fear of God removes the filthy residues
    of evil-mindedness.
O Nanak, those humble beings are beautiful
    who are imbued with the Lord's love. [52]

Farid, seek that sacred pool
    in which the genuine article is found.
Why do you bother to search in the pond?
    Your hand will only sink into the mud. [53]

fareedaa nandhee kant na raavio
vadee thee muee'aas.
dhan kookendee gor mein
tai sah naa milee'aas. [54] AG:1380

fareedaa sir paliaa daarree palee
muchhaan bhee palee'aan.
re man gahile baavle
maanah kiaa ralee'aan. [55] AG:1380

fareedaa kothe dhukan ketarraa
pir needarree nivaar.
jo deh ladhe gaanave
ga'e vilaarr vilaar. [56] AG:1380

fareedaa kothe mandap maarree'aa
et na laa'e chit.
mitee pa'ee atolavee
ko'e na hosee mit. [57] AG:1380

Farid, when she is young
   she does not enjoy her husband.
   When she grows up, she dies.
Lying in the grave, the soul-bride cries,
   "I did not meet you, my Lord."* [54]

Farid, your hair has turned grey,
   your beard has turned grey,
   and your moustache has turned grey.
O, my thoughtless and insane mind,
   why are you indulging in pleasures? [55]

Farid, how long can you run on the rooftop?†
You are asleep to your Husband Lord – give it up!
The days which were allotted to you are numbered
   and they are passing, passing away. [56]

Farid, the houses, mansions and balconies;
   to these, attach not your mind.
When unweighable dust falls upon you,
   then none of these shall befriend you. [57]

---

*Farid implies that youth is the time to turn to God – our health is good and we are in control of our faculties. In old age, the body becomes unsteady, the mind loses its focus, and one goes to the grave regretting that this precious life was wasted in worldly pursuits.

†Sheikh Farid likens a human life to a rooftop that has just a short span – before you know it, you are over the edge.

fareedaa mandap maal na laa'e
marag sataanee chit dhar.
saa'ee jaa'e samhaal
jithai hee tau vanjanaa. [58] AG:1380–1

fareedaa jinhee kammee naahe gun
te kammarre visaar.
mat sarmindaa theevahee
saa'een dai darbaar. [59] AG:1381

fareedaa saahib dee kar chaakree
dil dee laah bharaand.
darvesaan no lorree'ai
rukhaan dee jeeraand. [60] AG:1381

fareedaa kaale maide kaparre
kaalaa maidaa ves.
gunahee bhariaa mai phiraa
lok kahai darves. [61] AG:1381

tatee to'e na palavai
je jal tubee de'.
fareedaa jo dohaagan rab dee
jhooredee jhoore'. [62] AG:1381

jaan kuaaree taa chaa'o
veevaahee taan maamle.
fareedaa eho pachhotaa'o
vat kuaaree na thee'ai. [63] AG:1381

Farid, do not set your heart on palaces and wealth
    and think ever of the powerful death.
Contemplate that place alone where you have to go. [58]

Farid, the deeds which do not bring you any merit,
    leave those deeds
    lest you be put to shame at the Lord's Court. [59]

Farid, serve the Master,
    throw all doubt from your mind.
Men of God need to be forbearing like trees. [60]

Farid, my clothes are black and my outfit is black.
I wander around full of sins,
    and yet people call me a dervish – a holy man. [61]

The crop which is burnt will not bloom,
    even if it is soaked in water.
Farid, she who is forsaken by her Husband Lord
    grieves and laments. [62]

When the girl is a virgin, then she is full of desire;
    when she is married, then begin her troubles.
Farid, she has this regret
    that she cannot be a virgin again. [63]

kalar keree chhaparree
aa'e ulathe hanjh.
chinjoo borran naa peevah
udan sandee danjh. [64] AG:1381

hans udar kodhrai pa'iaa
lok vidaaran jaa'e.
gahilaa lok na jaanadaa
hans na kodhraa khaa'e. [65] AG:1381

chal chal ga'ee'aan pankhee'aan
jinhee vasaa'e tal.
fareedaa sar bhariaa bhee chalsee
thake kaval ikal. [66] AG:1381

fareedaa it siraane bho'e savan
keerraa larrio maas.
ketarriaa jug vaapare
ikat pa'iaa paas. [67] AG:1381

fareedaa bhannee gharree
savannavee tutee naagar laj.
ajraa'eel pharestaa
kai ghar naathee aj. [68] AG:1381

The swans have alighted
    on a small pond of dry saline soil.
They dip in their beaks but do not drink.
    Sick with thirst they fly away.[*] [64]

The swans fly away and land in the fields of grain. The
    people go to chase them away.
The thoughtless people do not know
    that the swans do not eat the grain.[†] [65]

Gone are the birds that brought life to the pools;
The entire pool will flow off,
    leaving alone the lotuses. [66]

Farid, in the grave a stone is your pillow,
    the earth your bed – worms will eat your flesh.
For aeons you will lie on one side, unchanging. [67]

Farid, your beautiful body shall break apart,
    and the subtle thread of the breath
    shall be snapped.
In which house will the Messenger of Death
    be a guest today? [68]

---

[*] For the true spiritual seekers and saints, this world is like a salt pond; it cannot assuage their thirst.

[†] Just as the people do not understand that swans will not eat the grains in the field, similarly they do not understand that true spiritual seekers and saints want nothing of this world.

fareedaa bhannee gharree
savannavee tootee naagar laj.
jo sajan bho'e bhaar the
se kio aavah aj. [69] AG:1381

fareedaa be nivaajaa kutiaa
eh na bhalee reet.
kab hee chal na aa'iaa
panje vakhat maseet. [70] AG:1381

uth fareedaa ujoo saaj
subah nivaaj gujaar.
jo sir saa'een naa nivai
so sir kap utaar. [71] AG:1381

jo sir saa'ee naa nivai
so sir keejai kaa'e.
kunne heth jalaa'ee'ai
baalan sandai thaa'e. [72] AG:1381

fareedaa kithai taide maapiaa
jinhee too janioh.
tai paasoh o'e lad ga'e
toon ajai na pateenoh. [73] AG:1381

Farid, your beautiful body shall break apart,
    and the subtle thread of the breath
    shall be snapped.
Those friends who were a burden on the earth –
    how can they come today?* [69]

Farid, O faithless dog,
    this is not a good way of life.
You never come to the mosque
    for your five daily prayers. [70]

Rise up, Farid, and cleanse yourself;
    chant your morning prayer.
The head which does not bow to the Lord –
    chop off and remove that head. [71]

The head that does not bow to the Lord,
    what is to be done with such a head?
Burn it
    under the earthen pot in place of firewood. [72]

Where are your parents, O Farid,
    whose offspring you are?
Before you, they've passed away;
    but you still believe not! [73]

---

*This appears to relate to people whose lives amount to nothing but a meaning-less existence between birth and death. They were given a beautiful human form which they could have employed in devotion to God, but lack of spiritual purpose made their lives worthless, a mere burden on the earth.

fareedaa man maidaan
kar to'e tibe laah.
agai mool na aavsee
dojak sandee bhaah. [74] AG:1381

mahlaa 5.
fareedaa khaalak khalak mah
khalak vasai rab maahe.
mandaa kis no aakhee'ai
jaan tis bin ko'ee naahe. [75] AG:1381

fareedaa je deh naalaa kapiaa
je gal kapah chukh.
pavan na itee maamle
sahaan na itee dukh. [76] AG:1381

chaban chalan ratann se
sunee'ar bah ga'e.
herre mutee dhaah se
jaanee chal ga'e. [77] AG:1381

fareedaa bure daa bhalaa kar
gusaa man na hadhaa'e.
dehee rog na laga'ee
palai sabh kichh paa'e. [78] AG:1381-2

fareedaa pankh paraahunee
dunee suhaavaa baag.
naubat vajee subah sio
chalan kaa kar saaj. [79] AG:1382

Farid, make your mind straight
    from the ups and downs of passions:
Then may you escape the furnace blast of hell. [74]

Fifth Guru
Farid, the Creator is in the creation,
    and the creation abides in God.
Whom can we call bad?
    There is none without Him. [75]

Farid, if instead of the navel-string
    the nurse had cut my throat,
    I wouldn't have been so badly involved with the
    world nor would pain have been my lot! [76]

My teeth, feet, eyes and ears have stopped working.
My body cries out,
    "Those whom I knew have left me!" [77]

Farid, answer evil with goodness;
    do not fill your mind with anger.
Your body shall not suffer from any disease,
    and you shall obtain everything. [78]

Farid, the bird is a guest
    in this beautiful world-garden.
The morning drums are beating –
    get ready to leave! [79]

fareedaa raat kathooree vandee'ai
sutiaa milai na bhaa'o.
jinnhaa nain neendraavle
tinnhaa milan kuaa'o. [80] AG:1382

fareedaa main jaaniaa dukh mujh koo
dukh sabaa'iai jag.
ooche charr kai dekhiaa
taan ghar ghar ehaa ag. [81] AG:1382

mahlaa 5.
fareedaa bhoom rangaavlee
manjh visoolaa baag.
jo jan peer nivaajiaa
tinnhaa anch na laag. [82] AG:1382

mahlaa 5.
fareedaa umar suhaavrree
sang suvannarree deh.
virle ke'ee paa'ee'anh
jinnhaa piaare neh. [83] AG:1382

kandhee vahan na dhaah
tau bhee lekhaa devnaa.
jidhar rab rajaa'e
vahan tidaa'oo gaun kare. [84] AG:1382

Farid, musk is distributed at night.
    Those who are asleep get not a share.
Those whose eyes are heavy with sleep –
    how can they be blessed with it? [80]

Farid, I thought I alone was in pain,
    but so is the world entire.
When I saw from the house-top,
    I saw the whole world on fire! [81]

Fifth Guru
Farid, in the midst of the beauteous world
    there is a thorny garden.
The persons who are blessed by the Guru
    suffer not even a scratch. [82]

Fifth Guru
Farid, life is blessed and beautiful,
    along with the beautiful body.
Only a rare few are found
    who love their beloved Lord. [83]

O river, break not your banks, for you too
    have to render account
    (to your God):
So flow (within your limits) as is the Lord's will. [84]

fareedaa dukhaa setee dih ga'iaa
soolaan setee raat.
kharraa pukaare paatnee
berraa kapar vaat. [85] AG:1382

lammee lammee nadee vahai
kandhee kerai het.
berre no kapar kiaa kare
je paatan rahai suchet. [86] AG:1382

fareedaa galeen su sajan veeh
ik dhoodhedee na lahaan.
dhukhaan jio maanleeh
kaaran tinnhaa maa piree. [87] AG:1382

fareedaa eh tan bhaunknaa
nit nit dukhee'ai kaun.
kannee buje de rahaan
kitee vagai paun. [88] AG:1382

fareedaa rab khajooree pakee'aan
maakhia na'ee vahannh.
jo jo vanjain deeharraa
so umar hath pavann. [89] AG:1382

fareedaa tan sukaa pinjar thee'aa
talee'aan khoondah kaag.
ajai so rab na baahurrio
dekh bande ke bhaag. [90] AG:1382

Farid, the day passes in agony, the night in woe,
    while the Boatman cries out:
    "O, thy boat is caught in the whirlpool!" [85]

The river flows on and on;
    it loves to eat into its banks.
What can the whirlpool do to the boat,
    if the Boatman remains alert? [86]

Farid, scores profess to be my friends;
    but true friends see I nowhere.
For one true Friend my heart yearns
    as in a smouldering fire. [87]

Farid, this body is ever barking;
    who can stand this continuous suffering?
I have put stoppers in my ears;
    I care not how much wind is blowing. [88]

Farid, God's dates have ripened
    and streams of honey flow.
Each day which passes
    steals away a mortal's age. [89]

Farid, my aged frail body has become a skeleton
    and the crows peck at my soles.
Even till now, God has not come to my aid;
    such is the fate of man. [90]

kaagaa karang dhadholiaa
saglaa khaa'iaa maas.
e' do'e nainaa mat chhuhau
pir dekhan kee aas. [91] AG:1382

kaagaa choond na pinjraa
basai ta udar jaahe.
jit pinjrai meraa sauh vasai
maas na tidoo khaahe. [92] AG:1382

fareedaa gor nimaanee sad kare
nighariaa ghar aa'o.
sarpar maithai aavnaa
maranoh naa dariaaho. [93] AG:1382

enee lo'inee dekhadiaa
ketee chal ga'ee.
fareedaa lokaan aapo aapnee
mai aapnee pa'ee. [94] AG:1382

aap savaarah mai milah
mai miliaa sukh ho'e.
fareedaa je toon meraa ho'e rahah
sabh jag teraa ho'e. [95] AG:1382

The crows have searched my skeleton
    and eaten up all flesh.
O crows, touch not these two eyes,
    as I hope to behold my beloved. [91]

O crow, do not peck at my skeleton;
    if you have landed on it, fly away.
Do not eat the flesh from that skeleton
    within which my Husband Lord abides. [92]

The humble grave calls me:
    "O homeless one, come to your home;
    when one day you must come to me,
    then why be afraid of death?" [93]

Within the sight of these eyes of mine
    a good many have departed.
Farid, people have their own anxieties
    and I have my own. [94]

(Says God): You meet me
    if you embellish yourself with merit,
    meeting me, you are at peace;
    for if you belong to me, O Farid,
    the whole world will belong to you. [95]

kandhee utai rukharraa
kichrak bannai dheer.
fareedaa kachai bhaandai rakhee'ai
kichar taa'ee neer. [96] AG:1382

fareedaa mahal nisakhan rah ga'e
vaasaa aa'iaa tal.
goraan se nimaanee'aa
bahsan roohaan mal.
aakheen sekhaa bandagee
chalan aj ke kal. [97] AG:1382–1383

fareedaa mautai daa bannaa evai disai
jio daree'aavai dhaahaa.
agai dojak tapiaa sunee'ai
hool pavai kaahaahaa.
iknaa no sabh sojhee aa'ee
ik phirde veparvaahaa.
amal je keetiaa dunee vich
se dargah ogaahaa. [98] AG:1383

fareedaa daree'aavai kannhai bagulaa
baithaa kel kare.
kel karede hanjh no
achinte baaj pa'e.
baaj pa'e tis rab de
kelaan visaree'aan.
jo man chit na chete san
so gaalee rab kee'aan. [99] AG:1383

How long can the tree remain stable
   on the riverbank?
O Farid, for how long can water be kept
   in an unbaked earthen vessel? [96]

Farid, the mansions are vacant;
   those who lived in them
   have gone to live underground.
   They remain there in those unhonoured graves.
O Sheikh, dedicate yourself to God;
   you will have to depart today or tomorrow. [97]

Farid! Death is visible
   as the river's opposite bank.
Beyond is flaming hell,
   resounding with loud shrieks.
Some have had realization;
   others go about wrapped in thoughtlessness.
Know, the deeds done in this world
   bear witness against us in the next. [98]

Farid, the crane, perched on the riverbank,
   enjoys (his hunt).
But, lo, while enjoying this,
   he is pounced upon by the hawks, unawares!
Yea, when the hawks of God pounce upon him,
   all his revelry goes,
   and what was never in his mind came to pass;
   such are the doings of God! [99]

saadhe trai man dehuree
chalai paanee ann.
aa'io bandaa dunee vich
vat aasoonee bannh.
malkal maut jaan aavsee
sabh darvaaje bhann.
tinhaa piaariaa bhaa'ee'aan
agai ditaa bannh.
vekhoh bandaa chaliaa
chahu janiaa dai kannh.
fareedaa amal je keete dunee vich
dargah aa'e kamm. [100] AG:1383

fareedaa hau balihaaree tin pankhee'aa
jangal jinnhaa vaas.
kakar chugan thal vasan
rab na chhodan paas. [101] AG:1383

fareedaa rut phiree van kambiaa
pat jharre jharr paahe.
chaare kundaan dhoondhee'aan
rahan kithaa'oo naahe. [102] AG:1383

This body weighing three and a half maunds*
   by food and water is sustained.
Man comes into the world
   with a vast store of hopes.
As approaches death's angel, crashing all doors,
   those loving friends and brothers
   perforce surrender to him.
Behold man, departing this world
   borne on the shoulders of four pallbearers.
Farid, only the good deeds done by us in this world
   stand by us in the next. [100]

Farid, a sacrifice am I to the birds
   who pass their days in solitary places,
Picking pebbles, living on sandy mounds,
   yet turning not away from God. [101]

Farid, the season has changed, the woods shake
   and the leaves continually drop off.
I have searched the four directions
   and have found not any abode anywhere. [102]

---

*A traditional unit of weight that ranged from 25 pounds (11 kg) to 160 pounds
(72.5 kg). The modern standard for India and Pakistan is about 37 kg.

fareedaa paarr patolaa dhaj karee
kambalrree pahire'o.
jinhee vesee sauh milai
se'ee ves kare'o. [103] AG:1383

mahlaa 3.
kaa'e patolaa paarrtee
kambalrree pahire'.
Nanak ghar hee baithiaa sauh milai
je nee'at raas kare'. [104] AG:1383

mahlaa 5.
fareedaa garab jinhaa vadiaa'ee'aa
dhan joban aagaah.
khaalee chale dhanee sio
tibe jio meehaah. [105] AG:1383

fareedaa tinaa mukh daraavne
jinaa visaarion naa'o.
aithai dukh ghaneriaa
agai thaur na thaa'o. [106] AG:1383

Farid, I have torn my clothes to tatters;
    now I wear only a rough blanket.*
I wear only those clothes which will lead me
    to meet my Lord. [103]

Third Guru
Why do you tear apart your fine clothes
    and take to wearing a rough blanket?
O Nanak, even sitting in your own home
    you can meet the Lord,
    if your mind is in the right place. [104]

Fifth Guru
Farid, those who are very proud
    of their greatness, wealth and youth,
    shall return empty-handed from their Lord,
    like sandhills after the rain.† [105]

Farid, dreadful are the faces of those
    who forget the Lord's Name.
Here, they undergo many troubles and,
    hereafter, find no abode and refuge. [106]

---

*A coarse woollen blanket, which is one of the few possessions of a *faqir*, signifies holiness and renunciation. He calls this blanket his *kambalrree*, a term of affection implying his dear, sweet little blanket. On the one hand, it is coarse and rough; on the other hand, it leads him to his Beloved.

†When the monsoon rains come in the Punjab, they wash away any hill of sand. However high you pile up sand, it will be lost to the rains.

fareedaa pichhal raat na jaagioh
jeevadrro mo'ioh.
je tai rab visaariaa
ta rab na visarioh. [107] AG:1383

mahlaa 5.
fareedaa kant rangaavlaa
vadaa ve-muhtaaj.
alah setee ratiaa
eh sachaavaan saaj. [108] AG:1383

mahlaa 5.
fareedaa dukh sukh ik kar
dil te laah vikaar.
alah bhaavai so bhalaa
taan labhee darbaar. [109] AG:1383

mahlaa 5.
fareedaa dunee vajaa'ee vajadee
toon bhee vajah naal.
so'ee jee'o na vajadaa
jis alah kardaa saar. [110] AG:1383

Farid, if you do not awaken
    in the early hours before dawn,
    you are dead while yet alive.*
Although you have forgotten God,
    God has not forgotten you. [107]

Fifth Guru
Farid, my Husband Lord is full of joy;
    He is great and self-sufficient.
To be imbued with the Lord God –
    this is the most beautiful decoration. [108]

Fifth Guru
Farid, look upon pleasure and pain as the same;
    eradicate corruption from your heart.
Whatever pleases the Lord God is good;
    understand this, and you will reach His Court. [109]

Fifth Guru
Farid, the world dances as it dances,
    and you dance with it as well.
That soul alone does not dance with it
    who is under the care of the Lord God. [110]

---

*Living in body, dead in spirit.

mahlaa 5.
fareedaa dil rataa is dunee sio
dunee na kitai kamm.
misal phakeeraan gaakharree
so paa'ee'ai poor karamm. [111] AG:1383–4

pahile pahrai phulrraa
phal bhee pachhaa raat.
jo jaagannh lahann se
saa'ee kanno daat. [112] AG:1384

daateesaahib sandee'aa
kiaa chalai tis naal.
ik jaagande naa lahanh
iknhaa sutiaa de' uthaal. [113] AG:1384

dhoodhedee'e suhaag koo
tau tan kaa'ee kor.
jinhaa naa'o suhaagnee
tinhaa jhaak na hor. [114] AG:1384

sabar manjh kamaan e' ·
sabar kaa neehano.
sabar sandaa baan
khaalak khataa na karee. [115] AG:1384

Fifth Guru
Farid, the mind is imbued with this world,
    but the world is of no avail.
Hard is the way of life of God's devotees.
    That position is obtained
    by supreme good fortune. [111]

The first watch of the night brings flowers,
    and the later watches of the night bring fruit.
Those who remain awake and aware,
    receive the gifts from the Lord. [112]

First Guru
The gifts are from our Lord and Master;
    who can force Him to bestow them?
Some are awake and do not receive them,
    while He awakens others from sleep
    to bless them. [113]

Those that are seeking conjugal bliss,
    what is lacking in you.
Those that are blessed in matrimony
    look to nothing but the spouse. [114]

O man, in your mind make patience your bow,
    of patience make your bowstring and
    of patience your arrows.
Thus the Creator shall not allow you
    to miss the mark. [115]

sabar andar saabree
tan evai jaalenh.
hon najeek khudaa'e dai
bhet na kisai den. [116] AG:1384

sabar eh suaa'o
je toon bandaa dirr karah.
vadh theevah daree'aa'o
tut na theevah vaahrraa. [117] AG:1384

fareedaa darvesee gaakharree
choparree preet.
ikan kinai chaalee'ai
darvesaavee reet. [118] AG:1384

tan tapai tanoor jio
baalan had balannh.
pairee thakaa sir julaa
je moon piree milannh. [119] AG:1384

tan na tapaa'e tanoor jio
baalan had na baal.
sir pairee kiaa pherriaa
andar piree nihaal. [120] AG:1384

hau dhoodhedee sajnaa
sajan maide naal.
Nanak alakh na lakhee'ai
gurmukh de' dikhaal. [121] AG:1384

Those who are patient abide in patience;
    in this way, they burn their bodies.
They are close to the Lord,
    but they do not reveal their secret to anyone. [116]

Let patience be your purpose in life;
    implant this within your being.
In this way you will grow into a great river;
    you will not break off into a tiny stream. [117]

Farid, know the ascetics' path is hard;
    Thy devotion is only of the surface.
Rare is the man who this path treads. [118]

I'd burn my body like a furnace
    and feed the fire with my bones;
Yea, I'll walk on my head if the feet tire,
    only if I were to meet with my love! [119]

Burn not your body like a furnace;
    feed not love's fire with your bones.
What wrong have your head and feet done to you?
    Pray, see your God within. [120]

I go searching for my Friend,
    but my Friend is ever with me.
Nanak, the unseen Lord is seen not;
    the exalted guru shows Him to the mortal. [121]

hansaa dekh tarandiaa
bagaa aa'iaa chaa'o.
dub mu'e bag bapurre
sir tal upar paa'o. [122] AG:1384

mai jaaniaa vad hans hai
taan mai keetaa sang.
je jaanaa bag bapurraa
janam na bherree ang. [123] AG:1384

kiaa hans kiaa bagulaa
jaa kau nadar dhare.
je tis bhaavai naanakaa
kaagoh hans kare. [124] AG:1384

sarvar pankhee hekarro
phaaheevaal pachaas.
eh tan lahree gad thiaa
sache teree aas. [125] AG:1384

The sight of the swans* swimming
    excited in storks the desire for emulation.
The poor storks got only drowned,
    head downwards. [122]

I knew him as a great swan,
    so I associated with him.
If I had known that he was only a wretched crane,
    I would never in my life
    have crossed paths with him. [123]

Talk not of swans and storks –
    His grace alone suffices.
Says Nanak, should He so wish,
    a crow He may turn into a swan. [124]

There is only one bird in the lake,
    but there are fifty trappers.
This body is caught in the waves of desire.
    O my true Lord, You are my only hope! [125]

---

*Swan: esoterically, a highly evolved soul. In Indian spiritual literature, a swan (*hansa*) is symbolic of grace and purity; it is believed that the natural drink of a swan is nectar (*amrit*), and its natural foods are pearls, diamonds and rubies, which signify the Beloved, the essence of the Divine. It is further believed that the beak of a swan has the unique ability to drink nectar after filtering out the dirty water or poison of maya with which it is mixed.

kavan so akhar kavan gun
kavan so manee'aa mant.
kavan so veso hau karee
jit vas aavai kant. [126] AG:1384

nivan so akhar khavan gun
jihbaa manee'aa mant.
e' trai bhaine ves kar
taan vas aavee kant. [127] AG:1384

mat hodee ho'e iaanaa.
taan hode ho'e nitaanaa.
anhode aap vandaa'e.
ko aisaa bhagat sadaa'e. [128] AG:1384

ik phikaa na gaalaa'e
sabhnaa mai sachaa dhanee.
hiaa'o na kaihee thaahe
maanak sabh amolve. [129] AG:1384

sabhnaa man maanik
thaahan mool machaangvaa.
je tau piree'aa dee sik
hiaa'o na thahe kahee daa. [130] AG:1384

What is that word, what is that virtue,
    and what is that magic mantra?
What are those clothes which I can wear
    to captivate my Husband Lord? [126]

Humility is the word, forgiveness is the virtue,
    and sweet speech is the magic mantra.
Wear these three robes, O sister,
    and you will captivate your Husband Lord. [127]

If one be innocent even when wise
    and be powerless even when blest with power,
    and share even when there is least to share,
    one is a true devotee of God;
    but rare is such a one, how rare! [128]

Speak never a rude word to any –
    the Lord eternal in all abides.
Break no heart –
    know each being is a priceless jewel. [129]

Each heart is a jewel;
    evil it is to break any.
Should you seek to find the Beloved,
    break no one's heart. [130]

Sheikh Farid's Verses
Outside the Adi Granth

WHILE SHEIKH FARID is best known for the slokas in the
Adi Granth, other verses attributed to him fill out a more
complete picture of his teachings and his manner of expression.
We include these little-known verses in the interest of shedding
light on the multi-faceted figure of the beloved *Ganj-i shakar*. To
the best of our knowledge, the poetry presented in this section
has never before appeared in English translation.

Persian Verses

Sheikh Farid's primary language was Persian. This was the language he spoke with his disciples, with his pir, and with his fellow
Sufis. In the period of Indo-Persian cultural fusion, Persian was
the cosmopolitan common language (*lingua franca*) among Sufis
across the vast stretches of land from present-day Turkey, Iran,
and Afghanistan to northern India.

From the recollections of his disciples, we know that Sheikh
Farid was familiar with a vast corpus of Persian poetry and could
recall at a moment's notice the appropriate verse to recite in
conversation. We also know that he gathered together with his
disciples to enjoy delightful evenings of hearing mystical verses,
whether sung or spoken. His deep pleasure in hearing Persian
mystical poetry sometimes carried him into ecstatic states. When

we consider his ability to make skilful editorial comments on his disciples' poems, it seems reasonable to assume that he also composed poetry in Persian.

Unfortunately, if he did compose Persian poems extensively, most of them have been lost to us. There is no complete collection of poems (*diwan*) by Sheikh Farid. Later writers produced *diwans* and attributed them to Khwaja Muinuddin Chishti and Sheikh Qutbuddin Bakhtiyar Kaki, the first two Chishti sheikhs in India. Scholars today are certain that these were not actually written by these two sheikhs. But in the case of Sheikh Farid, no such effort was made either to assemble his work or to produce a body of Persian poetry in his name. All we have are a few stray verses attributed to Sheikh Farid.

Still, these few verses are gems well worth reading and pondering. In them we may be hearing the Persian voice of the Sufi Sheikh Farid. The voice and tone, the delicate sensibility, is quite different from the voice of the slokas in the Adi Granth or in the other Multani verses from the oral tradition. Naturally, the spiritual message of his poems, regardless of language, is the same. We hear him sing of the pain of separation and longing; we hear him sing of a love for the divine Beloved. But his manner of expressing this love and longing has a different flavour in the Persian idiom.

The poems presented here begin with those Sheikh Farid is said to have composed and continue on to those he is said to have been fond of reciting. Reading the sources carefully, one cannot always say for sure whether the text implies that Sheikh Farid had composed the poem himself. *Siyar al-Auliya* is our earliest and most authoritative source for poetry by Sheikh Farid. When *Siyar al-Auliya* relates that someone posed a question to the sheikh and "Shaykh-i Shiyukh al-alam [Sheikh Farid] was quick to roll out the following couplet extempore,"[16] the implication seems clear that Farid created the poem on the spot.

Although other references to his authorship are ambiguous, Sheikh Farid's talent and natural ability for spontaneous composition of rhyming couplets was well known. When a poem is introduced with the words, "The moment this thought struck his mind, Shaykh-i Shiyukh al-alam [Sheikh Farid] had the following couplets rolling out of his lips,"[17] there is a question of whether he composed the verse or whether he was simply repeating a verse from another poet. Similarly, the phrase, "The following words of wisdom spoken by him too carry the seal of his astute knowledge and understanding,"[18] could imply that he composed the following couplet, since his poems were spoken, but they could also mean that he recalled a poem by another mystic poet. In the texts from the fourteenth century, this distinction regarding authorship seems not to have been considered important.

Rendering Persian poetry, especially the mystical poetry of the Sufis, into English is extremely challenging. The Persian language lends itself to complex layers of meaning difficult to capture in translation. Our translations strive to convey that meaning through the imagery of the poem, but in a free verse form. We have not attempted to duplicate the lyrical rhythm or the tight rhyming scheme of the original. The notes at the end of the poems show the sources for each verse.

Notes on Sources

The sources where these verses were recorded range from fourteenth-century texts – the memoir, *Siyar al-Auliya*, and the unpublished manuscript from the Chishti Sufis at Khuldabad – to modern scholarly articles. We are particularly indebted to Dr S.A.H. Abidi for his work in collecting Persian verses attributed to Sheikh Farid in numerous early texts.

- Poems 1–5 were recorded in *Siyar al-Auliya* on pages 139, 139, 141, 144, and 143, respectively. Amir Khurd presents these as having been composed by Sheikh Farid.

- Poem 6 was in the manuscript of a fourteenth-century text found in Khuldabad. As such, it represents one of the earliest written records of any words of Sheikh Farid, not long after *Siyar al-Auliya*.

- Poems 7–9 were collected by Abidi and published in G.S. Talib's compilation, *Baba Sheikh Farid: Life and Teachings*. Abidi's article "Baba Farid as Persian Poet" lists numerous medieval *tazkirat* (biographies of the saints) where Sheikh Farid is cited as the author of these poems.

- Poems 10–12 were included in Abidi's article, "Baba Farid as Persian Poet." Although poem 10 was cited in *Kalaam-i-Baba Farid Shakar Ganj* as a poem by Sheikh Farid and all these verses were attributed to Sheikh Farid by other modern scholars (including Mohan Singh Diwana, Mahmud Shairani, Miles Irving, and K.A. Nizami), Abidi himself doubts their authenticity.

- Poems 13 and 14 were recorded as couplets that were "often on his tongue." They appear on pages 126 and 202 in *Siyar al-Auliya*.

- Poems 15–20, according to Abidi, were recorded in the medieval text, *Rahat ul-Qulub*, as being frequently recited by Sheikh Farid.

du-sheena shabam dil-i hazeenam ba-girift,
wa andesha-i yaar naazneenam ba-girift.
guftam ba-saro deedah rawam bar dar-i tu,
ashkam ba-deed-o aasteenam ba-girift. [1]

ba-qadr-i ranj yaabi sarwari ra,
ba-shab bīdaar boodan behtari ra. [2]

ay mudda'i ba-da'wa chandeen makun dilbari,
yak harf-i raaz ma'ni mah sad jawaab baashad. [3]

Fareedoon farrukh farishtah na-buwad,
zi ood zi anbar sarishtah na-buwad.
zi daad-o dihish yaaft aan nekuwi,
tu daad-o dihish kun Fareedoon shawi. [4]

khwurish dih ba kunjishk-o kabk-o hamaam,
kih naa-gah humaa'i bar uftad ba-daam. [5]

Last night my grieving heart sank in melancholy,
    and yearning for my sweet Beloved filled my soul.
I wanted to rush and take refuge at Your gate,
    but my tears kept pouring and would not abate. [1]

The more suffering you endure the higher you rise.
Nightly vigils produce elevated souls. [2]

You who have claims,
    do not get carried away with your erudition,
for in inner meaning, a single word
    may have three hundred interpretations. [3]

King Fereydoon was not an angelic being,
    neither was he made of amber and incense.
He gained his fame by being just and generous.
Through justice and generosity,
    you too may become a Fereydoon. [4]

Feed birds small and large
    so mayhap someday
    you snare the Humā.* [5]

---

* The Humā is a mythical bird believed to raise to the throne anyone coming
under the shadow of its wings.

geeram kih ba-shab namaaz bisyaar kuni,
dar roz dawaay shakhsh beemaar kuni.
ta dil na-kuni zi ghussah-o keen khaali,
sad khirman-i gul bar sar-i yak khaar kuni. [6]

shab neest kih khoon-i dil ghamnaak na-rekht,
rozay na kih aabrooye man paak na-rekht.
yak sharbat-i aab-i khwush na-khuram har-giz,
ka-aan baaz zi raah-deedah bar khaak na-rekht. [7]

har sahar bar aastaan sar mi zanam,
bar tareeq-i doostan dar mi zanam.
hamchu murgh-i neem bismil pesh-i tu,
darmiyaan-i khaak-o khoon par mi zanam. [8]

siflah ra manzoor na-tawaan saakhtan go khoobar ast,
meekh ra dar deedah na-tawaan, koftan go az zar ast. [9]

o gadaay door baash az baadshaah,
ta na-baayad bar dar-i tu door baash.
gar wisaal-i shaah mi daari tam‘,
az wisaal-i khwayshtan mahjoor baash. [10]

You may attend to the sick all day
　　and pray all night long;
but if your heart is not empty of anger and malice,
　　to a single thorn
　　you sacrifice a hundred heaps of roses. [6]

No night goes by
　　that this stricken heart does not bleed.
No day goes by
　　that I am not robbed of my honour.
Not a single glass of water quenches my thirst
　　that does not return to earth as my tears. [7]

Every dawn I alight at Your door
　　as a hopeful friend
　　who comes to beg and implore.
Like a bird trailing in the dust only half alive,
　　I flutter in Your presence
　　hoping to surrender my life. [8]

Take not the ignoble one as your ideal,
　　though he may be distinguished.
One does not smite one's eye with a nail
　　even if it is made of gold. [9]

Keep your distance from kings, O mendicant! –
　　avoid them so they do not appear at your door.
Your desire for association with them
　　will obstruct you from reaching your self. [10]

oo dil ba-kas dih kih na-meerad ta tu,
naalah-i dard-i firaaq nigar mi yaarī. [11]

az noor-i jamaal mard-i mutlaq khezad,
waz shawq-i khuda nigar ba rawnaq khezad. [12]

har kih dar band naam-o aawaazah ast,
khaanah-i oo baroon darwaazah ast. [13]

khwaaham kih hameesha dar wisaal-i tu zaym,
khaaki shawam ba-zer-i paay tu zaym.
maqsood-i man khastah zi kawnayn tu'i.
az ba-har tu meeram wa baraay tu zaym. [14]

chun umr dar gushasht darweshi bih,
chun kaar-i ba-qismat ast kam koshi bih.
chun taras-i hayaat ast khuda baashi bih,
chun guftah nawishtah ast khaamoshi bih. [15]

Surrender your heart to one who does not die,
so you do not mourn in bitter separation. [11]

From the light of glory the Perfect One is born.
Behold what longing for God produces. [12]

Whoever chooses name and fame
finds his house outside the gate! [13]

I wish to turn into dust
    and find my abode under Your feet;
    I wish to live in union with You.
I am weary of both worlds
    and my sole purpose here is You –
    to live for You and die for You. [14]

Since life is a passing affair,
    those who live like a dervish are wise.
Since one's lot has been decided,
    running after the world is unwise.
Since existence is shrouded in fear,
    renouncing is the way.
Since utterances trap one in words,
    silence is wise. [15]

aan aql kuja kih dar kamaal-i tu rasad,
wa-aan deedah kuja kih dar jamaal-i tu rasad.
geeram kih tu pardah bar girifti zi jamaal,
aan rooh kuja kih dar jalaal-i tu rasad. [16]

tu raah na-raftah az aan na-namudand,
dard kih zad een dar kih baro na-gushoodand.
jaan dar rah-i dilhaast agar mi khwaahi,
tu neez chunaan shawi kih eeshaan boodand. [17]

ay basa dar dukkaan tura daroost,
ay basa sher ka-aan tura aahoost. [18]

afsos kih az haal-i minnat neest khabar,
aankih khabrat shawad kih afsos khudi. [19]

dar kooy aashiqaan chunaan jaan ba-dihand,
ka-aanja malak al-mawt na-gunjad hargiz. [20]

What intellect can dare
    to dream of Your perfection?
Where is there an eye
    worthy of beholding Your beauty?
Suppose You removed the veil,
    where is there a soul to bear Your glory? [16]

It was not opened unto you
    for you had not journeyed the distance.
Otherwise, who has ever been denied
    who has knocked on this door?
If your desire is to find your soul,
    look for it among the People of the Heart
    so you too may become what they are. [17]

Many fierce lions in your hands became tame gazelles.
From many ills You bring out cures. [18]

Alas, You pay no heed to my suffering.
There will be remorse when You do! [19]

In the lane of love
    where lovers surrender their souls,
    no Angel of Death need appear. [20]

Multani Verses

A rich oral tradition of poetry attributed to Sheikh Farid has continued to thrive throughout the seven centuries since his death. These poems in the Multani dialect have been sung, heard, remembered, and passed on over varying lengths of time before being first written down.

The earliest written evidence of poems in Multani believed to be by Sheikh Farid comes from a fourteenth-century text, *Hidayat ul-Qulub*. In the manuscript Carl Ernst discovered at the Chishti Sufi centre in Khuldabad, the text was written in Persian script, as were all Sufi writings of the period; but the seven *dohras*[*] in the manuscript – if one sounded them out from the Persian script – could be recognized as an archaic form of Multani. When Prof. Christopher Shackle was able to recognize one of the seven verses as a close variant of Sloka 7 of the Adi Granth, he provided the first clear evidence that Sloka 7 was in existence almost two centuries before Guru Nanak visited Sheikh Ibrahim at Pakpattan and received from him the collection of verses that were later incorporated into the Adi Granth.

In addition, the six other Multani *dohras* in the manuscript offer the first unambiguous evidence that there was in circulation at that early date – less than a century after Sheikh Farid's death – a body of poetry that the Chishti Sufis believed to be composed by Sheikh Farid. From this we might conclude that when Sheikh Ibrahim presented Guru Nanak with a collection of Sheikh Farid's poetry, it was only a selection of Sheikh Farid's verses then in circulation among Sufis. Alternatively, Guru Nanak could have selected among the slokas he was given and only retained a portion of the collection. In any case, it is clear that as early as the fourteenth century the oral tradition of verses by

---

[*] A two-line poem in which each line of the rhymed couplet has a division in the middle of the line; each couplet can stand alone as a complete unit; sometimes called a *doha*.

Sheikh Farid included *dohras* – at least six of them – that were not incorporated into the Adi Granth.

When it comes to the verses dating from the fourteenth century, the challenges of translating some of these very old verses are daunting. Of the six Multani verses in the Khuldabad manuscript, three were unintelligible. Whether due to stray marks on the manuscript, copyist errors or because this is a very old dialect that is spoken by a rare few today, no sense could be made of three of the verses.[19] It took the skills of Shackle, a world-renowned linguist, to render three of the verses into English:

> Alone, the one Lord's love fills the mind with pain.
> Will fire affect the heart which love has set ablaze?

> Today's the time for meeting, however far the way.
> These foolish folk know not, what will the morrow bring?

> Some knots may be clumsy, while others are well tied.
> Some are hidden in the pot, and some are fully cooked.

The third verse, above, seems mysterious or unfinished. According to Carl Ernst it appears to be a type of verse understood as riddling instructions given by a Sufi sheikh to his immediate disciple. It may have been addressed to a particular disciple, and perhaps was meant to be understood only by that disciple for his own spiritual development. Unfortunately, we have only a single verse of this type from Sheikh Farid. Nonetheless, this single verse may reveal a formerly unknown dimension of his way of teaching his disciples and, as such, is a valuable addition to our understanding of Sheikh Farid, *Ganj-i shakar*.

The oral tradition of poems attributed to Sheikh Farid has continued long past the fourteenth century and long past the compilation of the Adi Granth in the sixteenth century. Through the seventeenth, eighteenth, and even the nineteenth and twentieth centuries, poems by Sheikh Farid continued to surface, having been apparently passed down orally, and then appearing for the first time in writing. Naturally, many objective observers question whether these verses were actually composed by Sheikh Farid in the thirteenth century.

The verses that are included in the Adi Granth carry a unique authority. Not only were they composed by the beloved Baba Farid, they were also authenticated by the spiritual authority of Guru Nanak and his successors. However, Pritam Singh – after making an extensive study of primary sources – concluded that the verses in the Adi Granth are not a complete compilation of Sheikh Farid's poetry.* While admitting that not all the Multani verses attributed to Sheikh Farid are authentic, and expressing the hope that experts in linguistics may be able to "separate the chaff from the substance," Singh surmises that at least some authentic work outside the Adi Granth could have survived.[20]

Prof. Singh points to the clearly-recorded fact that Sheikh Farid readily spoke in the local language when conversing with people from the area, while speaking in Persian or Arabic when addressing literary Muslims. He notes further that the disciples of Sheikh Farid and those of his successors over the next two centuries wrote almost exclusively in Persian and placed no value on preserving any writings in the local language.

> From this I conclude that they [the disciples] considered his Punjabi works inconsequential ... and thus none of the writings in Punjabi were preserved by any learned person, whereas his works in Arabic and Farsi have been carefully recorded and conserved. If some Punjabi content was

---

*The texts consulted by Prof. Pritam Singh are listed in a footnote later in this chapter under the "Selection of Verses" discussion.

retained, it was merely as a gesture, a mere formality, as for them, it was only the writings in Persian and Arabic that were worth preserving.[21]

If, as he argues, only verses in Persian and Arabic were preserved in a formal way during the first few centuries after Sheikh Farid's lifetime, the rest of his compositions were kept alive through informal means:

> The end result was that Farid's work in Punjabi only stayed alive in the hearts and on the tongues of the local population or was recorded by the researchers of local languages like Rajab and Gopal Dass.[22]

Clearly, the longer any verse continued to be passed along orally, the greater the likelihood that changes were introduced. Language changes over time. To take an example familiar to most English speakers, Chaucer is virtually unintelligible to the modern reader. His original text, written in the English of the fourteenth century, must be translated into modern English before one can understand it. Suppose now that the English language of the fourteenth century had had no script and that Chaucer had composed *The Canterbury Tales* orally. Suppose those tales, in their poetic form, had been passed down the generations orally. One can guess that while it was passed along in this way, the language would have slowly and gradually transformed into something intelligible to today's reader.

Thus, while the slokas in the Adi Granth were frozen in written form in the sixteenth century, those in the oral tradition have probably gradually changed. Moreover, when these verses were first recorded, it was in manuscripts that were then copied by hand over a period of centuries in an informal process. This process leaves ample room for copyist errors. Later Chishti sheikhs could also have added verses written in a style reminiscent of Sheikh Farid, conveying, to the best of their understanding, his spiritual teachings.

With Sheikh Farid, as with other poet-saints who have inspired an extensive and long-lived oral tradition, scholars have long debated the question of whether each poem is actually by the original author. Simran Jeet Singh suggests in his invaluable paper that Sheikh Farid is the 'author,' not of a specific poem, but of a genre of poems transmitted orally and through performance – in this case, singing. When the pattern created by the original author is followed closely – in rhythm, rhyme, metre, imagery, performance style, and content or message – the original poet-saint may be said to have inspired, if not actually authored, the living tradition that thrives and grows long after him.[23]

Certainly, the Multani verses of Sheikh Farid from the oral tradition bear the stamp of his pattern of expression and his spiritual message. In these verses we encounter some poetic images that are similar to those in the Adi Granth, but also some that are not. Here also are images from the daily lives and struggles of common people.

> O Farid, cry and cry you must,
>   like the keeper of the barley field.
> Keep crying and wailing
>   till the barley ear ripens and drops.[24]

Just as farmers in the Punjab had to protect their fields of barley by shouting and making noise to keep the birds away, the reader is urged to stay alert and never slacken his vigilance until the spiritual purpose of life is achieved.

The work of overcoming the ego is described in gritty, down-to-earth terms. Just as hemp is beaten mercilessly to break down the fibres in preparation for rope-making, so also the ego must be beaten.

kkg2kkgght5k

O Farid, annihilate your ego,
    pound it to a pulp.
God's treasures are inexhaustible –
    grab as much as you wish.[25]

Once the ego has given up and submitted to annihilation, however, then one can fully relax and enjoy God's unlimited bounty:

Stretch your legs and sleep, O Farid,
    sleep all day and night.
If you only eliminate your ego,
    none will hold you accountable.[26]

Throughout these verses we hear the voice of one who sees past the superficiality of ceremonial forms. Lest anyone should imagine that having one's head shaved as a part of an initiation ceremony meant that he had achieved some spiritual elevation, we read:

O mind, shear yourself.
    What would you gain by shaving your head?
Countless sheep have been sheared,
    but none has made it to heaven.[27]

The verses from the oral tradition ring with the resounding message that the priceless pearl of spiritual realization is to be found within. Just as a pearl diver dives deep into the ocean, so the seeker must dive deep into the self.

An ocean is within your heart, O Farid,
    why do you trudge along the shore?
Dive into the depths;
    the pearl shall be found within.[28]

The verses from the oral tradition refer to the pir, the spiritual master, with diverse and intriguing metaphors. He is the true jeweller who knows the value of the pearl:

> O Farid, the gem is priceless;
>   the glass cutter knows not its value.
> Only the experienced merchant or a jeweller
>   knows its true worth.[29]

He is also the beloved doctor who can actually diagnose the ailment no one else can recognize, and he can cure it:

> Says Farid, my body has lost all strength
>   and my mind is restless.
> Come, my Beloved! Be my physician –
>   give me the medicine that will cure me.[30]

He is the guardian who protects and handles all of our affairs:

> I have taken refuge in my Beloved;
>   do not expose the account of my actions.
> Wedded to the True Sovereign,
>   this is how my affairs are handled.[31]

Above all, he is the one on fire with love for the Divine. By taking his protection, even a disciple who feels no love or longing can learn to love.

> Farid, either you suffer from longing or you learn from
>   those who nurture acute yearning.
> Do not take shelter from those
>   who know not the truth about longing.[32]

Selection of the Verses

The following selection of verses from the oral tradition comes
from three sources. Piara Singh Padam, after making an extensive
search, collected 72 verses. His sources range from *Masle Sheikh
Farid Ke* – published less than 35 years after compilation of the
Adi Granth – to an assortment of manuscripts dating from the
subsequent centuries.[*33] M. Asif Khan, in his book *Akhya Baba
Farid ne*, agrees with these 72 verses and adds another ten from
the Sarieki dialect to the list.[34] Prof. Pritam Singh collected a
total of 207 verses from ten books – some of which are the same
sources cited by both Padam and Khan – although, mostly, they
are sourced from Gurmukh Singh's book on Sheikh Farid.[†]

Of these, we have included a subset of 63 verses. To reach
a conclusion about which verses were likely to be the most
authentic, we consulted with a team of people from the Multan
region, including two elders who had grown up speaking the

---

[*]Dr Piara Singh Padam lists his sources as: Bhai Paindha's *Bir*, Rawalpindi
(now in Delhi); Ancient handwritten manuscript (two-hundred-fifty years
old manuscript from my own library); *Maslay Shaikh Farid Ji Kay* (vol. #359,
Library of the Language Department; *Sarbangi* (Vol. #11509, Mahindra College,
Patiala); The Old Janamsakhi; *Shabd Salok Bhagtan Kay* (book printed in 1901);
Irshadat-e-faridi by Pir Muhammad Hussain (1927); *The History of the Punjabi
Literature* by Prof. Pritam Singh (1958).

[†]Prof. Pritam Singh compiled his material through the efforts of Dr Gurmukh
Singh of Patiala who took the collection from the book (*Sheikh Farid: Bauhu
Pakhi Adhyan*, 1977, Patiala, Bhasha Vibhag, Language Department, Punjab)
edited by Ajit Singh Kakkar and himself. He [Dr Gurmukh Singh] writes
about his sources: *Shabad Shlok* (1901), *Sufiyan da Kalaam* by Dr Mohan Singh
Diwana, *Bole Sheikh Farid* by Dr Piara Singh Padam, *Aakhya Baba Farid Ne* by
Mohammed Aashiq Khan, *Punjabi Hath-Likhat Sahityaa*, *Khoj te Khoj Vidhi* by
Dr Gobind Singh Lamba, *Itihaas Shri Guru Granth Sahib: Bhagat Bani Bhaag*
by Giani Gurdit Singh, *Prachieen Bidanh* by GB Singh, *Bani Farid* by Dr Ratan
Singh Jaggi and *Punjabi Sahitya Da Itihaas*, Language Department, Punjab. In
addition to these sources, he notes that he had collected the material from many
handwritten books. Various slokas heard from elders, friends and *qawwals* were
also incorporated.

Multani dialect. They considered criteria such as the specific word usage, the tenor and sound of each sloka, relying on their personal knowledge of the dialect. They also turned to a dictionary for support with certain antique words long out of use. They recommended leaving out verses that had phrases inserted in a dialect other than Multani and also those where the first and second lines seemed unrelated to each other, thereby rendering the verse unintelligible. Certain verses that are very popular today, being performed in secular settings and familiar to contemporary audiences through recordings, were considered less likely to be authentic and, therefore, were left out.

With the Multani dialect still spoken only in a very circumscribed area, we were fortunate to find these elders who carry unique credentials. Far from the academic credentials of a linguistics scholar, they had been immersed both in the Multani dialect and the oral tradition since childhood. Sheikh Farid's verses are so integral a part of the Multani language that, as they remember it, their parents and grandparents often spoke to them not in sentences, but in verse. Much as Farid's terse two-lined slokas are bursts of thought conveyed in a lightning sharp colloquial usage, the Multani of their childhood had the flavour of – and frequent references to – Sheikh Farid's verses. As they put it, it is a language in which a seemingly simple phrase conveys a depth of meaning with 'razor-sharp directness.' With this background, the Multani elders we consulted read all the verses collected by Padam, Khan, and Pritam Singh, and identified the verses that they felt had 'the fragrance of Farid.'

While we cannot say with certainty that the 63 verses we present are absolutely authentic, nor that those left out are not, we believe this selection constitutes a representative sampling of the oral tradition of Sheikh Farid with a high degree of authenticity. In short, these verses ring true to those most deeply immersed in the tradition. Fully recognizing that some of the verses in this selection may not have been composed in the thirteenth century by Sheikh Farid himself, we present them here in part to convey the rich oral tradition of poetry that is the living legacy of Sheikh Farid, and in part simply to share the beauty of the spiritual message they convey. We believe these verses offer a meaningful addition to the body of Sheikh Farid's works available in English. It is our hope that this presentation may encourage scholars to continue the work of searching the manuscripts that could further verify the earliest date when each verse was recorded. Perhaps further scholarship will ascertain which verses belong to Sheikh Farid's legacy and which verses – in the words of *Siyar al-Auliya* – 'rolled off the tongue' of the great Sufi mystic, Sheikh Farid.

Notes on Sources

We have retained the numbering scheme used by both M. Asif Khan and Piara Singh Padam, although the collection in this edition is not contiguous. All but three slokas (67, 75, and 77) are also included in the collection by Prof. Pritam Singh.

fareedaa akai ta sikan sik,
akai ta puchh sikandee'aan.
tinhaa pichhe na luk,
jo sikan saar na jaananee. [1]

fareedaa sikaa sik sikandee'aan,
sikeen deehe raat.
maindee'aan sikaan sabh pujann,
jaa piree'aa paa'ee jhaat. [2]

fareedaa jit tan birahaa oopjai,
tit tan kaisaa maas.
ut tan eh bhi bahut hai,
haad chaam ar maas. [3]

fareedaa main tan augan etarrai
jete dhartee kakh.
tau jehaa main na lahaan,
main jehee'aan ka'ee lakkh. [4]

tan samund mansaa lahar
ar taaroo tarah anek.
te birahee kion jeevte,
je aah na karte ek. [5]

Farid, either you suffer from longing or you learn
    from those who nurture acute yearning.
Do not take shelter from those who know not
    the truth about longing. [1]

Farid, those who suffer in yearning for the Beloved
    pine day and night.
All my longings came to an end
    when my Beloved looked at me. [2]

O Farid, what extra flesh can there be
    on the body that fosters longing?
It is sufficient that such a body
    has bones, skin, and some flesh. [3]

O Farid, my bodily sins are as numerous
    as the blades of grass on this earth.
Another one like you I shall never find,
    though there are millions like me. [4]

Waves of desire surge in the ocean of this body –
    countless are the swimmers who try to swim across.
How do they manage to stay alive who are torn asunder
    and do not let out a single sigh in separation? [5]

asaan tusaadee sajjno,
athoh pahar sammaal.
deehe vasoh manai meh'i,
raatee supnai naal. [6]

preetam! tum mat jaanee'auh,
tum bichharat ham chain.
daadhe ban kee laakree,
sulgat hai din rain. [7]

vichhorraa buriaar
jit vichhrre tan dublaa.
se maahanoo hainsiaar
vichharr mete jo thee'an. [8]

jaa moo lagaa neh,
taan main dukh vihaajiaa.
jhuraan habho hee deh,
kaaran sache maa piree. [9]

fareedaa eh je jangal rukkhrre,
haree'al pat tinaah.
pothaa likhiaa arath daa,
ekas ekas maah. [10]

fareedaa akai ta lorr mukkadamee
akai ta alah lorr.
duh berree na latt dhar,
vanjah vakkhar borr. [11]

O my love! I am yours – I cherish you constantly.
You are in my thoughts during the day
    and in my dreams at night. [6]

Think not my love that I am restful
    in separation from you.
As burns the forest wood,
    I smoulder night and day. [7]

Separation is painful – it withers the body.
Even more cruel are they
    who remain unaffected in separation. [8]

Since the day I fell in love,
    I bartered to take on suffering.
Now I pine for my Beloved
    and suffer all day long. [9]

O Farid, the trees in the forest
    are laden with lush green leaves.
Meaningful scriptures are inscribed
    on every single leaf. [10]

O Farid, either pursue worldly glory
    or seek the Lord.
Place not your stake in both boats,
    else you may drown and lose everything. [11]

fareedaa choorrelee sion ratiaa,
dunee'aa koorraa bhet.
enee akkheen dekhadiaan
ujarr vanjah khet. [12]

fareedaa tan rahiaa man phatiaa,
taagat rahee na kaa'e.
uth piree! tabeeb thee'o,
kaaree daaroo laa'e. [13]

fareedaa paireen kande pandhrraa,
setee sujaanaa.
bhatth hindolah daa peenghana,
setee ajaanaa. [15]

fareedaa moo tan avgan etarre,
chammee andarvaar.
hik niree khuaaree thee rahah,
je disan baaharvaar. [16]

aasraa dhani manjhaahe,
ko'e na laahoh kaddh toon.
ve ion kaaj hathaahu,
variaane sacchaa dhanee. [17]

O Farid, the world is an illusion,
    yet you are possessed with this witch.
Before my very eyes fertile fields
    have become wastelands. [12]

Says Farid, my body has lost all strength
    and my mind is restless.
Come, my Beloved! Be my physician –
    give me the medicine that will cure me. [13]

O Farid, accompany the wise
    even if the path is thorny.
Avoid the thrill of a palanquin* ride
    if accompanied by an ignorant one. [15]

O Farid, there are as many sins in me
    as the hairs on my body;
    if exposed to the world,
    they would bring nothing but disgrace. [16]

I have taken refuge in my Beloved;
    do not expose the account of my actions.
Wedded to the True Sovereign,
    this is how my affairs are handled. [17]

---

*A covered canopy carriage with one seat in a decorated box, mounted on an elephant or carried on poles by four or more bearers.

fareedaa lahreen saa'ir khandee'aan,
bhee so hans tarann.
kiaa taren bag bapurre,
je pahilee lahar dubann. [19]

fareedaa jai dar lagai neh,
so dar naaheen chhadnaa.
aah pavah bhaavain meh,
sir hee upar jhalanaa. [20]

fareedaa ... tinne tol karen.
mithaa bolan, niv chalan,
hatthoh bhi kijh dey'n. [22]

fareedaa jitee khushee'aan keetee'aan
titee thee'am rog.
chhiloon kaaran maaree'ai,
khaadai daa kiaa hog. [23]

fareedaa paireen berraa thelh kai,
kandhee kharraa na ro'u.
vat na aavan theesee'aa,
et na neendrree sau. [24]

fareedaa sutiauh neend
mat pavande eev.
jinaa nain neendraavle,
dhanee milande keev. [25]

Farid, even if violent waves rise in the ocean,
   swans are able to swim across.
How will the helpless herons make it
   who drown in the very first wave? [19]

O Farid, never leave the door of the one
   who kindles love within you;
   endure even the downpour
   that batters mercilessly upon your head. [20]

O Farid, imbibe these three virtues:
   Sweetness of tongue, humility,
   and giving something in charity. [22]

O Farid, all your indulgences resulted in suffering.
If one is punished for eating the peel,
   what will be the lot of those
   who enjoy the fruit? [23]

Having kicked away the raft, O Farid,
   don't stand and cry on the riverbank.
Time once gone will not come back –
   waste not long hours in sleep. [24]

O Farid, you achieve nothing by sleeping.
How can the Lord be realized by those
   whose eyes are overwhelmed by sleep? [25]

fareedaa raateen sovah khatt,
deehe pitah pet koon.
jaa tau khatan vel,
tadaanhee te hoh rahiaa. [28]

fareedaa jaagnaa ee ta jaag,
raatrri habh vidhaanee'aan.
je moo matthe bhaag,
piree visaaran na karan. [29]

fareedaa so dar sachaa sev,
jit mukloobani jaahe.
rijmastak had khau,
amal na vikan khaahe. [31]

fareedaa jinee daa sabar kamaan,
atai zikar kaamaavan kaanee'aan.
onhaa mande baan,
khaalak khaalee naahe kare. [34]

fareedaa kadai aaho hekrraa,
atai hun thee'o pragat.
evee paav mashaaharo,
jaa laa'e baithoh hat. [36]

Farid, you sleep in your cot all night through
    and all day long hanker after your livelihood.
You remained asleep when it was time
    for you to strike the bargain.* [28]

O Farid, awaken! You must wake up now –
    the night is slipping away.
If it is so written in my destiny,
    I will never forget the Beloved. [29]

O Farid, serve at the true door
    that leads to salvation.
Toil and partake of that which is in your destiny –
    do not sacrifice your principles. [31]

O Farid, for those whose bow is patience,
    remembrance [*zikr*] is the arrow.
God does not let them miss their target
    even if the arrows are poorly aimed. [34]

Farid, at one time He was on His own –
    now he has manifested Himself.
He is accessible to all
    now that His shop is open. [36]

---

*When you should have made a deal (meditated), you were asleep.

buddhaa thee'aa shekh fareed,
kamban lage taalh.
tindarree'aan jal laanee'aan,
tutan lagee maahl. [38]

fareedaa damaamaa vajiaa maut daa,
charrhiaa malkul maut.
ghinnan vaahe jindarree,
dhaahan vaahe kot.
kot dhathaa garrh lutiaa,
dere pa'ee kahaah.
jeevandiaan de hor raah,
moi'aan de ehee raah. [39]

aj ke kall ke chahun diheen,
malak asaadee her.
kai jitaa kai haar oh,
saudaa ehee ver. [40]

Sheikh Farid has become old –
   his limbs are shaking.
The water scoops have emptied all the water
   and the chain is almost broken.* [38]

Farid, the death drum has sounded
   and the lord of death is advancing
   to capture your life
   and to demolish the fort of your body.
The fort has fallen,
   the castle has been plundered,
   and wailing fills the air;
   different are the ways of the living,
   but this alone is the way of the dead. [39]

Today, tomorrow or in another four days,
   the Angel of Death will look for us.
Whether you win or lose,
   now is the only chance for this transaction. [40]

---

*Using the metaphor of the Persian water wheel for the body.

fareedaa karan hakoomat dunee dee,
haakam naa'o dharann.
age dhaul piaadiaan,
pichhe kot chalann.
charrh chalan sukhvaasnee,
upar chaur jhulann.
sej vichhaavan paahroo,
jithe jaa'e savann.
tinaan janaan dee'aan dheree'aan,
door'hon pa'ee'aan disann. [41]

fareedaa eh mahjdeen aboothee'aan,
rakkhee'aan rabb savaar.
jaan jaan es jahaan mahan meh'i
taan taan dekhah jaar. [42]

fareedaa ucchaa na kar sadd,
rabb dilaan dee'aan jaanadaa.
je tudh vich kalabb,
so manjhaahu door kar. [45]

fareedaa dunee de laalach lagiaan,
mehnat bhull ga'ee.
jaan sir aa'ee apne,
taan sabho visar ga'ee. [46]

O Farid, they rule the world
    and call themselves monarchs.
Ahead of them march foot soldiers
    and behind them, mounted troops.
They ride in palanquins
    while hand-held fans are waved overhead.
The attendants prepare comfortable beds
    where they retire to sleep.
The mounds of the graves of such ones
    can be seen from afar. [41]

Farid, these mosques* of Adam,
    God has made and maintained well.
But as long as they are in this world,
    they are subject to decay. [42]

O Farid, call Him not loudly –
    God knows well our heart.
If there be a dog inside you,
    evict it from within. [45]

O Farid, lured by worldly greed,
    you neglected your spiritual practice.
When the time of trial comes,
    you will have no answer. [46]

---

*The mosque is the human body.

fareedaa jangal dhoonde sanghanaa,
lamme lurriaa na vat.
tan hujraa dargaah daa,
tis vich jhaatee ghat. [48]

fareedaa haathee sohan ambaaree'aan,
peechhe katak hazaar.
jaan sir aavee aapne,
taan ko meet na yaar. [49]

fareedaa je toon vanjen haj,
haj habho hee jee'aa mein.
laah dile dee laj,
sachaa haajee taan theeven. [50]

fareedaa manjh makkaa
manjh maarree'aa,
manjhah hee mehraab.
manjhe hee kaabaa thee'aa,
keende karee namaaz. [51]

fareedaa 'main' noon munj kar,
nikkee kar kar kutt.
bhare khazaane rabb de,
jo bhaavah so lutt. [52]

O Farid, you went searching in the thick forest
    and did not return for a long time.
Your body is the chamber of divinity –
    look within. [48]

O Farid, the decorated palanquin is on an elephant
    with thousands of soldiers following behind.
But when one is faced with adversity,
    there is no companion and no friend. [49]

O Farid, if you want to go on a *hajj*,
    hajj is all within.
A true *hajji* you would be
    if you could rid yourself of worldly shame. [50]

O Farid, Mecca is within; within are all the mansions
    and also the holy arch.
Ka'bah is within too –
    where have you been offering *namaz?*[*] [51]

O Farid, annihilate your ego,
    pound it to a pulp.
God's treasures are inexhaustible –
    grab as much as you wish. [52]

---

[*]Daily ritual prayers.

kook fareedaa kook too,
jion raakhaa juaar.
jab lag taandaa naa gire,
tab lag kook pukaar. [53]

fareedaa je too dil darvesh,
rakh akeedaa saahmanaa.
daraheen setee dekh,
matthaa morr na kand de. [54]

fareedaa darad na vanjam daaroo'en,
je lakh tabeeb lagann.
changee bhalee thee bahaan,
je moon piree milann. [55]

je je jeeven dunee te,
khuree'e kaheen na laa'e.
ikoh khaphan rakh ke,
hor sabhoh deh lutaa'e. [56]

fareedaa jaan jaan jeeven dunee te,
taan taan phir alakh.
dargaahe sacchaa taan theevai,
jaan khaphan mool na rakh. [57]

O Farid, cry and cry you must
   like the keeper of the barley field.
Keep crying and wailing
   till the barley ear ripens and drops.* [53]

O Farid, if you are a dervish at heart,
   be steadfast and firmly hold on to your faith.
Fix your gaze at the door,
   turn not your face away,
   and do not show your back. [54]

O Farid, no medicine will cure my pain
   although a million physicians may treat it.
If I am united with my Beloved,
   I will be cured forever. [55]

As long as you live in this world,
   do not get attached anywhere.
Except for a shroud,
   give away all your possessions. [56]

O Farid, remain completely detached
   while you live in this world.
You will be deemed true in God's court
   if you do not hold onto even a shroud. [57]

---

*The keeper of a barley field must ward off the birds that eat the immature grains by making noise. Similarly, one must remain on guard until one's spiritual development matures.

fareedaa maa'o mahindee kamlee,
jin 'jeevan' rakhio naa'on.
jaan din punne maut de,
na jeevan na naa'o. [58]

fareedaa dil andar daree'aa'o,
kandhee lagaa kee phirai.
tubbhee maar manjhaahe,
manjhoh hee maanak lahahn. [59]

tubbhee maaran gaakhrree,
saddhraan lakkh karen.
jinhaa daa man dhraapiaa,
se maanak labbhen. [60]

fareedaa maanak mol athaah,
kadar kee jaanah seesgar.
ike ta goorrhaa shaah,
ikai ta jaanah jauhree. [61]

fareedaa iknaa mat khudaa'e dee,
iknaa mang la'ee.
ik ditee mool na ghinnde,
(jion) patthar boond pa'ee. [62]

It was foolish of my mother
    to name me Jeevan, O Farid;
    as the day of death arrives,
    there is no *jeevan,** no name. [58]

An ocean is within your heart, O Farid,
    why do you trudge along the shore?
Dive into the depths;
    the pearl shall be found within. [59]

Difficult is the dive.
Millions cherish it,
    but only those whose minds are steadfast
    shall find the pearl. [60]

O Farid, the gem is priceless;
    the glass cutter knows not its value.
Only the experienced merchant or jeweller
    knows its true worth. [61]

Farid, some have God-given wisdom,
    some have begged for and received it.
Some refuse to take it when given,
    like a drop of water falling on a stone. [62]

---

*In Hindi, *jeevan* means life.

fareedaa vaddee eh bahaadree,
kar kusang ko tiaag.
dargah theevee mukh ujlaa,
ko'e na lagah daag. [63]

fareedaa aisaa ho'e raho,
jaisaa kakkh maseet.
pairaan talai lataarree'ai,
kade na chhodah preet. [64]

fareedaa paa'on pasaar kai,
atthe pahar hee saun.
lekhaa ko'ee na puchha'ee,
je vichoh jaavee haun. [65]

fareedaa kookendarraa ta kook,
kade ta rabb sunesee'aa.
nikal vaisee phook,
taan phir kook na hosee'aa. [66]

fareedaa khetee ujrree,
girvee par rahiaa maal.
saahib lekhaa mangsee,
bande kaun havaal. [67]

fareedaa khetee ujarree,
sache sion liv laa'e.
je adh khaadhee ubarah,
taan phal bahuteraa paa'e. [68]

Farid, it is an act of great valour
    to shun evil company.
You shall be exalted in the divine court;
    no blemish shall mar your honour. [63]

Farid, be like the grass around a mosque:
Trampled under feet,
    it never forsakes its love. [64]

Stretch your legs and sleep, O Farid,
    sleep all day and night.
If you only eliminate your ego,
    none will hold you accountable. [65]

O Farid, wail if you can,
    God will surely hear you one day.
For when you have no breath left,
    you can cry no more. [66]

O Farid, your crop is ruined
    and all your assets are mortgaged.
When the Lord holds you accountable,
    how will you explain? [67]

Farid, your crops are ruined;
    now kindle love for the true Lord.
Great will be your reward
    if you can be satisfied with half a loaf. [68]

fareedaa deh jar jar bha'ee,
nainee vahai sares.
sai kohaan manjaa bha'iaa,
angan thee'aa bides. [70]

fareedaa jaaganaa ee ta jaag,
hoee'aa ee prabhaat.
is jaagan no pachhtaahengaa
ghanaa savahengaa raat. [72]

aavo ladho saatharro
aivain vanaj kareen.
mool sambhaaleen aapnaa
paachhe laahaa la'een. [73]

saa'een sevee'aan gal ga'ee,
maas rihaa deh.
tab lag saa'een sevsaan
jab lag hosee kheh. [74]

manaan! munn munaa'iaan
sir munne kiaa ho'e.
ketee bhedaan munnee'aan
surag na ladhee ko'e. [75]

zindagee daa vasaah naheen,
samajh fareedaa toon.
kar lai achhe amal,
te ho jaa sarnaagoon. [77]

Farid, the body has decayed
  and water trickles down from my eyes.
My cot appears to be a hundred miles away
  and the courtyard seems like a foreign land. [70]

Wake up, O Farid, wake up! The day has dawned.
You will repent for not having awakened
  when the long night's sleep befalls you. [72]

Come, we have found a partner.
We shall conduct our business thus:
  First secure our capital, then collect our gain. [73]

Serving the Master I have become a skeleton –
  no flesh is left on my body.
I shall keep serving the Master till I turn to dust! [74]

O mind, shear yourself.
  What would you gain by shaving your head?
Countless sheep have been sheared,
  but none has made it to heaven. [75]

Understand this, O Farid,
  life cannot be taken for granted;
  perform virtuous deeds
  and surrender to the Lord. [77]

moosaa natthaa maut ton,
dhoonde kaa'e galee.
chaare koontaan dhoondiaan
agge maut khalee. [78]

kannaan dandaan akkhee'aan,
sabhnaa dittee haar.
vekh fareedaa chhad ga'e
mudh kadeemee yaar. [79]

Moses ran from death, looking for a lane.[*]
He looked in all four directions
    and found death standing in front of him. [78]

The ears, teeth, and eyes have all deserted me.
Look Farid, my companions have forsaken me. [79]

---

[*]Looking for a lane to hide in.

APPENDIX
Spiritual Practices Taught
by the Chishti Sheikhs

IN THE VERSES AND SAYINGS FROM SHEIKH FARID that have been preserved, there are almost no details about the spiritual practices he taught his disciples. His recorded words tell of love and longing for the Lord. They tell of the attitude of mind and the way of life required on the spiritual path. They urge the spiritual seeker to spend long hours in the night, not sleeping, but engaging in prayer and meditation. But they do not describe the specific meditation exercises to be done. We may assume that the needed instructions were given orally to disciples, but Sheikh Farid did not write any treatises about the method of meditation.

We do, however, know something about the meditation practices taught by the masters in the Chishti lineage, who placed great emphasis on performing spiritual exercises daily. According to the Chishti sheikhs, "Just as the body is developed, nourished and kept in health and vigour by physical exercises, in the same way the spirit, heart and mind are developed and made powerful by spiritual exercises."[1] These spiritual exercises centre on repetition (*dhikr* or *źikr*), contemplation (*shaghl*), and meditation (*muraqabat*). It is reasonable to assume that Sheikh Farid guided his disciples in these practices.

This first technique, *dhikr*, involves repeating a set of words, generally sacred words, such as names of God. These words are given to the disciple by his pir and are a means to bring the mind into a state of remembrance of Allah. For example, some of the sheikhs in the Chishti lineage have used the following as *dhikr*: *Allah Sami'* (Allah, All-hearing), *Allah Basir* (Allah, All-seeing), *Allah 'Alim* (Allah, All-knowing), *Allah Qadir* (Allah, All-powerful). This sequence of holy Names of God was to be repeated over and over. Such words, taken from the Qur'an, were seen as especially holy and imbued with power.

Interestingly, Baba Farid is known to have given non-Arabic words as *dhikr* to his Punjabi disciples who were not Muslims. Although we do not know the *dhikr* formula he used with his Muslim disciples, it was probably a set of words or phrases from the Qur'an, such as certain names of God. For his non-Muslim disciples, the *dhikr* formula seems to have been based on long-established mantras used by practitioners of yoga. Carl Ernst, a well-known scholar of Sufism in the Indian subcontinent, points out, "These phrases belong to a long tradition of adapting hatha yoga mantras to Islamic themes and Sufi practices."[2] Following Sheikh Farid's example, other sheikhs in both the Chishti and the Shattari lineages have also used *dhikr* formulas in Punjabi or Hindi. Awrangabadi, in his treatise on this unusual procedure, finds it to be perfectly valid: "It is right if one instructs the non-Arab disciple with expressions in Hindi or Persian or whatever he understands."[3]

Baba Farid's flexible use of *dhikr* formulas in the languages of, and from the cultures of, his disciples stands as a striking illustration of his broad-mindedness. While practising a Sufi path with deep roots in Islamic culture, his life and teachings indicated that the mystical path resided somewhere beyond and above religious and cultural distinctions. He understood that while outward observances were grounded in their particular socio-cultural context, the mystical path led to an inner reality which was universal.

Regardless of which *dhikr* formula he taught his disciples, Baba Farid told them that *dhikr* was the primary task and must take precedence over all other matters. According to the medieval text, *Rahat ul-Qalub*, Sheikh Farid used to say that one who befriends *dhikr*, in reality, befriends Allah.[4] Urging his disciples to practise *dhikr*, Sheikh Farid told them that *dhikr* is life and that to forsake it is to invite death.[5] Similarly, he told them that *dhikr* infuses life into the mind, which has otherwise gone dead with mundane thoughts.[6] For Sufis, the constant repetition of *dhikr* is the practical application of the words of the Qur'an: "Remember Allah while standing, sitting and lying (Q4:103)."[7]

According to the great Sufi philosopher, Abu Hamid al-Ghazali (d. 1111 CE), *dhikr* eventually can lead to a profound transformation of the practitioner. In the beginning it cleanses the mind of distracting, mundane thoughts; in the end it leads to the "naughting of all that is not God." He writes:

> In short, the very first condition of this holy way is the overcoming of the appetites of the flesh and getting rid of its evil disposition and vile qualities, so that the heart may be cleared of all but God; and the means of clearing it is *dhikr-i-Allah*, the remembrance of God and the concentration of every thought upon Him. The last stage of this way is complete effacement in Him, the naughting of all that is not God and persisting through what belongs to God.[8]

In the Chishti lineage, the practice of *dhikr* is a step-by-step process that begins simply. The disciple first learns to do *dhikr-i-jahri*, repeating the words aloud; then he moves on to *dhikr-i-khafi* (literally, hidden or secret *dhikr*), repeating the words silently. When the disciple is well versed in both of these practices, he may be taught the following method:

There is also another type of *dhikr* involving a different method: One sits quietly and closes the eyes and lips and recites with the tongue of his heart these words or phrases: *Allah Sami'* (Allah, All-hearing), *Allah Basir* (Allah, All-seeing), *Allah 'Alim* (Allah, All-knowing), *Allah Qadir* (Allah, All-powerful). It is done in this way that when saying *Allah Sami'* in imagination, one should take his breath from his navel to his chest; when saying *Allah Basir*, one should imagine to take his breath from his chest to his mind; when saying *Allah 'Alim* imagine the breath to be taken from the mind to the sky and lastly, saying *Allah Qadir* one should imagine one is taking one's breath from the sky to the throne of Allah.[9]

The next spiritual exercise widely mentioned among the Sufis is *shaghl* (contemplation), and there are references to Baba Farid practising *shaghl*. While we do not know the details of the type of *shaghl* that Baba Farid practised, in general among the Chishtis, the "disciple was to imagine that his Sheikh was personally present before him directing his contemplation."[10] The well-known scholar of Sufism, R.A. Nicholson, states:

The disciple must, mystically, always bear his *Murshid* in mind, and become mentally absorbed in him through a constant meditation contemplation of him. The teacher must be his shield against all evil thoughts. The spirit of the teacher follows him in all his efforts, and accompanies him wherever he may be, quite as a guardian spirit. To such a degree is this carried that he sees the Master in all men and in all things, just as a willing subject is under the influence of the magnetizer. This condition is called 'self-annihilation' in the *Murshid* or *Sheikh*.[11]

Another well-known spiritual exercise referred to at the time of Sheikh Farid is *muraqabat* (literally watching). This sometimes implies a practice of meditation in the sense this term is used in Christian contemplative practice; that is, quieting and centring the mind and then, in that stillness, pondering deeply on a particular idea or sacred phrase. One description of this type of practice of *muraqabat* is given by John Subhan:

> At the outset the worshipper performs *dhikr* by repeating the phrases: *Allahu hadiri*, i.e. "God who is present (with me)." *Allahu naziri*, "God who sees me." *Allahu Shahidi*, "God who witnesses me." And *Allahu ma'i*, "God who is with me." Having recited this *dhikr*, either loudly or mentally, the worshipper proceeds to meditate upon some verse or verses of the Qur'an.[12]

On the other hand, sometimes the term *muraqabat* is used to mean a particularly deep level of concentration, arrived at as a result of *dhikr* practice:

> The seeker of the truth, when he becomes coloured with the light of remembrance (*dhikr*) of Allah, is then instructed by his spiritual guide and teacher to take to *muraqabat* (meditation). *Muraqabat* means and implies that there is no other idea in the mind, except the one meditated upon. No rival thought should confuse, puzzle, disturb or distract the one undergoing meditation. The one treading the spiritual path keeps a vigilant eye upon his heart and protects it from undesirable thoughts, notions and feelings.[13]

Speaking of this type of *muraqabat* – which he calls *muraqaba-e-qalb* (literally watching in the heart) – Hazrat Nizamuddin

Auliya explained the importance of inner mystical practice, as opposed to outward ritualistic forms. He made an analogy to curing a disease. If the disease to be healed is inside, the medicine also must be taken inside:

> A patient suffering from a stomach ache gets relief by taking medicine through the mouth as per the doctor's advice. If he, on the other hand, makes a paste of this medicine and applies it on his belly, it is not going to work on the disease inside his belly. It is on this simple logic that the Dervishes of all times have adopted and considered *muraqaba-e-qalb*, the supreme of all meditational practices.[14]

The practices of repetition, contemplation, and meditation gradually lead into a practice called the '*sultan-ul-adhkar*' – the 'king of all practices.' (*Adhkar* is the plural of *dhikr*, so a literal translation would be the king or sultan of all *dhikrs*.)[15] This spiritual practice is a great mystery, and little is written to explain its nature. However, it is believed that not only the sheikhs of Sufism, but also the Prophet Muhammad himself, practised this *sultan-ul-adhkar*:

> Hazrat Mianji used to say that Ghau-us-Saqlain related, "Our Prophet was in the cave of Hurrah [Ḥirā'] for six years plunged in this meditation of *sultan-ul-adhkar*, and I myself have been in that cave for twelve years engaged in the practice of this meditation, and many wonderful and mighty things have been revealed to me."[16]

Secrecy about the *sultan-ul-adhkar* is one face of the 'silence of the friends.' Ever since Mansur al-Hallaj (d. 922) was tortured and executed for declaring his oneness with the Lord, Sufis began to adhere to the principle of keeping the mystical teachings secret (*isharat*).

Disciples recalling the daily practices of Baba Farid say that each evening, after finishing the evening ritual prayer, he would retire to his room to practise repetition and contemplation (*dhikr-o-shaghl*).[17] Similarly, Nizamuddin's disciples also say he practised *dhikr-o-shaghl*, but that he firmly believed that people should not know about this practice. He withdrew and kept his practice hidden from the curious crowd.[18] This sense of the urgent need for secrecy is an example of *isharat*. This need for secrecy may be part of the reason that these early Chishti sheikhs avoided writing, and passed on their teachings only orally.

And so, although there are frequent references in *Fawa'id-ul-Fu'ad*, *Siyar al-Auliya*, *Hasht Bihisht*, *Rahat ul-Qalub*, and *Jawahar-e Faridi* to Baba Farid entering deep meditative states, details as to the nature of the practice – or of the experience – are missing. We might assume that these deep meditative states were evidence of the practice of *sultan-ul-adhkar*, or evidence of reaching a spiritual station that went beyond *dhikr*, *shaghl*, and *muraqabat*.

Disciples describe how Sheikh Farid would continue to lie motionless for hours and sometimes for days together at a stretch. Once he remained in this deep meditative state for seven days without feeling any need for food or water.[19]

Sama

The most controversial of the spiritual practices engaged in by Sheikh Farid and other Sufis is *sama*. It is also the most baffling to outside observers. Scholars and historians regularly translate *sama* as 'musical assemblies' or even 'musical concerts' – terms that fall far short of conveying the esoteric connotations of the practice.

In *sama* a group of disciples gather together with their pir to listen to mystical verses sung by a *qawwal* (singer, chanter, reciter).* The subject is divine love and yearning for union; the verses are replete with the praises of God or of some spiritual master.[20] In the spiritualized atmosphere created by focused attention on these elevating subjects, as well as by the presence of the pir, the Sufis find themselves drawn towards a higher state of consciousness.

However, as the Sufis have repeatedly explained, there are two types of *sama*. According to Chishti teachings, these two types depend on whether the music is heard outwardly or in a subtle form, inwardly: "When it is heard through a singer it is concealed, latent and invisible, but when it is heard from Allah, it is presence."[21] Nizamuddin describes the outward type of *sama* as "invasive" – it invades the body through the ears. But the "non-invasive" type of *sama* links the hearer to the higher realms:

"*Sama* is of two kinds," he remarked. "One is invasive, the other is non-invasive. The former invades (the body). For instance, on hearing a voice or a line of poetry, one experiences great agitation. This is called invasive *sama*, and it cannot be explained. As for non-invasive *sama*, it happens like this: When one hears a verse in *sama*, (one is drawn out of one's self). One links that verse to another realm, whether to God, or to one's spiritual master, or to some other realm that rules the heart."[22]

These two types of *sama* might be thought of as two different levels of consciousness at which one might experience *sama*. For this reason, Nizamuddin's disciple Amir Hasan Sijzi wrote that

---

* The practice of *sama* in different Sufi Orders may vary. For the Chishti Sufis of this era the focus was on listening. In other Sufi Orders, such as the Mevlevis, sama involves ecstatic dancing.

it was nearly impossible for one who experienced ecstasy in the inner or "non-invasive" *sama* to explain what it was to someone who was not at that level of consciousness:

> One who has experienced ecstasy in *sama* (*sahib e-sama*) finds it difficult to answer questions about *sama* posed by an enquirer. Why? Because (1) the enquirer is in a state of distraction (*tafriqah*) while the respondent combines in himself all the qualities of love (*'ishq*); (2) the enquiry comes from the outer mouth, while the reply pertains to the heart; (3) the enquiry concerns the external reasons for listening to *sama*, while the reply relates to its inner secrets; and (4) the enquiry is based on the exercise of intellect (*'aql*), while the reply reflects the outpouring of love (*'ishq*).[23]

The Chishti sheikhs describe this higher level of sama as listening to the 'Voice of God.' In the Qur'an it is stated that the creation was brought into being by Allah saying, "Be!" The word, "Be!" is *kun*. According to Chishti teachings, "The origin of *sama* is the voice or sound of the word *kun*, which means 'be!' The Sufis treat this voice as the reality of all voices and the soul of the *sama*."[24] Therefore, "*sama* in fact to the Sufis constitutes communion with Allah."[25] Sheikh Sharib goes so far as to say, "In the *sama* you are united with Allah." He writes:

> Some say that the *sama* is a source of presence and that a complete and abundant love is obtained from it, so much so that the lover is united with the Beloved.... By the *sama* manifold union is achieved, for it gives a place to sincere love in the heart and confers observation on the head, union to the soul, service to the body, vision to the eye and the voice of the Friend to the ear.[26]

According to Khwaja Muinuddin Chishti, hearing the "voice of the Friend" deepens love and awe, and sometimes leads to ecstatic dancing:

> The *sama* is a means of knowing the divine secrets. With the removal and uprooting of carnal desires, love appears, followed by awe. The inner secrets come to be understood. As soon as the secrets appear, one is seized by fondness, leading to a state of ecstasy and inducing one to dance.[27]

In *sama*, everything depends on the level of consciousness of the listener. As Sheikh Sharib says, "A beginner, under no circumstances is capable of hearing the voice of God."[28] For the beginner, *sama* necessarily meant hearing – with the physical ears – mystical verses sung by a *qawwal*. Because this type of musical concert could easily degenerate into a sensual experience, music enjoyed for its entertainment value, the Sufis were clear that worldly people, people "engrossed in worldly affairs," should not be permitted to attend such a gathering.[29]

Jamaluddin Hansawi, Sheikh Farid's disciple, described three levels of listeners: those who enjoy this world; those who renounce this world and seek the next; those who renounce both this world and the next and seek only God. The subtleties of *sama* are revealed, he said, only to the third group.[30] Similarly, Hazrat Zunnun* stressed the spiritual orientation of the listeners: "The one who hears it [*sama*] for the sake of God, finds a way towards God. But the one who hears it for his own self falls in trouble."[31]

And indeed, *sama* did lead some to fall into trouble. *Sama* drew criticism from many quarters. Stirring the emotions, *sama* sometimes excited wild behaviour, dancing, and tearing

---

*The spelling of the name of this famous early Sufi from Egypt is often given as Dhu'l Nun.

of clothes. Religious scholars and judges debated whether the ecstatic, uncontrolled dancing and the trances induced by *sama* were or were not lawful. And so, the Sufis established rules for *sama*. First and foremost, the sheikh must be present. As it says in *Siyar al-Auliya*, "As the presence of a Sheikh in *sama* was mandatory, it goes without saying that the *sama* was conducted under his guidance and instructions and hence, it could not be *haram* (unlawful)."[32]

Secondly, the listeners must all be pursuing the spiritual path. According to the Chishtis, ideally, the listeners should all be disciples of the same pir, or of the same lineage.

By Community of interest is meant that those participating in the music concert should be the disciples of the one spiritual guide, or the Dervishes, having common affiliations, or the Sufis of the same stock.[33]

Thirdly, while listening, the disciples should not talk with one another or bring up other subjects. "But, instead, they should sit and watch, and wait for the blessings of God." And finally, the subject matter of the verses being sung must be spiritual. That is, the singer was supposed to focus the couplets and his art of singing or recitation on Love, the Lover, and the Beloved.[34] In general, these were Persian poems (*ghazals*) mostly from well-known masters, though Nizamuddin began using popular Hindi devotional songs. However, he never allowed any instruments to be played, just the human voice.[35] The addition of musical instruments distracted from the simple focus on the mystical verses.

The most controversial aspect of *sama* was dancing. The early Chishti sheikhs did not strictly forbid dancing, yet they were also not wholeheartedly in favour of it. Unlike the Mevlevis, the lineage of Sufis established by the successor of Rumi, where dancing is a central aspect of *sama*, the Chishtis saw dancing as permissible only as long as it was strictly involuntary. As Nizamuddin said, "As for dancing and movements and tearing of clothes, if the person is truly overcome, then he is not answerable; and if the movements are voluntary, made in order to show to the people, then this is *haram* (unlawful, not permitted)."[36] However, he also indicated that sitting still – that is, being in control of oneself enough to be able to sit still – allowed the passion or ecstasy to reach a deeper level:

> When a dervish claps his hands during *sama*, the *shahwat* (passion) in his hands falls off (that is, gets dissipated); and when he dances (literally beats the floor with his feet) the *shahwat* in his feet vanishes; and when he shouts, the *shahwat* inside him disappears.[37]

Given the controversy over *sama*, several eminent Sufis wrote extensive treatises, attempting to establish a legal basis for it. Simnani (1287–1386 ce), for example, defined three levels of ecstasy: empathetic ecstasy, momentary ecstasy, durative ecstasy.[38] Empathetic ecstasy was the lowest level of ecstasy, reached by the stirring of emotions in *sama*, yet it could lead to the flashes of a higher type of ecstasy (momentary ecstasy), and eventually to durative ecstasy. Similarly, the three levels of ecstasy were also described as *tawajud, wajd,* and *wujud*: induced ecstasy, real ecstasy, and finding (meaning: finding God).[39] Again, "induced ecstasy" came first and could be induced by hearing *sama*, but it could also lead to the deeper levels of ecstasy. However, the pretence of ecstasy – as must have happened – was the most deplorable.

Despite all the arguments for and against *sama*, its value was beyond question for Sheikh Farid.

Once the question of the permissibility of *sama* was discussed in the presence of Sheikh Farid. "God be praised!" he exclaimed.

"One gets burnt up and is reduced to ashes, and the others are arguing about the permissibility of the matter!"[40]

Similarly, the value of *sama* was crystal clear to Amir Hasan, the disciple of Nizamuddin. Its simplest value was that it produced a spiritual atmosphere that he found extremely helpful in his devotional life. It was, he said, like the atmosphere he always found in the presence of his pir. One time he was with Nizamuddin and told him:

> "As for that obedience to prayer, ritual observance, and recitation of litanies that mark a true devotee, I am lacking. But when I listen to *sama*, I am overcome with delight and I experience inner comfort in the same way that, when I am in the purifying presence of my Master, I am released from selfish desires, worldly pursuits, and the claim of others upon me." "Are you free of such attachments this very moment?" asked the Master. "Yes, I am," I replied.[41]

ENDNOTES

A FULL LISTING OF ALL REFERENCE MATERIALS can be found in the Bibliography. The shortened forms used here are listed primarily by author. When there are multiple works by an author, the specific work cited follows the author's name.

Santha Sanchiaan Sri Guru Granth Sahib Ji published by Shiromani Gurdwara Prabandhak Committee in Amritsar, India is the source for the Adi Granth (AG) quotations; and translations used throughout this book have been taken from approved English-language versions. References cite the Adi Granth page followed by sloka number; e.g. AG:1379, Sloka 8.

Baba Sheikh Farid: Life and Teachings, edited by G.S. Talib, is a volume of short essays in English, Punjabi, Urdu and Hindi published by the Baba Farid Memorial Society. References cite author names followed by 'in Talib.'

Introduction

1. Suvorova, p. 89
2. Anand, p. 15
3. Kirmani, *Siyar*, p. 202
4. Nasr, p. 189
5. Abidi in Talib, p. 59
6. Suvorova, p. 84
7. Suvorova, p. 213
8. Lawrence, *Notes*, p. 40

Life & Teachings

1. Aquil, p. 138
2. Nizami, *Life and Times*, p. 1
3. Nizami, *Life and Times*, p. 2

4. Hadrat, p. xviii
5. Nizamuddin, *Morals*, p. 221
6. Nizami, *Life and Times*, p. 155
7. AG:1379, Sloka 27
8. Nizami, *Life and Times*, p. 10
9. Nizami, *Life and Times*, p. 9
10. Nizami, *Life and Times*, pp. 10–11
11. Sharib, *Culture*, p. 188
12. Sharib, *Mystical*, p. 29
13. Sharib, *Mystical*, pp. 42–3
14. Sharib, *Mystical*, p. 35
15. Sharib, *Mystical*, p. 43
16. Nizami, *Life and Times*, p. 9

17. Nizami, *Life and Times*, p. 13
18. Sharib, *Sufi*, p. 24
19. Islam, *Sufism*, p. 242
20. Nizami, *Life and Times*, p. 14
21. Nizami, *Life and Times*, pp. 14–15
22. Currie, p. 31
23. Ibid.
24. Nizami, *Life and Times*, p. 11
25. Sharib, *Mystical*, p. 35
26. Khan, *Sufi Message*, p. 84
27. Sharib, *Mystical*, p. 46
28. Nizami, *Life and Times*, pp. 11–12
29. Taher, *Sufi Saints*, p. 219
30. AG:1378, Sloka 20
31. Nizamuddin, *Morals*, pp. 148–9
32. Nizamuddin, *Morals*, p. 291
33. Nizami, *Life and Times*, p. 18
34. Nizamuddin, *Morals*, p. 304
35. Sharib, *Mystical*, pp. 39–41
36. Abidi in Talib, p. 61
37. Nizamuddin, *Morals*, pp. 129–30
38. Currie, p. 28
39. Sharib, *Mystical*, p. 36
40. Nizami, *Life and Times*, p. 16
41. Nizami, *Life and Times*, p. 50
42. Nizamuddin, *Morals*, pp. 108–9
43. Ibid.
44. Nizami, *Life and Times*, p. 18
45. Ibid.
46. Nizami, *Life and Times*, p. 22
47. Suvorova, p. 88
48. Ibid.
49. Nizami, *Life and Times*, p. 22
50. Kirmani, *Siyar*, p. 139
51. Nizami, *Life and Times*, p. 16
52. Ibid.
53. Nizami, *Life and Times*, p. 17 (quoting *Siyar al-Auliya*, p. 72)
54. Sharib, *Sufi Saints*, pp. 307–8 (quoting *Siyar-ul-Aqtab*, p. 73)
55. Nizami, *Life and Times*, p. 32
56. Nizamuddin, *Morals*, p. 140
57. Nizamuddin, *Morals*, p. 304
58. Lawrence, *Notes*, p. 22
59. Lawrence, *Notes*, pp. 22–3
60. Nizamuddin, *Morals*, pp. 291–2
61. Nizamuddin, *Morals*, p. 166
62. www.en.wikipedia.org/wiki/Fariduddin_Ganjshakar
63. Taher, *Sufi Saints*, pp. 216–17
64. AG:1379, Slokas 24 and 25
65. Abidi in Talib, p. 60
66. Sharib, *Mystical*, p. 29
67. Sharib, *Mystical*, p. 26
68. Sharib, *Mystical*, p. 29
69. Nizami, *Life and Times*, p. 114
70. Nizamuddin, *Morals*, p. 233
71. AG:1379, Sloka 36
72. AG:1382, Sloka 91
73. Abidi in Talib, p. 61
74. Sharib, *Mystical*, p. 48
75. Sharib, *Mystical*, p. 26
76. AG:1382, Sloka 87
77. AG:794, *Raag Soohi*
78. Abidi in Talib, p. 62
79. Sharib, *Mystical*, p. 33
80. Sharib, *Mystical*, p. 51
81. Sharib, *Mystical*, pp. 54–5
82. Sharib, *Mystical*, p. 50
83. Sharib, *Mystical*, p. 58
84. Sharib, *Mystical*, p. 52
85. Sharib, *Mystical*, p. 55
86. Nizami, *Life and Times*, pp. 114–15
87. Sharib, *Culture*, p. 49

88. Sharib, *Mystical*, p. 50
89. Sharib, *Culture*, p. 193
90. Sharib, *Culture*, p. 181
91. Kirmani, *Siyar*, p. 169
92. Sharib, *Culture*, p. 71
93. Sharib, *Culture*, p. 69
94. *Rahat ul-Qalub*, pp. 63–4
95. Sharib, *Culture*, p. 70
96. *Rahat ul-Qalub*, p. 65
97. *Rahat ul-Qalub*, p. 60
98. Rizvi, pp. 146–8
99. Kirmani, *Siyar*, p. 202
100. Nizami, *Life and Times*, p. xvi
101. Sharib, *Mystical*, p. 59
102. Sharib, *Mystical*, p. 66
103. Sharib, *Mystical*, p. 59
104. Sharib, *Mystical*, p. 66
105. AG:1380, Sloka 42
106. AG:1377, Sloka 2
107. Abidi in Talib, p. 61
108. Sharib, *Meditations*, p. 63
109. Sharib, *Mystical*, p. 58
110. Sharib, *Mystical*, p. 61
111. Sharib, *Culture*, p. 41
112. Sharib, *Culture*, p. 23
113. Sharib, *Culture*, p. 71
114. AG:1382, Sloka 88
115. Rizvi, pp. 146–8
116. AG:1378, Sloka 10
117. AG:1379, Sloka 37
118. Christopher Shackle's paper.
119. AG:1383, Sloka 99
120. AG:1382, Sloka 79
121. AG:794, *Raag Soohi Lalit*
122. AG:1384, Sloka 112
123. Kirmani, *Siyar*, p. 139
124. AG:1382, Sloka 80
125. AG:1381, Sloka 67
126. Abidi in Talib, p. 61

127. Sharib, *Culture*, p. 188
128. Sharib, *Mystical*, p. 88
129. Sharib, *Mystical*, pp. 53–4
130. Sharib, *Mystical*, p. 94
131. Sharib, *Mystical*, p. 85
132. Kirmani, *Siyar*, p. 127
133. Nizami, *Life and Times*, p. 28
134. Ernst and Lawrence, *Sufi Martyrs*, p. 67
135. Diwane-Garib Nawaz, p. 34
136. Sharib, *Culture*, p. 157
137. Maneri, p. 26
138. Maneri, p. 27
139. Vaughan-Lee, p. 35
140. Ernst, *Teachings of Sufis*, p. 152
141. Nizamuddin, *Morals*, p. 258
142. Sharib, *Mystical*, p. 68
143. Sharib, *Mystical*, p. 48
144. Sharib, *Mystical*, p. 70
145. Kirmani, *Siyar*, p. 127
146. Sharib, *Mystical*, p. 92
147. Sharib, *Mystical*, pp. 56–7
148. Sharib, *Mystical*, p. 31
149. Sharib, *Mystical*, p. 52
150. Sharib, *Mystical*, pp. 51–2
151. Sharib, *Mystical*, p. 56
152. Sharib, *Mystical*, p. 49
153. AG:1382, Sloka 84
154. *Tales of the Mystic East*, p. 42
155. Nizami, *Life and Times*, pp. 78–9
156. Rizvi, pp. 146–8
157. AG:1380, Sloka 50
158. www.unc.edu/~cernst/ FaridMss.pdf (scan of Khuldabad manuscript)
159. Smith, p. 104
160. Islam, *Sufism*, prologue.
161. Kirmani, *Siyar*, p. 171

162. Kirmani, *Siyar*, p. 506
163. Sharib, *Mystical*, p. 18
164. Sharib, *Mystical*, p. 19
165. Nizami, *Life and Times*, p. 90
   (quoting *Siyar al-Auliya*, p. 74)
166. Taher, *Sufi Saints*, pp. 215–16
167. Kirmani, *Siyar*, p. 144
168. Kirmani, *Siyar*, p. 144
169. Aquil, pp. 11–12
170. Nizamuddin, *Morals*, p. 140
171. Sharib, *Culture*, p. 83
172. Sharib, *Mystical*, pp. 83–4
173. Nizamuddin, *Morals*, p. 144
174. AG:1379, Sloka 29
175. Rizvi, pp. 146–8
176. Islam, *Sufism*, p. 372
177. Nizami, *Life and Times*, p. 44
178. Sharib, *Mystical*, p. 60
179. Sharib, *Mystical*, pp. 57–8
180. Sharib, *Sufi Saints*, p. 113
181. Nizamuddin, *Morals*, p. 166
182. Islam, *Sufism*, p. 78
183. Nizamuddin, *Morals*, p. 200
184. Kirmani, *Siyar*, p. 143
185. Rizvi, pp. 146–8
186. Nizamuddin, *Morals*, pp. 247–8
187. Nizami, *Life and Times*, p. xiv
188. Nizamuddin, *Morals*, p. 166
189. Nizami, *Life and Times*, p. 147
190. Aquil, p. 134
191. Nizami, *Life and Times*, p. 152
192. Nizami, *Chist*, p. 93
193. Nizami, *Chist*, p. 92
194. Nizami, *Life and Times*, p. xiv
195. Islam, *Sufism*, p. 448
196. Aquil, p. 94
197. Rizvi, p. 147
198. Aquil, p. 44
199. Islam, *Sufism*, p. 448

200. www.khwajagharibnawaz.com/
   chishtyorderofsufis.htm
201. Ibid.
202. Islam, *Sufism*, p. 448
203. Aquil, pp. 84–5
204. Ibid.
205. Suvorova, p. 211
206. Suvorova, p. 83
207. Ibid.
208. Ibid.
209. Sharib, *Culture*, p. 61
210. Sharib, *Culture*, p. 60
211. www.khwajagharibnawaz.com/
   chishtyorderofsufis.htm
212. Suvorova, p. 95
213. Nizamuddin, *Morals*, p. 27
214. AG:1381–2, Sloka 78
215. AG:1378, Sloka 6
216. Rizvi, pp. 142–3
217. Nizamuddin, *Morals*, p. 361
218. Nizamuddin, *Morals*, pp. 180–1
219. Nizamuddin, *Morals*, p. 192
220. Nizamuddin, *Morals*, pp. 256–7
221. Sharib, *Culture*, pp. 65–6
222. Rizvi, pp. 146–8
223. Ibid.
224. Nizamuddin, *Morals*, p. 35
225. Abidi in Talib, p. 62
226. Kirmani, *Siyar*, p. 141,
   aphorism 45
227. Nizami, *Life and Times*, p. 118
228. Nizamuddin, *Morals*, p. 172
229. Taher, *Sufi Saints*, pp. 215–16
230. Suvorova, p. 101
231. Nizamuddin, *Morals*, pp. 108–9
232. Islam, *Sufism*, pp. 104–5
233. Islam, *Sufism*, p. 97
234. Nizamuddin, *Morals*, p. 288
235. Islam, *Sufism*, p. 97

236. Nizamuddin, *Morals*, pp. 136
237. Nizamuddin, *Morals*, pp. 136–7
238. Nizamuddin, *Morals*, p. 129
239. Currie, p. 31
240. Nizami, *Life and Times*, p. 11
241. Kirmani, *Siyar*, p. 151
242. Aquil, p. 127
243. Nizamuddin, *Morals*, p. 84
244. Nizamuddin, *Morals*, p. 184
245. Ibid.
246. Rizvi, p. 147
247. Nizamuddin, *Morals*, p. 292
248. Ibid.
249. Nizamuddin, *Morals*, pp. 292–3
250. Nizamuddin, *Morals*, p. 322
251. Nizamuddin, *Morals*, pp. 220–1
252. Nizamuddin, *Morals*, pp. 171–2
253. Nizamuddin, *Morals*, pp. 154–5
254. Nizamuddin, *Morals*, p. 326
255. Nizamuddin, *Morals*, pp. 197–8
256. Nizamuddin, *Morals*, pp. 252–3
257. Nizamuddin, *Morals*, p. 227
258. Ibid.
259. Nizamuddin, *Morals*, pp. 227–8
260. Rizvi, pp. 146–8
261. Nizamuddin, *Morals*, pp. 114–15
262. Nizamuddin, *Morals*, p. 346
263. Nizamuddin, *Morals*, pp. 346–7
264. Nizamuddin, *Morals*, p. 170
265. Nizamuddin, *Morals*, p. 275
266. Ibid.
267. Nizamuddin, *Morals*, p. 147
268. Ibid.
269. Suvorova, p. 97
270. Nizami, *Life and Times*, p. 129
271. Nizami, *Chist*, p. 95
272. Taher, *Sufi Saints*, pp. 215–16
273. Nizami, *Chist*, p. 93
274. Nizamuddin, *Morals*, pp. 141–2
275. Nizamuddin, *Morals*, p. 252
276. Ibid.
277. Ibid.
278. Lawrence, *Notes*, pp. 23–4
279. Nizamuddin, *Morals*, p. 113
280. Nizamuddin, *Morals*, p. 25
281. Ibid.
282. Ernst and Lawrence, *Sufi Martyrs*, p. 73
283. Nizamuddin, *Morals*, pp. 241–2
284. Nizamuddin, *Morals*, p. 242
285. Ibid.
286. Sijzi, *Fawa'id al-Fu'ad*, p. 334
287. Nizamuddin, *Morals*, pp. 26–7
288. Nizamuddin, *Morals*, p. 27
289. Ibid.
290. Nizamuddin, *Morals*, p. 28
291. Nizamuddin, *Morals*, p. 137
292. Nizamuddin, *Morals*, pp. 137–8
293. Nizamuddin, *Morals*, pp. 109–10
294. Nizamuddin, *Morals*, p. 26
295. Nizamuddin, *Morals*, p. 167
296. Nizamuddin, *Morals*, p. 168
297. Nizamuddin, *Morals*, pp. 266–7
298. Nizamuddin, *Morals*, p. 192
299. Nizamuddin, *Morals*, pp. 27–9
300. Nizamuddin, *Morals*, p. 141
301. Nizamuddin, *Morals*, pp. 172–3

Poetry
1. Rakshat Puri
2. Rakshat Puri
3. Syed, p. 36
4. Shackle.
5. AG:1379, Sloka 38
6. AG:1378, Sloka 17
7. Shackle.
8. Rakshat Puri.

9. Shackle.
10. Shackle.
11. Shackle.
12. Nazeer, p. 11
13. Shackle.
14. Shackle.
15. Ernst, *Eternal Garden*, pp. 167, 329
16. Kirmani, *Siyar*, p. 143
17. Kirmani, *Siyar*, p. 144
18. Kirmani, *Siyar*, p. 141
19. Shackle.
20. Singh, p. 275
21. Singh, p. 274
22. Ibid.
23. Simran Jeet Singh.
24. Padam in Talib, sloka 53
25. Padam in Talib, sloka 52
26. Padam in Talib, sloka 65
27. Khan, sloka 75
28. Padam in Talib, sloka 59
29. Padam in Talib, sloka 61
30. Padam in Talib, sloka 13
31. Padam in Talib, sloka 17
32. Padam in Talib, sloka 1
33. Padam in Talib, pp. 48–57
34. Khan, pp. 99–109

Appendix

1. Sharib, *Culture*, p. 41
2. Ernst and Lawrence, *Sufi Martyrs of Love*, p. 33
3. Ibid. (quoting Awrangabadi)
4. *Rahat ul-Qalub*, p. 65
5. *Rahat ul-Qalub*, p. 39
6. *Rahat ul-Qalub*, p. 17
7. Sharib, *Culture*, p. 42
8. Sharib, *Reflections*, p. 54
9. Sharib, *Culture*, pp. 42–3

10. Rizvi, p. 218
11. Nicholson, p. 140
12. Subhan, p. 100
13. Sharib, *Culture*, p. 44
14. *Siyar al-Auliya*, p. 705
15. Subhan, p. 100
16. Dara Shikoh, pp. 16–19
17. *Siyar al-Auliya*, p. 156
18. *Siyar al-Auliya*, p. 221
19. Israrul-Auliya, *Hasht Bihisht*, p. 22
20. *Siyar al-Auliya*, p. 751
21. Sharib, *Culture*, p. 110
22. Nizamuddin, *Morals*, p. 212
23. Lawrence, *Notes*, p. 40
24. Sharib, *Culture*, p. 103
25. Sharib, *Culture*, p. 104
26. Sharib, *Culture*, p. 110
27. Sharib, *Culture*, p. 104
28. Sharib, *Mystical*, p. 92
29. Sharib, *Mystical*, p. 91
30. Ernst and Lawrence, *Sufi Martyrs*, p. 43 (quoting *Lata'if-i Ashrafi*, pp. 45–6)
31. Sharib, *Mystical*, p. 91
32. *Siyar al-Auliya*, p. 751
33. Sharib, *Mystical*, p. 90
34. *Siyar al-Auliya*, p. 751
35. *Siyar al-Auliya*, p. 502 (quoting Islam, *Sufism*, p. 431)
36. Ibid.
37. *Siyar al-Auliya*, pp. 513–14 (quoting Islam, *Sufism*, p. 431)
38. Ernst and Lawrence, *Sufi Martyrs*, pp. 43–4
39. Lawrence, *Notes from a Distant Flute*, p. 48
40. *Siyar al-Auliya*, p. 502
41. Nizamuddin, *Morals*, p. 212

GLOSSARY

Adi Granth   Primal (*adi*) book or scripture (*granth*); also called the Granth Sahib; the name given to the scripture that brings together the poetry of the first five Gurus and the ninth Guru in the line of Guru Nanak, as well as numerous saints from different parts of India. The Adi Granth was compiled by Guru Arjun Dev, the fifth Guru, and was completed in 1604 CE. The hymns of Guru Tegh Bahadur, the ninth Guru, were added by Guru Gobind Singh. The followers of the teachings of the Gurus have adopted the Adi Granth as their most sacred scripture. See also Guru Nanak.

alms   Currency used to show gratitude. Under *shariah*, a person was to give two and a half percent of unexpended income each year as a charity offering to the poor. See *shariah*.

Auliya   The plural form of *wali* is an Arabic word meaning custodian, protector, helper, friend of God; someone who has authority or guardianship over somebody else. In Islam, the term can be used to denote one vested with the authority of God. In English, it most often means a Muslim saint or holy person. Also spelled Awliya.

Balban, Sultan   Ruler of Delhi from 1266–1287 CE, he was the ninth Sultan of the Mamluk Sultanate. Originally known as Ulugh Khan, he changed his name to Balban when, through craft and an assassination, he became the Sultan.

Chishti, Muinuddin (1143–1236 CE)   A renowned Persian Sufi saint whose spiritual master was Usman Harooni, the fourteenth sheikh in the Chishti lineage. After many years of travelling, Khwaja Chishti settled in Ajmer, Rajasthan, where he established his *khanqah*. Founder of the Chishti Order in India, his spiritual descendants include renowned masters such as Sheikh Qutbuddin Bakhtiyar Kaki, Sheikh Farid, Hazrat Nizamuddin Auliya, and others. Also known as Khwaja Gharib Nawaz (lit. Helper of the Poor) and the Khwaja of Ajmer.

Chishti Order   The Chishti Order was founded by Abu Ishaq Shami (d. 940 CE), who came from Syria and established his centre in the village of Chisht, near Herat, Afghanistan. The Chishti Order traces its lineage back to Ali, the cousin of the Prophet Muhammad. In the seventh generation of successors after Shami, Khwaja Chishti brought the Order to India at the close of the twelfth century CE and established its centre in Ajmer, from whence it spread. The Chishti Order was the first of the four main Sufi Orders in India, the others being Qadiri, Suhrawardi, and Naqshbandi. The Chishti Order is particularly known for its dedication to serving the poor and needy.

dervish   A practitioner of the Sufi path, particularly known for extreme poverty and asceticism. From the Persian word for door (*dar*), the term dervish carries the connotation of one who goes door to door, one who has no material possessions. In some Sufi circles the disciples are called dervishes, though a Sufi sheikh may sometimes call himself dervish out of humility. Sometimes spelled *darvish* or *darvesh*.

dhikr   Repetition. Among Sufis, a spiritual discipline typically involving the repetition of the Names of God or of some other invocation. See also *sama*.

dirams   Currently, one United Arab Emirates dirham equals $.27 USD. In Sheikh Farid's day, 1 alm (for example, *jital*) for gratitude equalled 10 *dirams*.

Disposition of the Saints (*Siyar al-Auliya*)   Written by Sayyid Muhammed Kirmani, better known as Amir Khurd, this book was compiled between 1351 and 1382 CE and represents one of the few accounts of the sheikhs of the early Chishti lineage.

faqir Literally a pauper, mendicant. From the Arabic word *faqr*, poverty, a faqir means a poor person. Among Sufis, the term faqir connotes saint, sage or master. Refers to one who has achieved the state of *faqr* or spiritual poverty and understands that everything belongs to God. A true *faqir* is God-realized.

futuh Unasked-for donations, charity. For Sheikh Farid, the principles were that whatever was freely given should be accepted as a gift from God, but the thought of wishing for anything to be given should not even cross the mind. Moreover, whatever was received in a day must be used or given away in the same day; nothing should be kept for the next day.

hajj Pilgrimage to the Ka'bah, in Mecca, Saudi Arabia. There are specific rules and regulations that must be observed, Muslims believe, in order for the pilgrimage to be acceptable to God. One who has successfully completed the *hajj* is called a *hajji*.

Ishaq, Badruddin Sheikh Farid's son-in-law and a scholar, he was also one of Sheikh Farid's disciples. When asked by Sheikh Farid to equally distribute tankahs to the poor and the needy, he mistakenly withheld one coin until daylight, causing the sheikh some discomfort. See *tanka.*

jama'at khanah Congregational or gathering place, specifically in the Chishti line of Sufis. *Khanqah* is a more general term for Sufi centres, but the centres established by Chishti Sufis are often termed *jama'at khanah* because of their emphasis on communal living.

jital A copper coin introduced by Sultan Iltutmish worth about 10 *dirams.* See *tanka.*

Ka'bah Also known as the Sacred and the Ancient House, the Ka'bah is a cuboid building at the centre of Islam's most sacred mosque, Al-Masjid al-Haram, in Mecca, Saudi Arabia.

Kaki, Qutbuddin Bakhtiyar (1173–1235 CE) An important mystic of the twelfth century CE and the master or pir of Baba Farid, who became his chief spiritual successor.

khalifa   Among Sufis, the disciple of a Sufi master or pir who is entrusted with the right to teach and initiate by the master. The successor of a Sufi pir. Literally, *khalifa* means substitute.

khanqah   Literally, a house of prayer; a Sufi gathering place or a hostel where disciples and visitors can stay. Also see *jama'at khanah.*

khilafat   Literally, to succeed or follow, lineage, successorship; in certain Islamic or Sufi circles it means a chain of command or authority. The *khilafat nama* is the certificate that authorizes someone to initiate disciples.

khilafat nama   See *khilafat.*

Khwaja   An honorific used in the Middle East, South Asia, and Central Asia that means master or lord. Etymologically related to the Persian word *hodja,* meaning one who has inner wisdom. See also sheikh.

Morals for the Heart (*Fawa'id-ul-Fu'ad*)   A book comprised of notes from 188 days of discourses of (conversations with) Hazrat Nizamuddin Auliya that were transcribed and compiled by Amir Hasan Sijzi. This comprehensive record of the notable Chishti sheikh established records of conversations with a sheikh (*malfuzat*) as a popular literary form for conveying Sufi teachings.

Muhammad   Abu al-Qasim Muhammad ibn 'Abd Allah ibn 'Abd al-Muttalib ibn Hashim (c. 570–c. 632 CE), was born in Mecca and lived in what is now Saudi Arabia. Called 'the Messenger,' he brought the Muslim teachings to the people of his time and taught the importance of worshipping the one God, Allah. The message revealed to him is recorded in the Qur'an, and traditions concerning his life and teachings are found in the Hadith.

Multani   A Sanskrit-based language that is classified as a dialect of Sarieki, Punjabi or Sindhi and is sometimes referred to as Multani-Sarieki. Multani was primarily spoken in the southern Punjab, originated around the city of Multan, and covered an area of approximately 26,000 square miles that included Multan, Muzafargarh, Dera Ghazi Khan, Bahawalpur and southern parts of Dera Ismail Khan and Jhang (now in Pakistan).

murshid Literally, guide. Among Sufis, a term for a spiritual guide, a teacher or master. See also pir.

Nanak, Guru (1469–1539 CE) Born near Lahore (now in Pakistan), Guru Nanak spent a large part of his life travelling to teach the underlying unity of all religions. In days when there was no mechanized form of transport, legend says that he went as far as the south of India and to Mecca in the West. He was the first in the line of the ten Gurus whose teachings are recorded in the *Adi Granth*.

Chiragh Dehlavi, Nasiruddin (1274–1356 CE) A Sufi saint in the Chishti Order, the successor of Hazrat Nizamuddin Auliya.

Nizamuddin Auliya (1238–1325 CE) A saint of northern India whose ancestors came to India from Bokhara in Persia. Born in Uttar Pradesh, Hazrat Nizamuddin Auliya was a disciple of Baba Farid and his chief successor. His tomb in Delhi is still revered today.

pir Literally, an elder, an old man or a man of experience and knowledge. Among Sufis, pir denotes a spiritual guide, a teacher or a master.

qalandars Wandering ascetic Sufi dervishes who may or may not be connected to a specific Order (*tariqah*). Some *qalandars* deliberately flout social norms, inviting the censure of society as a part of their spiritual practice.

Qasur A city in the Punjab province of Pakistan. Sometimes spelled Kasur.

qāzi Administrator of Islamic religious law, a magistrate. Sometimes spelled *qaḍi*.

sama Listening to the singing of mystical poetry as a means to enter deep meditative states: the subject is divine love and yearning for union, and the verses are filled with praises of God or of a spiritual master. *Sama* means 'listening,' while *dhikr* means 'remembrance.' These rituals often include singing, playing instruments, dancing, recitation of poetry and prayers, and wearing symbolic attire. It is a particularly popular form of worship in the Chishti Order of the Indian subcontinent. See also *dhikr*.

shariah   Islamic code of conduct, law, and justice; Qur'anic law. See also alms.

sheikh   Literally, learned man, teacher, professor, old man, chief. Among Sufis, sheikh denotes the master, murshid, pir, and one who has become perfect in *shariah* (religious law), *tariqah* (the path), and *haqiqah* (the truth).

sloka   A couplet; verse; stanza.

Sufi   A seeker of God; someone who follows a mystical path through the religion of Islam. Regarding the etymology of the word, there are diverse views. Some believe the root of Sufi is the Greek word *sophia* (wisdom) whereas others say it is *soffeh* (a corridor or verandah) because there was a verandah at the Prophet's mosque in Medina, where some of his poor followers lived. *Soof* (wool) is the root according to others, who reason that the Prophet, Jesus, and some ascetics of old wore woollen gowns. Finally, *safā* (purity, cleanliness) is tenable because the seeker of God must go through extensive mental purification.

tanka   A silver coin introduced by Sultan Iltutmish to replace a grain-based currency that was minted to correspond with the current local harvest. The higher value occurred immediately after harvest when the crop was fresh and available, and therefore heavier, and lower value when the harvest was dry and mouldy. Both the *tanka* and the *jital* equalled the weight of 178 grains.

tawakkul   Trust in God. *Tawakkul* implies gratefully and gladly accepting whatever God sends; it means neither expecting nor wishing for anything more or less than whatever He provides.

tazkirat   A collection of sayings and deeds of a given saint, pieced together into a biographical sketch/account. These anecdotes are presented as traditions that have been passed down orally through the centuries until the time when the *tazkirat* is published.

źikr   See *dhikr*.

BIBLIOGRAPHY

English

Anand, Balwant Singh. *Baba Farid*. New Delhi: Sahitya Akademi, 1975.

Aquil, Raziuddin. *Sufism and Society in Medieval India*. Debates in Indian History and Society Series. New Delhi: Oxford University Press, 2010.

Chishti, Muinuddin. *Diwan-i Gharib Nawaz*. Compiled by Muslim Ahmad Nizami. Delhi: Kutub Khanah Naziriyah, 1958.

Currie, P.M. *The Shrine and Cult of Muin al-Din Chishti of Ajmer*. New Delhi: Oxford University Press, 1989.

Dara Shikoh, Muhammed. *Risala-i-Haq-Numa, The Compass of Truth*. (English rendering by Srisa Chandra Vasu). Allahabad: Panini Office, Bhuvaneshwari Ashrama, 1912.

Encyclopædia of Islam, 2nd Edition, 12 vols. with indexes and etc., Leiden: E. J. Brill, 1960–2005.

Ernst, Carl W. *Eternal Garden: Mysticism, History and Politics at a South Asian Sufi Center*. Albany: SUNY, 2004.

———. *Teachings of Sufis*. Selected and translated by Carl W. Ernst. Boston: Shambhala, 1999.

Ernst, Carl W. and Bruce B. Lawrence. *Sufi Martyrs of Love: The Chishti Order in South Asia and Beyond*. New York: Palgrave Macmillan, 2002.

Islam, Riazul. *Sufism in South Asia: Impact on Fourteenth Century Muslim Society*. Karachi: Oxford University Press, 2002.

al-Jilani, Hadrat Abd al-Qadir. *The Secret of Secrets*. Interpreted by Shaykh Tosun Bayrak al-Jerrahi al-Halveti. Islamic Texts Society, Golden Palm Series, 1992.

Khan, Inayat. *The Sufi Message of Hazrat Inayat Khan*. London: Barrie and Rockliff, 1964.

Lawrence, Bruce B. *Notes from a Distant Flute: Sufi Literature in Pre-Mughal India*. Tehran: Imperial Iranian Academy, 1978.

Maneri, Sharafuddin. *The Hundred Letters*. Translated by Paul Jackson. Classics of Western Spirituality. New York: Paulist Press, 1980.

Nasr, Seyyed Hossein. *The Garden of Truth: The Vision and Promise of Sufism, Islam's Mystical Tradition*. New York: HarperOne, 2007.

Nicholson, R.A. *Mystics of Islam*. London: Routledge, 1914.

Nizami, Khaliq Ahmad. *The Life and Times of Shaikh Baba Farid-u'd-din Ganj-i-Shakar*. New Delhi: Idarah-i Adabayat-i Delhi. Revised and enlarged edition, 1998.

Nizamuddin Awliya. *Morals for the Heart: Conversations of Shaykh Nizam ad-din Awliya Recorded by Amir Hasan Sijzi*. Translated and annotated by Bruce B. Lawrence. Classics of Western Spirituality. New York: Paulist Press, 1992.

O'Brien, Edward. Edited by James Wilson and Hari Kishan Kaul. (1st ed. 1903) 5th ed. *Glossary of the Multani Language or South-Western Punjabi*. Language Department, Punjab. Chandigarh: Bharti Printers, 2001.

Puri, Rakshat. "Love is His Own Power: The Slokas of Baba Farid." A paper by Rakshat Puri presented at The Writers Workshop, Calcutta, 1990.

Rizvi, Saiyid Athar Abbas. *A History of Sufism in India. Vol. 1, Early Sufism and its History in India to AD 1600*. New Delhi: Munshiram Manoharlal Publishers Pvt. Ltd, 1986.

Shackle, Christopher. "Sikh and Muslim Understandings of Baba Farid." The 2008 Amrit Kaur Ahluwalia Memorial Lecture, delivered Saturday, April 19, 2008, UC Berkeley.

Sharib, Zahurul Hassan. *The Culture of the Sufis*. Southampton: Sharib Press, 1999.

———. *Khawaja Gharib Nawaz*. Ajmer: Asma Publications, 2007.

———. *The Meditations of Khwaja Muin ud Din Chishti*. Southampton: Sharib Press, 1994.

———. *The Mystical Philosophy of Khawaja Moinuddin Hasan Chisti*. Ajmer: Khawaja Publishers, 1959.

———. *The Reflections of the Mystics of Islam*. Southampton: Sharib Press, 1995.

———. *The Sufi Saints of the Indian Subcontinent*. New Delhi: Munshiram Manoharlal, 2006.

Sijzi, Amir Hasan. *Fawa'id al-Fu'ad: Spiritual and Literary Discourses of Shaikh Nizāmuddin Awliyā*. Translated by Ziya-ul-Hasan Furuqi. Islamic Heritage in Cross-Cultural Perspectives, no. 2. New Delhi: DK Printworld (P) Ltd, 1995.

Singh, Simran Jeet. "Farid Bani: Sufi Verses in Early Sikh Literature." A paper presented at the AAR 2011 Annual Conference, November 19–22, 2011.

Smith, Margaret. *Al-Ghazali, The Mystic*. London: Luzac and Co, 1943.

Subhan, John A. (Bishop). *Sufism: Its Saints and Shrines*. Lucknow: The Lucknow Publishing House, 1960.

Suvorova, Anna Aronovna. *Muslim Saints of South Asia: The eleventh to fifteenth centuries*. London: Routledge Curzon, 2004.

Syed, Najm Hosain. *Recurrent Patterns in Punjabi Poetry*. Lahore: Justin Group Printers, 2003.

Taher, Mohamed. *Sufi Saints*. New Delhi: Anmol Publications Pvt. Ltd, 1998.

Tales of the Mystic East. (1st ed. 1961) 5th ed. Beas, Punjab: Radha Soami Satsang Beas, 1983.

Talib, G.S., ed. *Baba Sheikh Farid: Life and Teachings*. New Delhi: Baba Farid Memorial Society, 1973.

Vaughan-Lee, Llewellyn. *Traveling the Path of Love: Sayings of Sufi Masters*. Inverness, Calif: Golden Sufi Center, 1995.

Persian
Diwan-e Gharib Nawaz, compiled by M.A. Nizami. Delhi: Jama Masjid, 1958.

Punjabi

 Santha Sanchiaan Sri Guru Granth Sahib Ji. 2 vols. Amritsar: Shiromani Gurdwara Prabandhak Committee, 1997.

Singh, Pritam. *Shri Guru Granth Sahib Vale Sheikh Farid di Bhal.* Amritsar, India: Singh Brothers, 2008.

Urdu

Ahmad, Sayyid Nazeer. *Kalaam-i-Baba Farid Shakar Ganj.* Lahore: Packages Ltd, 1984.

Hasht Bihisht, Malfuzat-e Khwajgan-e Chisht. Delhi: Maktabah-Jaam-e Noor, (n.d.).

Khan, M. Asif. *Akhya Baba Farid ne.* Lahore: Pakistan Panjabi Adabi Board, 1978.

Kirmani, Muhammad ibn Mubarak. *Siyar al-awliya.* Lahore: Urdu Science Board, 2004.

———. *Siyar al-awliya.* Lahore: Mustaq Book Corner, Urdu Bazaar, 1978.

Nizami, Khaliq Ahmad, *Tarikh Mashaikh Chist,* Delhi: Nadohal Musanfin, Urdu Bazaar (n.d.).

Rahat ul-Qalub (attributed to Nizamuddin Auliya). New Delhi: Jamnur, Kucha Chilan, Dariya Ganj (n.d.).

ACKNOWLEDGEMENTS

WE OFFER OUR GRATITUDE to the many contributors who helped with this labour of love. Our special thanks to Vraje Abramian for his renditions of the Persian poetry; to our team from Ajmer for their tireless review of the vast amount of Multani material attributed to Sheikh Farid; and to the many scholars and experts who regularly contribute to our publications for their guidance on Muslim culture and Sufi insight.

INDEX

grasping the hand of the sheikh, 32,
48, 126, 127. *See also* initiation
gratitude, 79, 85, 89
Guru Nanak, 155, 158, 240, 242

H

hajj. See pilgrimage
heart
furnace of love, 56
jewel, 159, 160, 227
ocean within, 245, 269
throne of Allah, 72, 74, 280, 284
historical context
Delhi Sultanate, 7, 29, 50, 97
free kitchen, 93
itinerant mystics, 23
Memoirs of the Saints, 11
Mughal Empire, 12, 155
Muslim immigration, 7
Muslim passion for poetry, 7, 10
north India Sufism, 9, 40, 100,
228, 278
oral tradition, 4, 10, 14, 53, 154, 240,
241, 243, 247, 283
Punjab in turmoil, 6
scholarship honored, 8, 19, 20, 33, 83
Sikh tradition, 156
humility, 13, 29, 39, 50, 105, 106, 134,
151, 173, 175, 179, 195, 227, 257

I

Ibrahim, Sheikh, 157, 240
illusory world, 4, 225, 255
imagery
aging, 169, 197, 253, 261, 273, 275
autumn, 215
barking dog, 67
bedding, 189
beggar, 64

birds, 57, 69, 95, 165, 169, 201, 205,
215, 225, 233, 235, 257
blacksmith, 191
blood of greed, 195
boatman, 167, 209
bow and arrow, 221, 259
bride, 165, 173, 185, 187, 197
burnt crop, 199
business partnership, 273
daily activities, 244
dog of ego, 263
doorstep of the Lord, 64
downpour, 54, 257
dry bread, 185
dry wood, 38
dust, 4, 181, 237, 273
farmer, 183, 189, 244, 267
ferrying across, 171
fire, 35, 37, 56, 207, 209, 253
flesh-eating crows, 56, 209, 211
flowers and fruit, 171, 209, 221, 235
fortress of the body, 193, 261
fragrance of musk, 71, 187, 207
furnace of hell, 205, 213
gong, 189, 191
grass underfoot, 179, 271
graveyard, 165, 201
guest in the garden, 69, 205
hawks of God, 69, 213
head that doesn't bow, 203
Husband Lord, 149, 165, 175, 185,
197, 199, 211, 219, 221, 227, 255
jeweller, 269
lamps of the eyes, 193
lane of love, 71, 239
leaky roof, 181
lightning, 165
lush forest, 253
morning ritual, 203

submission, 26, 40, 43, 64, 191, 245
successor. *See* Nizamuddin, Hazrat
  Auliya
suffering, 189, 233, 239, 251, 253, 257
Sufi mystic. *See* pir
Sufism. *See also* Chishti lineage
  action not intellect, 26, 61, 83
  friends of God, 59, 62, 279, 286
  importance of integrity, 82
  mutual respect among Orders, 112
  nightly prayers, 21, 70, 221, 233, 235,
    265, 277, 283
  people of the heart, 37, 239
  pir's informal conversations, 12
  power of love, 78
  principle of forgiveness, 107
  role of Orders, 5, 112, 115
  role of pirs, 5, 25, 60, 75, 121,
    141, 241
  role of poetry, 27
  teaching through poetry, 14
  true pilgrimage, 74, 76
  views on holy men, 39
Suhrawardi, Sheikh Shihabuddin, 6,
    27, 114, 139
surrender, 71, 79, 84, 85, 207, 219, 223,
    235, 237, 239, 273
Suvorova, Anna, 9
Syed, Najm Hosain, 148, 153

T

Tabrizi, Sheikh Jalaluddin, 22, 27,
    28, 115
Taher, Mohamed, 33, 53
tanka, 302
teachings, 53–80, 141
time for change, 179, 199, 205, 213, 219
transformation, 78, 225, 279
translation approach, 151–53, 230, 241
trust in God, 83, 90, 138

U

uniqueness of God, 251
urgency, 68, 69, 169, 175, 177, 197, 205,
    209, 241

V

virtues, 33, 79, 82, 89, 91, 112, 142, 151,
    175, 205, 211, 227, 233, 235, 257,
    271, 273

W

worldly pursuits, 4, 20, 29, 31, 45, 63,
    65, 69, 113, 121, 125, 138, 149, 165,
    173, 179, 183, 219, 221, 235, 237, 253,
    255, 259, 263, 265, 286

Z

Zakariya, Sheikh Bahauddin, 23, 37,
    112, 114, 115

BOOKS ON SPIRITUALITY

RSSB TRADITION

Sar Bachan Prose – *Soami Ji Maharaj*
Sar Bachan Poetry – *Soami Ji Maharaj*

Spiritual Letters – *Baba Jaimal Singh*

The Dawn of Light – *Maharaj Sawan Singh*
Discourses on Sant Mat, Volume I – *Maharaj Sawan Singh*
My Submission – *Maharaj Sawan Singh*
Philosophy of the Masters (5 volumes) – *Maharaj Sawan Singh*
Spiritual Gems – *Maharaj Sawan Singh*

Discourses on Sant Mat, Volume II – *Maharaj Jagat Singh*
The Science of the Soul – *Maharaj Jagat Singh*

Die to Live – *Maharaj Charan Singh*
Divine Light – *Maharaj Charan Singh*
Light on Saint John – *Maharaj Charan Singh*
Light on Saint Matthew – *Maharaj Charan Singh*
Light on Sant Mat – *Maharaj Charan Singh*
The Path – *Maharaj Charan Singh*
Quest for Light – *Maharaj Charan Singh*
Spiritual Discourses (2 volumes) – *Maharaj Charan Singh*
Spiritual Heritage – *Maharaj Charan Singh*
Spiritual Perspectives (3 volumes) – *Maharaj Charan Singh*

Call of the Great Master – *Daryai Lal Kapur*
Heaven on Earth – *Daryai Lal Kapur*
Honest Living – *M. F. Singh*
In Search of the Way – *Flora E. Wood*
The Inner Voice – *C. W. Sanders*
Liberation of the Soul – *J. Stanley White*
Life Is Fair: The Law of Cause and Effect – *Brian Hines*
Living Meditation – *Hector Esponda Dubin*
Message Divine – *Shanti Sethi*
The Mystic Philosophy of Sant Mat – *Peter Fripp*
Mysticism: The Spiritual Path – *Lekh Raj Puri*
The Path of the Masters – *Julian P. Johnson*
Radha Soami Teachings – *Lekh Raj Puri*
A Soul's Safari – *Netta Pfeifer*
A Spiritual Primer – *Hector Esponda Dubin*
Treasure beyond Measure – *Shanti Sethi*
With a Great Master in India – *Julian P. Johnson*
With the Three Masters (3 volumes) – *Rai Sahib Munshi Ram*

MYSTIC TRADITION

Bulleh Shah – *J. R. Puri and T. R. Shangari*
Dadu: The Compassionate Mystic – *K. N. Upadhyaya*
Dariya Sahib: Saint of Bihar – *K. N. Upadhyaya*
Guru Nanak: His Mystic Teachings – *J. R. Puri*
Guru Ravidas: The Philosopher's Stone – *K. N. Upadhyaya*
Kabir: The Great Mystic – *Isaac A. Ezekiel*
Kabir: The Weaver of God's Name – *V. K. Sethi*
Many Voices, One Song: The Poet Mystics of Maharashtra –
    Judith Sankaranarayan

Mira: The Divine Lover – *V. K. Sethi*
Saint Namdev – *J. R. Puri and V. K. Sethi*
Sant Charandas – *T. R. Shangari*
Sant Paltu: His Life and Teachings – *Isaac A. Ezekiel*
Sarmad: Martyr to Love Divine – *Isaac A. Ezekiel*
Shams-e Tabrizi – *Farida Maleki*
Sheikh Farid: The Great Sufi Mystic – *T. R. Shangari*
Sultan Bahu – *J. R. Puri and K. S. Khak*
The Teachings of Goswami Tulsidas – *K. N. Upadhyaya*
Tukaram: The Ceaseless Song of Devotion – *C. Rajwade*
Tulsi Sahib: Saint of Hathras – *J. R. Puri and V. K. Sethi*
Voice of the Heart: Songs of Devotion from the Mystics

MYSTICISM IN WORLD RELIGIONS

Adventure of Faith – *Shraddha Liertz*
Buddhism: Path to Nirvana – *K. N. Upadhyaya*
The Divine Romance – *John Davidson*
The Gospel of Jesus – *John Davidson*
Gurbani Selections (Volumes I, II)
The Holy Name: Mysticism in Judaism – *Miriam Caravella*
Jap Ji – *T. R. Shangari*
The Mystic Heart of Judaism – *Miriam Caravella*
The Odes of Solomon – *John Davidson*
One Being One – *John Davidson*
The Prodigal Soul – *John Davidson*
The Song of Songs – *John Davidson*
Tales of the Mystic East
A Treasury of Mystic Terms,
    Part I: The Principles of Mysticism (6 volumes) – *John Davidson, ed.*
Yoga and the Bible – *Joseph Leeming*

VEGETARIAN COOKBOOKS

Baking Without Eggs
Creative Vegetarian Cooking
The Green Way to Healthy Living
Meals with Vegetables

BOOKS FOR CHILDREN

The Journey of the Soul – *Victoria Jones*
One Light Many Lamps – *Victoria Jones*

MISCELLANEOUS THEMES

Empower Women: An Awakening – *Leena Chawla*
Equilibrium of Love: Dera Baba Jaimal Singh

For Internet orders, please visit: www.rssb.org

For book orders within India, please write to:
Radha Soami Satsang Beas
BAV Distribution Centre, 5 Guru Ravi Dass Marg
Pusa Road, New Delhi 110 005

ADDRESSES FOR INFORMATION AND BOOKS

INDIAN SUB-CONTINENT

INDIA
The Secretary
Radha Soami Satsang Beas
Dera Baba Jaimal Singh
District Amritsar,
Punjab 143 204

NEPAL
Mr. S.B.B. Chhetri
RSSB - Kathmandu
Gongabu 7 P.O. Box 1646
Kathmandu
☎ +977-01-435-7765

SRI LANKA
Mrs. Maya Mahbubani
RSSB - Colombo
No. 47/1 Silva Lane
Rajagiriya, Colombo
☎ +94-11-286-1491

SOUTHEAST ASIA

Mrs. Cami Moss
RSSB - Hong Kong
T.S.T., P.O. Box 90745
Kowloon, Hong Kong
☎ +852-2369-0625

Mr. Manoj Sabnani
RSSB - Hong Kong
27th Floor, Tower B
Billion Centre
1 Wang Kwong Road
Kowloon Bay, Hong Kong

Mrs. Ivy Sabnani
Unit D, 22nd Floor, Tower A
Billion Centre
1 Wang Kwong Road
Kowloon Bay, Hong Kong

HONG KONG
RSSB - Hong Kong
27th Floor, Tower B
Billion Centre
1 Wang Kwong Road
Kowloon Bay
☎ +852-2369-0625

GUAM
Mrs. Rekha Sadhwani
625 Alupang Cove
241 Condo Lane
Tamuning 96911

INDONESIA
Mr. Ramesh Sadarangani
Yayasan RSSB - Jakarta
Jl. Transyogi Kelurahan
Jatirangga
Pondok Gede 17434
☎ +62-21-845-1612

Yayasan RSSB - Bali
Jalan Bung Tomo
Desa Pemecutan Raya
Denpasar, Bali 80118
☎ +62-361-438-522

JAPAN
Mr. Jani G. Mohinani
RSSB - Kobe
1-2-18 Nakajima-Dori
Aotani, Chuo-Ku,
Kobe 651-0052
☎ +81-78-222-5353

KOREA
Mr. Haresh Buxani
SOS Study Centre - Korea
638, Hopyeong-Dong
R603-1 & 604
Sungbo Building
Nam Yangju, Gyeong Gi-Do
☎ +82-231-511-7008

MALAYSIA
Mr. Bhupinder Singh
RSSB - Kuala Lumpur
29 Jalan Cerapu Satu,
Off Batu 3¼, Jalan Cheras
Kuala Lumpur 56100
Wilayah Persekutuan
☎ +603-9200-3073

PHILIPPINES
Mr. Kay Sham Buxani
SOS Study Centre - Manila
9001 Don Jesus Boulevard
Alabang Hills, Cupang
Muntinlupa City, 1771,
Metro Manila
☎ +63-2-772-0111 / 0555

SINGAPORE
Mrs. Asha Melwani
RSSB - Singapore
19 Amber Road
Singapore 439868
☎ +65-6447-4956

TAIWAN, R.O.C.
Mr. Haresh Buxani
SOS Study Centre - Taiwan
Aetna Tower Office
15F., No. 27-9, Sec.2,
Jhongjheng E.Rd.
Danshuei Township,
Taipei 25170
☎ +886-2-8809-5223

THAILAND
Mr. Harmahinder Singh Sethi
RSSB - Bangkok
58/32 Thaphra
Ratchadaphisek Road,
Soi 16, Wat Thapra
Bangkok Yai District,
Bangkok 10600
☎ +66-2-868-2186 / 2187

ASIA PACIFIC

AUSTRALIA
Mrs. Jill Wiley
P.O. Box 1256
Kenmore 4069, Queensland

SOS Study Centre - Sydney
1530 Elizabeth Drive
Cecil Park,
New South Wales 2178
☎ +61-2-9826-2564

NEW ZEALAND
Mr. Tony Waddicor
P.O. Box 5331, Auckland

SOS Study Centre - Auckland
80 Olsen Avenue
Hillsborough, Auckland
☎ +64-9-624-2202

CANADA & UNITED STATES

CANADA
Mr. John Pope
5285 Coombe Lane, Belcarra,
British Columbia V3H 4N6

SOS Study Centre - Vancouver
2932 -176th Street
Surrey, B.C. V3S 9V4
☎ +1-604-541-4792

Mrs. Meena Khanna
149 Elton Park Road
Oakville, Ontario L6J 4C2

SOS Study Centre - Toronto
6566 Sixth Line, RR 1
Hornby, Ontario L0P 1E0
☎ +1-905-875-4579

UNITED STATES

Northeastern USA
Dr. Frank E. Vogel
275 Cutts Road
Newport, NH 03773

Southeastern USA
Dr. Douglas Torr
529 Carolina Meadows Villa
Chapel Hill, NC 27517

North Central USA
Mr. Gaurav Chawla
36689 Rolf St.
Westland, MI 48186

South Central USA
Mr. Hank Muller
P.O. Box 1847
Tomball, TX 77377

Northwestern USA
Mr. James Rosen
6710 Round Oak Road
Penngrove, CA 94951

Southwestern USA
Dr. Vincent P. Savarese
2550 Pequeno Circle
Palm Springs, CA 92264-9522

SOS Study Centre -
Fayetteville
4115 Gillespie Street
Fayetteville, NC 28306-9053
☎ +1-910-426-5306

SOS Study Centre - Petaluma
2415 Washington Street
Petaluma, CA 94954-9274
☎ +1-707-762-5082

MEXICO & CENTRAL AMERICA

Dr. Servando Sanchez
16103 Vanderbilt Drive
Odessa, Florida 33556 USA

MEXICO
Mr. Francisco Rodriguez Rosas
RSSB - Puerto Vallarta
Circuito Universidad S/N
Lomas Del Progreso El Pitillal
Puerto Vallarta, CP 48290
☎ +52-322-299-1954

RSSB - Guadalajara
Efrain Gonzalez Luna
2051 Col. Americana
Guadalajara, Jalisco 44090
☎ +52-333-615-4942

BELIZE
Mrs. Milan Hotchandani
4633 Seashore Drive
P.O. Box 830, Belize City

PANAMA
Mr. Ashok Tikamdas Dinani
P.O. Box 0302-01000, Colon

SOUTH AMERICA

ARGENTINA
Ms. Fabiana Shilton
Leiva 4363 Capital Federal
C.P. 1427 Buenos Aires

BRAZIL
Mr. Guillerme Almeida
RUA Brasilla 131/21
Sao Paulo 0454-040

CHILE
Mr. Vijay Harjani
Pasaje Cuatro No. 3438
Sector Chipana, Iquique

Fundacion RSSB - Santiago
Av. Apoquindo 4775,
Oficina 1503
Las Condes, Santiago

COLOMBIA
Mrs. Emma Orozco
Asociacion Cultural
RSSB - Medellin
Calle 48 No. 78A-30
Medellin 49744
☎ +574-234-5130

ECUADOR
Mr. Miguel Egas H.
RSSB - Quito
Calle Marquez de Varela
OE 3-68y Avda. America
P.O. Box 17-21-115, Quito
☎ +5932-2-555-988

PERU
Mr. Carlos Fitts
Asociacion Cultural
RSSB - Lima
Av. Pardo #231, 12th Floor
Miraflores, Lima 18
☎ +511-651-2030

VENEZUELA
Mrs. Helen Paquin
RSSB - Caracas
Av. Los Samanes con
Av. Los Naranjos Conj
Res. Florida 335
La Florida, Caracas 1012
☎ +58-212-731-2208

CARIBBEAN

Mr. Sean Finnigan
SOS Study Centre - St. Maarten
P.O. Box 978, Phillipsburg
St. Maarten, Dutch Caribbean

Mrs. Jaya Sabnani
1 Sunset Drive South
Fort George Heights
St. Michael BB111 02
Barbados, W.I.

BARBADOS, W.I.
Mr. Deepak Nebhani
SOS Study Centre - Barbados
No. 10, 5th Avenue, Belleville
St. Michael BB11114
☎ +1-246-427-4761

CURACAO
Mrs. Hema Chandiramani
SOS Study Centre - Curacao
Kaya Seru di Milon 6-9
Santa Catharina
☎ +599-9-747-0226

ST. MAARTEN
Mr. Prakash Daryanani
SOS Study Centre - St. Maarten
203 Oyster Pond Road
St. Maarten, Dutch Caribbean
☎ +1-721-547-0066

GRENADA, W.I.
Mr. Ajay Mahbubani
P.O. Box 820, St. Georges

GUYANA
Mrs. Indu Lalwani
155, Garnette Street
Newtown Kitty, Georgetown

HAITI, W.I.
Ms. Monique Finnigan Pierre
Route de Camp Perrin
Lamartiniere, HT 8140

JAMAICA, W.I.
Mrs. Shamni Khiani
37A Leader Drive
Montego Bay

ST. THOMAS
Mr. Rajesh Chatlani
5178 Dronningens Gade, Ste2
US Virgin Islands,
VI00801-6145

SURINAME
Mr. Ettire Stanley Rensch
Surinamestraat 36,
Paramaribo

TRINIDAD, W.I.
Mr. Chandru Chatlani
20 Admiral Court
Westmoorings-by-Sea,
Westmoorings

EUROPE

AUSTRIA
Mr. Hansjorg Hammerer
Sezenweingasse 10
A-5020 Salzburg

BELGIUM
Mr. Piet J. E. Vosters
Driezenstraat 26
Turnhout 2300

BULGARIA
Mr. Deyan Stoyanov
Foundation RSSB - Bulgaria
P.O. Box 39, 8000 Bourgas

CYPRUS
Mr. Heraclis Achilleos
P.O. Box 29077
1035 Nicosia

CZECH REPUBLIC
Mr. Vladimir Skalsky
Maratkova 916
142 00 Praha 411

DENMARK
Mr. Tony Sharma
Sven Dalsgaardsvej 33
DK-7430 Ikast

SOS Study Centre - Denmark
Formervangen 36
Glostrup 2600

FINLAND
Ms. Anneli Wingfield
P.O. Box 1422
00101 Helsinki

FRANCE
Mr. Pierre de Proyart
7 Quai Voltaire
Paris 75007

GERMANY
Mr. Rudolf Walberg
P.O. Box 1544
D-65800 Bad Soden

Mr. Stephan Zipplies
Auf der Platt 20
61479 Glashuetten im Ts

SOS Study Centre - Frankfurt
In den Ensterwiesen 4+9
Weilrod-Riedelbach 61276
☎ +49-6083-959-4700

GIBRALTAR
Mr. Sunder Mahtani
RSSB Charitable Trust -
Gibraltar
15 Rosia Road
Gibraltar GX11 1AA
☎ +350-200-412-67

GREECE
Mr. Themistoclis Gianopoulos
6 Platonos Str.
17672 Kallithea, Attiki

SOS Study Centre - Athens
10 Filikis Etaireias Street
14234-Nea Ionia, Attiki

ITALY
Mrs. Wilma Salvatori Torri
Via Bacchiglione 3
00199 Rome

NETHERLANDS
Mr. Henk Keuning
Kleizuwe2
3633 AE Vreeland

RSSB - Netherlands
Middenweg 145 E
1394 AH Nederhorst den Berg
☎ +31-294-255-255

NORWAY
Mr. Manoj Kaushal
Langretta 8
N - 1279 Oslo

POLAND
Mr. Vinod Sharma
P.O. Box 59
Ul. Szkolna 15
05-090 Raszyn

PORTUGAL
Mrs. Sharda Lodhia
CRCA Portugal
Av. Coronel Eduardo Galhardo
No.18 A-B, Lisbon 1170-105

ROMANIA
Mrs. Carmen Cismas
C.P. 6-12, 810600 Braila

SLOVENIA
Mr. Marko Bedina
Brezje pri Trzicu 68
4290 Trzic

SPAIN
Mr. J. W. Balani
Fundacion Cultural RSSB -
Malaga
Avenida de las Americas s/n
Cruce Penon de Zapata
29130 Alhaurin de la Torre,
Malaga
☎ +34-952-414-679

SWEDEN
Mr. Lennart Zachen
Norra Sonnarpsvägen 29
SE-286 72 Asljunga

SWITZERLAND
Mr. Sebastian Züst
Weissenrainstrasse 48
CH 8707 Uetikon am See

UNITED KINGDOM
Mr. Narinder Singh Johal
SOS Study Centre -
Haynes Park
Haynes Park, Church End
Haynes
MK45 3BL Bedford
☎ +44-1234-381-234

Mr. Douglas Cameron
25 Rosebank Cottages
Woking GU22 9Q2

Mr. Bill Kahn
Haynes Park, Church End
Haynes
MK45 3BL Bedford

AFRICA

BENIN
Mr. Jaikumar T. Vaswani
01 Boite Postale 951
Recette Principale,
Cotonou 01

BOTSWANA
Dr. Krishan Lal Bhateja
P.O. Box 402539, Gaborone

DEM. REP. OF CONGO
Mr. Prahlad Parbhu
143 Kasai Ave., Lubumbashi

GHANA
Mr. Murli Chatani
RSSB - Accra
P.O. Box 3976, Accra
☎ +233-242-057-309

IVORY COAST
Mr. Veerender Kumar Sapra
Avenue 7, Rue 19, Lot 196
Trechville,
05 BP 1547 Abidjan 05

KENYA
Mr. Amarjit Singh Virdi
RSSB - Nairobi
P.O. Box 15134
Langata 00509, Nairobi
☎ +254-20-210-2970

LESOTHO
Mr. Sello Wilson Moseme
P.O. Box 750, Leribe 300

MADAGASCAR
Mrs. I. Rakotomahandry
BP100 Airport d'Ivato
Antananarivo 105

MAURITIUS
Dr. I. Fagoonee
RSSB Trust - Mauritius
69 CNR Antelme /
Stanley Avenues
Quatre Bornes
☎ +230-454-3300

MOZAMBIQUE
Mr. Mangaram Matwani
Av Josina Machel,
1st floor No. 376
Maputo 190

NAMIBIA
Mrs. Jennifer Carvill
P.O. Box 449
Swakopmund 9000

NIGERIA
Mr. Nanik N. Balani
G.P.O. Box 5054
Marina, Lagos

RÉUNION
Ms. Marie-Lynn Marcel
5 Chemin 'Gonneau, Bernica
St Giles-Les-Hauts 97435

SIERRA LEONE
Mr. Kishore S. Mahboobani
82/88 Kissy Dock Yard,
P.O. Box 369, Freetown

SOUTH AFRICA
Mr. Gordon Clive Wilson
P.O. Box 1959
Randpark Ridge
Gauteng 2156

SOS Study Centre - Bush Hill
24 Kelly Road
Bush Hill, Johannesburg
☎ +27-11-025-7655

SWAZILAND
Mr. Mike Cox
Green Valley Farm
Malkerns

TANZANIA
Mr. Manmohan Singh
99 Lugalo Street
Dar-Es-Salaam 65065

UGANDA
Mr. Sylvester Kakooza
RSSB - Kampala
P.O. Box 31381, Kampala

ZAMBIA
Mr. Surinder Kumar Sachar
2922 Mutondo Crescent
Copper Belt, Kitwe 212

ZIMBABWE
Mr. Gordon Clive Wilson
P.O. Box 1959
Randpark Ridge
Gauteng 2156, South Africa

MIDDLE EAST

BAHRAIN
Mr. Sameer Deshpande
Flat No.55, Bldg No. 781
Rd. No. 3630, Block 336
AL Adliya, Manama

ISRAEL
Mr. Michael Yaniv
Moshav Sde Nitzan 59
D.N. Hanegev 85470

KUWAIT
Mr. Jayakara Shetty
P.O. Box 22223
13083 Safat

U.A.E.
Mr. Daleep Jatwani
P.O. Box 37816, Dubai
☎ +971-4-339-4773